WHEN WOMEN PLAYED HARDBALL

•••

SUSAN E. JOHNSON

SEAL PRESS

Design by Clare Conrad

Cover photos: Upper left, Fans entering the ticket gate at Rockford's Beyer Stadium; courtesy of Dorothy Key. Upper right, The Fort Wayne Daisies pose for a photo, 1950; Northern Indiana Historical Society collection. Lower right, Betty Weaver Foss, the Fort Wayne Daisies' "clean-up" batter; Northern Indiana Historical Society collection. Lower left, Dorothy "Snookie" Doyle was a Rockford Peaches team leader; courtesy of Dorothy Doyle.

Library of Congress Cataloging-in-Publication Data

Johnson, Susan E., 1940-
    When Women Played Hardball / Susan E. Johnson
        p.   cm.
    ISBN 1-878067-43-5
    1. All-American Girls Professional Baseball League — History. 2. Women baseball players — United States — Biography. I. Title.
GV875.A56J64 1994
796.357'64'093 — dc20   93-23645
                                                                   CIP

Printed in the United States of America
First Printing, April 1994
10 9 8 7 6 5 4 3 2 1

Distributed to the trade by Publishers Group West
Foreign Distribution:
    In Great Britain and Europe: Airlift Book Company, London

Photo and permissions acknowledgments appear on page 289 which constitutes a continuation of the copyright page.

Acknowledgments

My thanks go first to my heroes, the women who played baseball for the All-American Girls Professional Baseball League, 1943 to 1954. You were so important to me, and this book is my gift back.

Special thanks to those players from the 1950 Rockford Peaches and Fort Wayne Daisies who during the interviews gave me so generously of their time and their memories: Amy Irene Applegren, Kay Blumetta, Wilma Briggs, Dottie Collins, Alice Pollitt Deschaine, Snookie Doyle, Marilyn Jones Doxey, Tiby Eisen, Betty Foss, Nickie Fox, Rose Gacioch, Fran Janssen, Dottie Kamenshek, Vivian Kellogg, Dottie Key, Helen Ketola LaCamera, Marie Mansfield Kelley, Norma Metrolis, Evie Wawryshyn Litwin Moroz, Maxine Kline Randall, Ruth Richard, Mary Rountree, Lou Erickson Sauer, Dottie Schroeder, Kate Vonderau, Jo Weaver and Helen Waddell Wyatt.

I am also grateful to other people who talked with me at length: Peoria Redwings Manager Leo Schrall, Rockford Peaches Chaperone Millie Lundahl, Peaches fan Coleen Holmbeck, and players Isabel Alvarez, Faye Dancer and Jean Weaver.

Dottie Collins, Treasurer of the All-American Girls Professional Baseball League Players' Association, answered many questions over many months. I was also helped in a variety of ways by past Association President Joan Holderness, current Association President Mary Baumgartner, Executive Director (1987-1992) Karen Kunkle, Secretary Jean Geissinger Harding, and newsletter founder June Peppas.

League historian and statistician Sharon Roepke talked with me and compiled many of the statistics used in the book. I am also grateful to Sharon for allowing me to reprint several of the baseball cards she has created and made available to players and the public.

Diane Barts and Carol Pickerl of The Northern Indiana Historical Society, the repository of the official AAGPBL Collection, helped me find the materials I needed and provided many of the fine pictures included in this book. I am grateful also to the many players who loaned me pictures and other memorabilia.

Ted Spencer, Curator at the National Baseball Hall of Fame, was most helpful. Player Rossey Weeks gave me permission to quote her poem "Play Ball." The *Rockford Register-Star*, the *Fort Wayne News-Sentinel* and the *Fort Wayne Journal-Gazette* gave me permission to reprint complete accounts of the seven 1950 championship series games.

Other people interested in the League generously shared their time and materials: Janis Taylor, producer and director of two videos about the League; Barbara Gregorich, author of *Women at Play*, a history of women and baseball; Sue Macy, author of *A Whole New Ball Game*, a history of the League for young adults; and Karen Weiller and Catriona Higgs, researchers examining the social history of the League.

The manuscript was read by several people whose suggestions have been invaluable. None of these people are responsible, of course, for any errors of fact or judgment. My wholehearted thanks to Holly Morris, my editor at Seal Press, and to Clare Conrad, Ingrid Emerick, June Thomas and all the other women of Seal who have so enthusiastically worked on the collective project that is this book. Thanks also to my other readers: Kim Severson, my friend in Anchorage; Ruth Baetz, my friend and editor in Seattle; and Martin Cobb, my copyeditor.

Faith Conlon of Seal Press thought the book was a good idea, and I am enormously grateful to her. Claudia Ehli in Anchorage kept saying I needed to write this book so she could read it. Patricia Huling in Seattle meticulously transcribed hours of taped interviews. Bucky Dennerlein of the Anchorage chapter of The Audubon Society was supportive on a daily basis. Sharon Woods, Secretary of the Anchorage Glacier Pilots college summer league team, asked me to throw out the first pitch at a Pilots game, one of the highpoints of my baseball career. Dave Foreman, Pilots' team statistician, answered some complicated technical questions.

And my special personal thanks go to my partner, Constance Wolfe, who always asks the right questions and whose love and support make my writing possible; and to her mother, Mathilda Congdon, my favorite baseball fan.

To my mother, Margaret,
who took me to the library;
and
To my father, Harold,
who took me to the ballpark

Contents

Rockford fans at a night game at "the Peach Orchard" in 1950. Fans and players are applauding a Rockford strikeout or critical defensive play. Left to right in the dugout: Marilyn Jones, Louise Erickson, Lois Florreich, Irene Applegren, Helen Waddell and Edna Scheer.

Preface

Baseball season is always bittersweet for me. Sweet because I am a true baseball fan. I love to watch women's softball live and the men's major leagues on television. I even toss the ball around a bit myself. The bitter comes because what's missing from each season is my team: the Rockford Peaches. They haven't played since 1954.

The Peaches were a women's professional team that played hardball (yes, hardball) during the twelve years of the All-American Girls Baseball League, 1943 to 1954. No other women's professional team sport in the United States has survived as long. The calibre of play was excellent and the pay was good. At its height in 1948, the League consisted of ten teams and entertained nearly a million fans in middle-sized Midwestern cities. The Rockford Peaches (Illinois) battled teams like the South Bend Blue Sox (Indiana), the Racine Belles (Wisconsin), and the Grand Rapids Chicks (Michigan). When I became a fan, at age ten in 1950, the Peaches were fighting for the pennant in a close race with the Fort Wayne Daisies (Indiana).

My idea of heaven was to sit in the stands and watch my heroes play. In my memory the weather is always warm, slightly muggy. The air smells of farm land and peanuts or Cracker Jack. Because the League played mostly night games, I am watching in a pool of artificial light surrounded by dimness, accentuating my feeling of being in a special world.

My Dad is with me, teaching me to keep score. I like keeping track, but even better I like being a happy sponge, absorbing the feel of women playing a difficult game with obvious skill and love of the sport and each other.

I remember my attention being riveted; the players and the play constituted my world. Dottie Key roamed centerfield and pilfered bases once she got on. "Squirt" Callow, Rockford's leftfielder, was a flashy hitter; I always hoped she would drive in those baserunners. "Snookie" Doyle patrolled shortstop, snuffing out enemy rallies. And Dottie Kamenshek, solid and imperturbable at first base, was sure to get a hit when we most needed one.

I paid less attention to pitching and catching than would an older, more sophisticated fan. I knew who the pitchers were, but didn't keep track of their win-loss records or their earned-run averages. In fact, I wasn't interested in statistics. I was caught up in the rhythm of play, my fantasized personalities of the girls, the way my body internalized what their bodies were doing, the joy of seeing women do something I, as a tomboy, could identify with and respect.[1]

The play was unpredictable. Anything could happen, though usually routinely competent plays were made on routinely well-hit balls. You know the pace of good baseball: Everything is going along in a comforting way, the reliable excellence almost lulling you to sleep, your attention beginning to waver a wee bit, when suddenly the opposition has runners on first and third, no one out, and their main woman at bat. Main woman, that was perfect.

This is still my idea of heaven.

◆◆◆

I've reflected since on why watching these women play baseball was so significant for me. I know I could identify with them easily. Many of the girls were only ten years or so older than I, young enough that I could relate to them, yet old enough that I was in awe. I watched them with wonder and an excitement that was close to erotic. My heart was in my throat much of the time.

My family took me to booster picnics where I could see my heroes wearing street clothes, walking about in the sun, drinking cokes and eating potato salad. I bought black-and-white glossy photos of the players and shyly asked for their autographs. But being this close to them was almost too much. My worship was so intense that I needed them to remain at a distance, lest the energy they were radiating toward me—and reflecting back upon me—vaporize my ten-year-old self. I also needed them to stay larger than life, so that I could project upon them the qualities of courage and resourcefulness and strength that I as a girl growing up needed women to show me.

As a young adolescent I was already learning that ladies properly stayed behind the scenes. The Peaches were a startling exception; here, the women were the scene. I remember how good it felt to join with other fans in cheering for our team. Sports can unite a city in a way unmatched by any other community event. To have Rockford's attention focused upon a women's team, upon my team, gave me a special connection to civic pride, a feeling that my community valued what my sex could do.

The All-Americans were heroes for all their fans, but especially for their little-girl fans. They showed us women doing something difficult and dangerous, something that took physical courage, intelligence and a fighting spirit. Moreover, the ballplayers were doing this as a team, working hard with other women to achieve something worthwhile, a game well played, and—if dedication, hard work, luck and the umpires cooperated—a victory. And they did all this with a lightheartedness that told me struggle, even combat, could be fun.

◆◆◆

I was fourteen when, after the 1954 season, the League died, the victim of management missteps, increased fan mobility, the growing popularity of television, and a cultural message that women should return to the kitchen, leaving factories, offices and ballparks to the men.

I was left to struggle with the transition from tomboy to early adolescent girl all on my own. Out of loyalty both to my team and to a compelling era in my own personal history, I kept my autographed pictures and my scrapbooks. I had carefully clipped the accounts of each game from the newspaper and Scotch-taped them onto lined school paper. I didn't date anything, because at that age everything happened today, or at most last night. And I didn't throw anything away, because that would have meant the true disappearance of my team, its death in my heart.

I've carried these mementoes with me for nearly forty years. Three years ago, as I reached fifty years old, I became aware that not only do I age, but so do those who are important to me: my partner, my parents, my brother and sister, my friends and my heroes. If I was fifty, my baseball heroes must be at least ten years older than I. If I was ever to "do anything" with my material and my memories, now was the time.

The result is this book.

◆◆◆

I went in search of my heroes. What better way, after all, to find out about baseball and the women who played baseball than to talk with the women themselves. What I found were not goddesses, but real women, now in their later years, who told me what playing professional women's baseball was really like, both the good and the not-so-good, both the wins and the losses.

I have tried to capture the lives of the players themselves, how they came to play ball, what their daily life and the daily game was like, how they felt about their manager and chaperone, their teammates, their opponents, and their fans. I was interested in how they adapted to the image the League organizers created for them, that they should "look like girls and play like men." I wanted to know what their lives were like after baseball, and what they think and feel now—nearly forty years later—looking back.

I have also tried to bring alive a sense of the game itself. I asked the players to recall specific games and particular moments within games. How did a game go? What did they think about as the game progressed? Which skills were most important? What was distinctive about the women's game compared to how men play baseball? And how important was it to them who won and who lost?

This is a book based on interviews with twenty-six of the women who played for the 1950 Rockford Peaches and Fort Wayne Daisies.[2] 1950 was the year I became a fan and the year these two teams, after struggling for the pennant through more than one hundred regular season games, fought each other for seven more heart-stopping contests in a compelling championship series. An account of this series forms the baseball context for the women's stories.

The other sources I used included yearbooks, memoranda, letters, contracts and other official papers from the time; magazine and newspaper articles then and now; pamphlets and books from the present (none were written at the time); and my own and the players' scrapbooks and memorabilia.

There is a distinct advantage to concentrating on only one year and two teams. It is too easy, in reporting on a branch of public entertainment like sports, to focus only on the "stars," the few people whose extraordinary qualities or special good luck have brought them much media attention. As a result, the vast majority of players are, relatively speaking, ignored. My commitment to interviewing everyone I could find on these two teams meant I searched out all the players, not just the most prominent. In this book we hear from rookies and utility players and second-stringers, those whose roles are important if secondary and whose experiences are just as exciting, funny and worthy of note as the oft-quoted. There are plenty of stars here—you don't field winning teams without some top players, and the 1950 Peaches and Daisies were both winning teams—but the whole team is suited up, not just the starting line-up.

While the method chosen has the advantage of comprehensiveness and intimacy, there is a corresponding sacrifice of generalizability. Every All-American is unique, but of course I could not talk with everyone. Collectively, the players I interviewed played for many teams, knew most of the other players in the League, and played all twelve years. Their experiences, or others very like them, are shared by many other players.

Nonetheless, precisely speaking this book tells of the experiences, attitudes, beliefs and memories of the twenty-six players on the 1950 Peaches and Daisies. It is their story, not necessarily everyone's.

The interviews depend on memory, an essential feature of which is memory's creative nature. The women whose stories are featured in this book clearly remember a great deal about their experience, even while they disclaim complete accuracy. Many factors, however, make remembering a perilous and less-than-completely-accurate venture for these women. The women themselves are older, and they played a great deal of baseball—over one hundred games per season—a long time ago. And at the time the women played, they didn't know, of course, that fifty years later they would be asked to tell us what happened.

Perhaps the most significant reason the players may have trouble remembering is that their playing days—until very recently—have been subject to the silence that blankets much of women's experience. Once the League folded, scarely anyone—neither the media, management, the players, nor organized men's baseball—mentioned it again. As Nickie Fox says, "In 1954, when the League ended, it fell off the face of the earth."[3]

Most of the players simply stopped talking about their baseball experience, some because of the reputation they thought they might acquire if people knew they'd been ballplayers, others because no one they talked to could grasp just what they'd accomplished.

Vivian Kellogg, the Daisies' first baseman, puts it this way:

You see, when I quit and came home I never said anything to anybody because nobody believed that there was a girls' baseball team. And so rather than be embarrassed by talking of something that it seemed no one had ever heard of, I never said anything.

Yet with all these challenges, the women do remember a lot, and some remember in considerable detail. Every player—I found no exceptions—has kept scrapbooks and other memorabilia from her playing days. These are vivid reminders of what happened. Over and over again during the interviews, players would jog their memories by referring to yellowed clippings. Once their memories had a little boost, they could recreate entire scenes.

The biggest help the players have in remembering, however, is a significant recent development; in the past decade, the League has come alive again. The women of the All-American Girls Baseball League have rediscovered each other, and have in turn been given a second life by both professional baseball and the movies. In the late 1970s, fan Sharon Roepke and player June Peppas, along with several others, began an organized effort to contact all the women who had ever played in the League. Gradually women were located, and a newsletter was circulated. In 1982 a fortieth anniversary reunion was held in Chicago, the first time since 1954 that All-Americans had officially been called together. The former "girls of summer" wore nametags so they could recognize their mature incarnations. Many issues of the newsletter and many reunions followed, and in1987 a Players' Association was established to promote recognition of the League and manage current affairs.

Now the public has become involved. With much encouragement from the reunited League and its friends, in 1988 the National Baseball Hall of Fame in Cooperstown, New York unveiled an exhibit honoring "Women and Baseball." Many All-Americans congregated to congratulate themselves and enjoy a recognition long withheld by history. In 1992 a full-length feature film, "A League of Their Own," which told a fictionalized, sympathetic, and largely accurate story of the first year of the League, became the year's seventh top money-maker. Helen "Sis" Waddell[4] and I discussed the movie and the League's previous period of quiescence:

Susan: Now before "A League of Their Own," for all those years . . .

Sis: I was dead. If there's a resurrection, why this is the resurrection.

◆◆◆

These pages are what the women of the All-American Girls Baseball League remember and want to share with you and me about the highpoint of their lives, their chance to play professional baseball. The book is organized around an account of the seven games of the 1950 championship series between the Rockford Peaches and the Fort Wayne Daisies. Each description of a game is followed by a profile of a particular player so that you can get to know several players in depth and detail. Each profile is then followed by a chapter focused on some significant aspect of these women's experience.

◆◆◆

Miracles play a big part in this story. The All-Americans regard their rediscovery and belated recognition as a miracle, an unanticipated and total surprise. In 1992 the Women's Sports Foundation's annual formal banquet honored three All-Americans (Marilyn Jenkins, Betty Trezza and Jean Faut Eastman) whom the Players' Association had chosen to represent the whole League. Marilyn Jenkins described the event:

> The Parade of Athletes included all the famous athletes, like Billie Jean King and Jackie Joyner-Kersee, but it wasn't 'til they brought out the three All-Americans that everybody in the place stood up. We were the only athletes there that got a standing ovation. Billie Jean King wanted my autograph! They kept calling me a pioneer. I gotta think about this.

The All-Americans also regard as a divine gift the original opportunity they had to play professional baseball. Never before or since in the history of women's sports has a team sport enjoyed the support and lasted as long as did the All-American Girls Baseball League. The marvel for these women is that the League was formed and that they were in the right place at the right time, blessed with the right skills, willing to make the right sacrifices, and in love with the right sport.

This book is the story of these women and their experience with professional baseball. It is a story of memories and miracles.

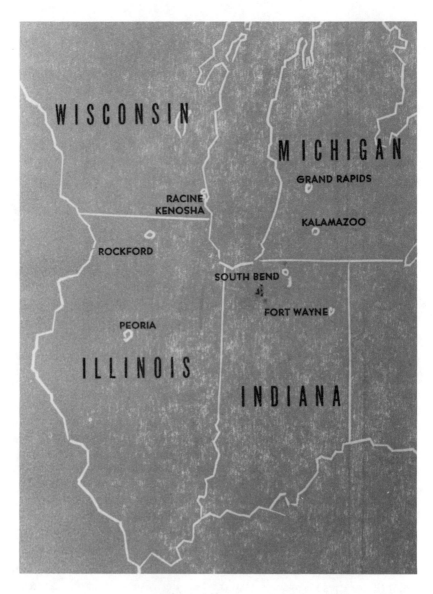

Map showing the eight cities where All-American teams were located in 1950.

A Short History of the League

The All-American Girls Baseball League[5] was the brainchild of Philip Wrigley, owner of the Chicago Cubs. In the fall of 1942 the Office of War Information had informed Wrigley and other big-league owners that it might be necessary to cancel the 1943 major-league baseball season. While the war had wrenched the country out of the economic depression of the 1930s, its impact on men's professional baseball had not been as salubrious. The men's minor leagues, the farm teams upon whom they depended for new talent, had been largely wiped out by the military draft. Half of the players for the sixteen big-league teams had joined the war effort, and stars like Joe DiMaggio were putting on Army uniforms.

Even if the 1943 major-league season was not cancelled (which in fact it was not), Wrigley became concerned that player quality would be lowered and fans would lose interest. Always a creative marketing intelligence, he went in search of an idea that could tide baseball over this crisis. Wrigley, along with Brooklyn Dodgers general manager Branch Rickey and others, decided to create a women's professional ball league.

The war years were a time when, in the interests of patriotism, women were encouraged to do all the things normally reserved for men: to work in factories or in offices or to join the armed services. It was the era of Rosie the Riveter. What more timely idea than to invite women to go to work on the ballfields of the country as well. The All-American Girls Baseball League was born, an innovation that was to change the lives of the girl ball-players of that time.

The Wrigley organization chose four medium-sized cities close to the parent group in Chicago to introduce the League: Racine (the Belles) and Kenosha (the Comets) in Wisconsin, South Bend (the Blue Sox) in Indiana and Rockford (the Peaches) in Illinois. Wrigley's assistants had convinced the civic fathers of all four cities that for a mere $22,500 they could buy a team franchise, thereby demonstrating their patriotism by providing wholesome entertainment for war workers and their families. A non-profit corporation was formed uniting the four clubs' Boards of Directors with the Wrigley organization leadership. Wrigley matched each city's contribution, took care of all publicity and provided everything needed to field a team: the players, coaches, chaperones, umpires, uniforms and so forth. The cities were to provide the fans.

Players were the property of the League, not of their individual teams, an organizational arrangement that had considerable impact on the lives of the players themselves. The League recruited, trained and signed the players, then evaluated and assigned them to various teams according to their abilities with the purpose of creating teams of equal strength at the beginning of each season. Players signed one-year contracts with the League itself. At the end of each season, they decided whether to continue with the League and then were available for assignment to the same team or another team. This allocation rule, while sensible for the League as a whole, created havoc for the players and their loyalties.

The Wrigley organization was aware of the tremendous popularity of softball at this time in the United States and Canada. Both during the Depression and the War that followed, money, leisure time and gasoline were hard to come by. People—potential fans—needed recreational activities close to home. An inexpensive and quick form of entertainment in an era before television was to stroll over to the ballpark and catch the local team's game. Women's teams attracted the loyalty of fans as successfully as did the men. In Chicago itself a women's amateur softball league was drawing many spectators. On the West Coast, Wrigley contacts had discovered 1,000 women's softball teams in or near Los Angeles alone. Dottie Collins, a Fort Wayne pitcher, remembers playing in the final game of the1936 Southern California Women's Softball Championship that drew 25,000 people.

Clearly, competent women players were available to play the game. Wrigley's scouts visited ballparks all over the U.S. and Canada (and later Cuba), watched girls play softball and recruited them into the League.

The girls were asked to do more, however, than simply play good ball. Ken Sells, a Wrigley assistant and first President of the League, described management's multiple intentions: not only did they promise to provide women of "professional ballplayer calibre," but, they assured city backers, these women were to have "high moral standing," and "femininity was to be stressed at all times."[6]

The organizers believed that fan appeal could be guaranteed only if these female players, who were expected to play ball with the skill of men, also looked and acted distinctly like women. The reasoning was explicitly stated in the League manual:

> Every effort is made to select girls of ability, real or potential, and to develop that ability to its fullest power. But no less emphasis is placed on femininity, for the reason that it is more dramatic to see a feminine-type girl throw, run and bat than to see a man or boy or a masculine-type girl do the same things. *The more feminine the appearance of the performer, the more dramatic her performance.* (emphasis in the original)[7]

In the interests of both "high moral standing" and "femininity," rules of dress and deportment were promulgated and enforced by chaperones assigned to each team. Hair must show under the baseball cap, skirts are to be worn in public, make-up must be used, destinations for dates and other entertainment must be approved, and so on. Early recruits to the League attended pre-season Charm Schools where Helena Rubinstein and other specialists instructed them in ladylike behavior.

The baseball uniform itself—a one-piece tunic-like dress with the skirt above the knee—was designed to attract fans to the ballpark and to remind them once they were there that they were watching not only real baseball, but real girls. Observers and players alike agree that, especially in the early years, fans were initially drawn to the park for the unusual spectacle, but they returned and developed a loyalty to the team, not because of the coiffures, but because of the class and the clout.

Furthermore, chaperones were integral parts of the teams, not just enforcers of the feminine code. Often ex-players, they were the girls' confidantes, moral support, mother figures, friends and for many matters the communication link between manager and players.

The League invited male sports figures, some with considerable baseball experience, some without, to manage the teams. Stars like Baseball Hall of Famers Max Carey and Jimmie Foxx and hockey player Johnny Gottselig joined competent but more obscure coaches like Bill Allington and Leo Schrall to teach the women the game. Some of these men turned out to be excellent, dedicated coaches, and the women are forever grateful for their guidance. Others could at best lend their famous names to the enterprise; the girls played despite their manager's questionable influence.

In 1943, when the average salary was between $10 and $20 a week, the All-American players received $45 to $85 a week for a regular season that lasted four months. They played nearly every day, with double-headers on many weekends—a total of over one hundred games—travelling from city to city by bus.

At first the women played softball, but by the 1948 season the basepaths had lengthened, the distance from pitcher's rubber to plate had grown, and the pitchers were hurling overhand a ball that had shrunk from 12 to 10-⅜ths inches.[8] The women were playing professional baseball in a league of their own for the first and only time in the history of sports in the United States.

The calibre of play was excellent. Max Carey, an able League President for five years and skilled manager of two All-American teams, had played major-league baseball for the Pittsburgh Pirates for seventeen years. Later Hall of Famer Carey evaluated the final game of the1946 championship series, a 14-inning contest between the Rockford Peaches and the Racine Belles, "Barring none, even in the majors, it's the best game I've ever seen."[9]

In this game the Peaches pitcher, Carolyn Morris, pitched a no-hitter for nine innings. The Belles pitcher, Joanne Winter, allowed thirteen hits, but the Peaches couldn't combine them into a run. The scoreless nail-biter of a game went into extra innings. Then, in the bottom of the 14th, Sophie Kurys of Racine got a hit, stole second, and, in the midst of stealing third, saw her teammate Betty Trezza hit the ball to right field. Kurys slid home to win the game.

That same year Kurys, the "Flint Flash," stole 201 bases. Her career tally of 1,114 stolen bases is still a professional baseball record.[10]

My hero was Dottie Kamenshek, the Peaches' first baseman. When she retired at the beginning of the 1952 season, she had led the league for one or more seasons in: at-bats, runs scored, hits, singles, fewest strikeouts and batting average, .316 in 1946, .306 in 1947.

In 1950 Dottie turned down a chance to be the first woman to play professional baseball with men. The Fort Lauderdale team in the Florida International (minor)League wanted her to try out, but she declined saying, "I want to finish out my career with the Peaches." Wally Pip, himself a great fielding first baseman for the

New York Yankees in the 1920s, called Dottie "the fanciest fielding first baseman I've ever seen—man or woman."

The best single-season batting average for an AAGBL player was achieved by Joanne Weaver, who connected for an astounding .429 average (in 333 at-bats) in 1954. If we compare her average to major league and Negro League male single-season batting averages (for players with at least 300 at-bats), we find Weaver's accomplishment is historic for the game as a whole. She is tied for the fourth best batting average in the history of professional baseball, and she is the last player in the history of the game to bat over .400.[11]

Matching records with male major-league players and recounting the opinions of male experts speaks well for the quality of play of the All-American Girls Baseball League. But fans like me weren't there to compare; we were there to enjoy. We were a mixture of men, women and children, mostly white, middle- or working-class families, there to savor an afternoon or an evening at the ballpark, to watch our girls hit the ball hard, pitch well, make some good plays, and, with any luck, win.

By 1954, however, not as many of us were showing up; attendance dwindled to 270,000, the lowest total in ten years and only 60,000 more than had enjoyed the League's very first season.

There were many factors that contributed to the League's demise. People were increasingly mobile, no longer dependent on local entertainment, and now had available to them the television, a medium that threatened the existence of all live entertainment. With aggressive leadership, though, the League might have made television work for it, using televised games to increase fan interest, as men's baseball has done so successfully.

But League management was in disarray. Beginning with the 1951 season, the clubs had acquired ownership of their teams and begun to look out for their own interests, to the neglect of the League as a whole. Decentralized ownership proved increasingly erratic, its quality varying hugely from city to city, and promotion of the League suffered accordingly. To add to these problems, the League had never established a farm system to identify and develop new talent. As a result it was becoming increasingly difficult to find women who had the skill and flexibility to move directly from softball to baseball.

At the same time, social propaganda strongly suggested that, since World War II and the Korean War were over, women were dispensable in paid public life. They should leave the factories, offices, and ballparks to the men and return to their proper place, the kitchen and the nursery.

At the end of the 1954 season, the All-American Girls Baseball League played its last games. The girls found work back home or in the cities where they'd played ball. Some married and raised children. Others devoted themselves to friends and careers. All that remained of girls' baseball were yellowing newspaper clippings, uniforms that no longer fit, trophies tarnishing in the attic, and scars and aching knees. And, occasionally, the sharp memory of a crucial run batted in, a perfect throw, the roar from the crowd, and that thrilling call: "Play ball."

THE 1950 CHAMPIONSHIP SERIES
Player Positions

ROCKFORD PEACHES

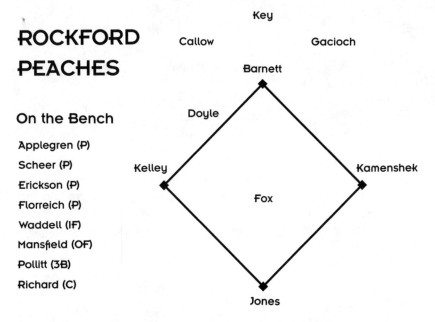

Key

Callow   Gacioch

Barnett

Doyle

Kelley   Kamenshek

Fox

Jones

On the Bench

Applegren (P)
Scheer (P)
Erickson (P)
Florreich (P)
Waddell (IF)
Mansfield (OF)
Pollitt (3B)
Richard (C)

FORT WAYNE DAISIES

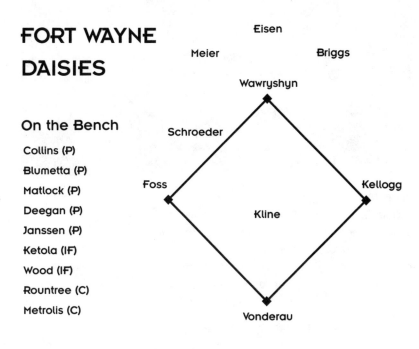

Eisen

Meier   Briggs

Wawryshyn

Schroeder

Foss   Kellogg

Kline

Vonderau

On the Bench

Collins (P)
Blumetta (P)
Matlock (P)
Deegan (P)
Janssen (P)
Ketola (IF)
Wood (IF)
Rountree (C)
Metrolis (C)

The 1950 Rockford Peaches team picture: Front row, left to right: Irene Applegren, Helen Waddell, Nickie Fox, Dorothy Kamenshek, Charlene Barnett, Eleanor Callow, Marie Mansfield, Dorothy Key, Louise Erickson. Second row: Chaperone Dorothy Green, Marilyn Jones, Dorothy Doyle, Alice Pollitt, Ruth Richard, Jackie Kelley, Lois Florreich and manager Bill Allington.

The 1950 Fort Wayne Daisies team picture: Front row, left to right: Thelma Eisen, Helen Ketola, Joanne Weaver, Maxine Kline, Ruth Matlock. Second row: Wilma Briggs, Evelyn Wawryshyn, Fran Janssen, Betty Weaver Foss, Kate Vonderau, Mary Rountree, Sally Meier. Back row: Manager Max Carey, coach/chaperone Doris Tetzlaff, Dorothy Schroeder, Trois Wood, Vivian Kellogg, Kay Blumetta, Dorothy Collins. Not pictured: Millie Deegan, Norma Metrolis and Betty Luna.

Full team rosters appear on pages 271 through 275.

GAME ONE

Saturday, September 9, 1950

There was little in the close of the 1949 All-American Girls Base-ball League season to suggest the fierce battle between the Rockford Peaches and the Fort Wayne Daisies that would erupt at the end of 1950.

The Peaches were the League's Yankees, the dominant team in the All-American League. In the seven years since Rockford had entered the League as one of the four original teams, they had won more pennants (two) and post-season championships (three) than any other team. In 1949 they ended the season tied with the South Bend Blue Sox for first place with 75 wins and 36 losses, a .676 winning percentage, and went on to win the championship series.

The Daisies, on the other hand, finished a distant fifth in 1949, twenty-two games out of first place, playing three games short of .500 ball (52 wins, 57 losses). They had entered the League in 1944 as the Minneapolis Millerettes, but when it became apparent that girls' baseball did not draw fans in big cities, the franchise moved to Fort

Wayne. For five years the team had struggled to no avail to bring a pennant home for their many enthusiastic supporters.

But two things happened to the Daisies in the off-season. Max Carey, a famous Pittsburgh Pirate, major-league base-stealing champion and former President of the All-American League, agreed to manage the team. Even more important, Betty Weaver Foss, the first of three powerful Weaver sisters to play for the Daisies, joined the team at third base.

The Peaches and the Daisies projected contrasting images. Rockford was a serious team, known for its excellent pitching, consistently fine defensive play and discipline. When the Peaches took the field in their sparkling white-and-black home uniforms, fans knew they would see a sharply played game. Their manager Bill Allington looked stern, suggesting in his face the no-nonsense approach that his teams brought to the game. He was known as "the Silver Fox" because he'd taught the Peaches trick plays intended to catch other teams off-guard. Allington, said opponents, "knew a lot of ways to win."

The Daisies were a more relaxed, casual team. A rookie described their mood and that of their new manager, Max Carey, as "jovial." Their yellow travelling uniforms, trimmed in brown, gave a sprightly impression that was confirmed by their play. The Daisies' shortstop, Dottie Schroeder, personified the team. Tall and slim, attractive, sporting blond pigtails, Dottie was widely photographed and acknowledged to be the League's most graceful player, simply beautiful in motion.

Her team had no lack of talent, but they did need Carey's coaching. With it, Fort Wayne fielded a winning team in 1950, potentially the League's winningest unless wily Rockford somehow derailed them.

As the 1950 season drew to a close, Rockford and Fort Wayne were locked in what sports editor Dick Day of the *Rockford Register-Republic* called "the most sizzling pennant race in the eight-year history of the All-American Girls Baseball League."[12]

Halfway through the season Rockford, plagued with injuries, had looked to be well out of it. Day reported, "In midsummer the pennant had appeared hopelessly out of Rockford's reach. Fort Wayne was breezing along at the head of the pack with plenty of daylight between it and its closest rival, and the Peaches were struggling under the impact of an injury pox that had kept one or more regulars benched for all but a few of their games this season."[13]

By the end of the season, however, Rockford was back in contention. The lead changed hands several times late in the season, and by September first, the two teams were about as close as you could get without being tied. With four games remaining for Rockford and five for Fort Wayne, Rockford trailed the Daisies by .001215 percentage points, but led by half a game when the race was figured on a won-lost basis. (The two teams had played a different number of total games, which made deciding who was ahead by how much a matter for higher mathematics.)

Rockford won all of its last four games to finish the season with 67 wins and 44 losses. Fort Wayne won three out of its five games, but the two losses left the Daisies finishing the season two games behind the Peaches. Again Rockford had managed to come out on top, but barely.

Fort Wayne Journal-Gazette sportswriter Bob Reed was pleased, however. In his "Sports Roundup" of September 6, 1950, headlined "Daisies Had Great Year," he concluded, "Regardless of how they fare in the current play-offs, the Fort Wayne Daisies have had their best season in six years of membership in the All-American Girls Baseball League, both on the field and at the gate. The Fort Wayne club finished second, two games behind, in a race that was decided on the final day of the schedule, after leading the pack for a large part of the season."[14]

It was well-deserved praise, but the All-Americans did not play to come in second. Fort Wayne looked forward to the playoffs as a chance to recapture glory snatched from them at the last moment.

Both teams dispatched their respective rivals in the first round of the playoffs: Rockford beat the Kenosha Comets and Fort Wayne defeated the Grand Rapids Chicks. Rockford's Dick Day crowed, "The 1950 crop of Rockford Peaches probably will go down in local baseball history as the most remarkable team the AAGBL ever produced. They frequently get more errors and fewer hits than the teams they beat. They've left a prodigious number of runners stranded on the bases. They've been playing all season long with a patched-up lineup. But here they are, pennant winners once again—and now first-round play-off victors."[15]

Game One began the championship confrontation the Daisies and the Peaches had been fighting toward all season. Fort Wayne's Maxine Kline, one of the League's best pitchers in 1950, did not have a good day in this first game. The Peaches' pitcher Nickie Fox, a winner during the season though with a record not nearly as impressive as Kline's, won Game One. The Peaches' Dottie Kamenshek and Rose Gacioch hit well, as did Fox, Dottie Key and Snookie Doyle. Doyle batted in two of the three Rockford runs.

The Peaches' pitcher hit well, 2-for-4 in this game with a double. Many All-American pitchers were consistently good batters. Maxine Kline batted .309 in 1950 (in 94 at-bats), and another Fort Wayne pitcher, Ruth Matlock, batted .361 (in 36 at-bats). The specialization that is true of men's baseball, where most pitchers concentrate solely on pitching and are feeble at bat, did not dominate girls' baseball.

The Daisies' graceful Dottie Schroeder stole two bases, typical of her quickness, as did Helen Ketola. Doyle and Key stole bases for Rockford. For the Daisies Wilma Briggs, a .275 hitter in 1950, and Evie Wawryshyn, batting an excellent .311 that year (third in the League) combined to take advantage of Marilyn Jones' throwing error to score the Daisies' only run.

Fortunately for Jones, this run was not critical to the outcome of the game. Jonesy, the Peaches' backup catcher and a rookie, would not normally have been playing in this crucial series, but Ruth Richard, the regular catcher, whom many believe was the best in the League, had broken her ankle the last day of the regular season. This series was Jonesy's chance to prove herself, the moment all backup players wait and hope for.

♦♦♦

Descriptions of these seven championship games have been taken from the newspaper accounts of the day. Although the Rockford-Fort Wayne series was broadcast on local radio, most fans turned to the morning sports pages—or, after work, to the reports in the evening edition—to find out how their team had fared the night before. (There was, of course, no television.)

The style of sports writing here is itself notable. There are no gimmicks or flourishes and no condescending sexism, no "cute young thing tosses winning ball." It's the straight-ahead, just-the-facts style that characterized serious sports writing at the time. As such, it indicates the respect that the All-American game was accorded by its closest observers.

15-Hit Attack Hands Daisies 3 to 1 Defeat

Staff Sports Writer
Rockford Morning Star, September 10, 1950

Launching a 15-hit attack on Maxine Kline, the league's second high average pitcher during the regular season with a 23-9 record, the Rockford Peaches defeated Fort Wayne, 3-1, Saturday night at Beyer Stadium in the first game of the A.A.G.B.L. championship playoffs with the Daisies.

Nickie Fox, who closed the regular season with a 14-12 record, gave the Daisies only four hits. Two of these came in the first inning, when the visitors scored their only run of the game.

The Peaches and Daisies will meet in the second game of the seven-game set at the stadium tonight at 8 o'clock. Manager Bill Allington of Rockford named Louise Erickson, with a 16-10 record, to take over the mound duties tonight. Manager Max Carey undoubtedly will select Millie Deegan, who finished the league schedule with a 16-9 record, as his pitcher in an effort to even the series. Deegan was effective against the Peaches during the season.

Saturday night the Peaches made hits in all eight innings, but got a number of their safe blows after two were out. They bunched three for a run in the third, two for a run in the fifth, and three for their third and last run in the eighth. In the last two playoff games the Peaches have made a total of 29 hits, getting 15 Saturday night and 14 Friday night in Kenosha.

Dottie Kamenshek and Rose Gacioch each hit safely three times in four official trips to the plate. Snookie Doyle got two for four, as did Nickie Fox and Dottie Key. One of Fox's hits was a two-bagger.

Daisies Score First

Fort Wayne scored first in the first inning. With one out, Wilma Briggs doubled down the third base line. Evelyn Wawryshyn singled, Briggs stopping at third base. As Wawryshyn went down to second, Marilyn Jones threw to second with nobody covering the bag, and Briggs scored. Wawryshyn was thrown out at third by Key while trying to reach third base on the error. Betty Foss flied out to end the inning.

In only two other innings did the Daisies have a scoring chance. In the fifth Dottie Schroeder led off with a walk and stole second, but the next three batters were easy outs. In the eighth Fox walked Millie Deegan, batting for Mary Rountree. Helen Ketola, running for Deegan, stole second, but Kline struck out and Thelma Eisen and Briggs flied out to end the threat.

The Peaches tied the score in the last of the third when Key led off with a single. She stopped at second on Kamenshek's second straight hit. Snookie Doyle singled over Schroeder's head to drive in Key with the tying run. The Peaches went out in front in the fifth inning when Kamenshek led off with her third single. Kamenshek stole second as Doyle flied out to left and Kelley grounded out, short to first. Gacioch singled to left to score Kamenshek with the lead run.

Fox Doubles

In the eighth, with two out, Fox doubled off Sally Meier's glove, going to third on Key's second hit of the night. Key stole second and Kamenshek walked to load the bases. Doyle singled Fox home with a base blow to left, but Key was thrown out at the plate, Meier to Kate Vonderau, while trying to score on the hit.

Summary

Runs - Briggs, Kamenshek, Key. Errors - Schroeder, Jones. Runs batted in - Doyle 2, Gacioch. Doubles - Briggs, Fox. Sacrifice hits - Barnett, Jones. Stolen bases - Schroeder 2, Ketola, Doyle, Key. Double play - Kline to Kellogg to Foss. Runners left on base - Fort Wayne 5, Rockford 11. Base on balls - off Kline 1, Fox 2. Strike outs - Kline 1, Fox 2. Winning pitcher - Fox. Losing pitcher - Kline. Time - 1:31. Attendance - 2,598.

▲ Marilyn "Jonesy" Jones during
her first year in the League. Chet
Grant, her manager in Kenosha,
said, "She's got a lot of spirit. I'm
gonna keep her."

▶ Marilyn Jones Doxey in 1992
showing off a newspaper account
of one her favorite memories, the
no-hit game she pitched in 1952
against the Rockford Peaches,
her team in 1950.

MARILYN "JONESY" JONES
Rockford, Catcher

Statistics: Born, 1927. Home town: Providence, Rhode Island. Height: 5 feet 5 inches. Playing weight: 130 pounds. Bats: Right. Throws: Right. Entered League: 1948 at age 21. Teams: Kenosha, 1948; travelling team, 1949; Rockford, 1950-52; Battle Creek, 1952-53; Fort Wayne, 1954. Lifetime totals: Batting average: .160. Fielding percentage: as catcher .890; as pitcher .880. Pitching statistics: Games won 31; games lost 26; winning percentage .544; earned-run average: 2.79.

Marilyn Jones was not the girl that manager Bill Allington expected to catch the 1950 championship series for the Peaches. His regular catcher, Ruth Richard, a five-time All Star (1949-53), would have caught the series had she not broken her ankle. Rockford fans collected $600 to help Richie recover, but no amount of money or hospital visits from teammates would put her back behind the plate. When the lights came up for the playoffs with the Kenosha Comets, a series Rockford had to win to advance to the championship, Marilyn Jones was Rockford's catcher. Marilyn remembers her feelings that night: "It was thrilling, but I was scared to death. I always had trouble catching pop flies. I couldn't get under them right."

She gets up from the kitchen table in her Michigan trailer home where we are talking, looks up far beyond the low ceiling into lights that shone down on her forty-two years ago, and weaves uncertainly under an imaginary ball. "It was really difficult for me 'cause they'd turn a different way. I'd always get under them the wrong way."

She sighs and sits down again, "I mean, I did catch some, but I really missed a lot."

The 1950 season saw the introduction of the "rookie rule" into the League. In the interests of developing new players, each team was required to field at least one rookie at all times. Jones had only played a few games in 1948 and had been on a "development team" in 1949 (teams of rookies who travelled, playing exhibition games), so she qualified.

> When we went to Fort Wayne later in the championship series, I can remember a fan challenging Allington, "Where's your rookie? Where's your rookie?" I was missin' all these pop-ups and shouted back at him, "Can't you tell where the rookie is?"

Marilyn was one of many players for whom getting into the League and staying there was a lot of hard work. But hard work, flexibility, a realistic attitude, a sense of humor and courage kept her going. In the 1950 playoffs and championship series it was her courage that would have to substitute for pressure-situation playing time.

> He always gave you experience, Bill did. Maybe when the game was lost or something, he'd put me in to give me a coupla innings. It was a good thing he did too.

Allington acquired Peoria's Rita Briggs, a veteran catcher, as backup should Jones herself be injured during the championship series.

> I said to Bill, "How much will you pay me to get hurt?" Because he couldn't use her unless I got hurt. He just laughed. And she never caught a game.
>
> He was behind me though. I mean, he had to be behind me, and he had to tell me to do well because he had to use me. He didn't have any alternative. It was help me or lose.

◆◆◆

I found Marilyn Jones, now Marilyn Doxey, in South Haven, Michigan, a resort community on the eastern shore of Lake Michigan. Marilyn is sixty-five and retired now after managing various aspects of Michigan Bell Telephone's operations for thirty-one years. She is stocky, of medium height, and has short, straight, grey hair, an open direct manner and a frequent smile. She lives with her husband Bud, a former fast-pitch softball player and umpire, who works part-time at the marina. Before he retired, Bud was a parts manager for a trucking components company. They live modestly in a well-kept trailer court. It was September when I visited, a clear, crisp fall day, and they were making plans to leave for Florida where they have another trailer set up for the winter months.

Marilyn began playing organized softball when she was twelve years old in playground leagues in her hometown of Providence, Rhode Island. By the time she was fifteen she was good enough to be given a summer job so that her employer could use her talents on the company softball team. Her family was working-class, her father a supervisor in the city water department, her mother a housewife. She had two older brothers and a younger sister. "I had a brother only twenty-two months older than I. I competed with him in sports my whole life."

Marilyn looked outside her immediate family, though, for her most important sources of support.

> When I was fourteen or so there was this one pitcher in town, he got paid $10 to pitch every Saturday, he'd pick me up and take me to the ballgames. My mother says, "What in the world is he picking you up for?" 'cause I was only a kid, you know.
>
> Well, he was interested in me because I enjoyed going to the ballgames, and I'd shag fly balls, and I'd play catch. We were friends.
>
> I was kind of a little tomboy I guess. I always wanted to be playing kick the can and ball and such things. I played with my brother and his friends rather than with girlfriends playing with dolls. I was more interested in going to the ballpark.
>
> I did babysit occasionally. [She laughs at the memory.] My mother said that one time, when I was supposed to be watching this baby in a carriage, I got on my bike, attached the carriage to the bike, and was pulling the baby around. Until my mother saw me, that is. I wasn't gonna just sit there and watch that baby.

Marilyn graduated from high school and worked three years for the telephone company. Then, in 1948, when she was twenty, she heard from another player about local try-outs for some league in the Midwest that was paying money for girls to play baseball. "My Dad didn't want me to go, he didn't want me to give up the secure job I had, so he said, 'I'm not gonna sign for you.'" Parents had to give their permission for girls under age twenty-one to play for the League. "Well, Dad," I said, "It's March. If you don't sign for me now, in April I'm gonna be twenty-one, and I'm gonna go anyway."

Her father signed, and the company gave her a leave of absence, which they later revoked because she was being paid to play. "They sent me a telegram while I was in spring training, so I just resigned. It's easy to do when you're away from home and havin' fun." Her starting salary of $55 a week, standard for that time, was more than double what she was making at the telephone company.

Marilyn played for several different teams in her career, and thus worked with different managers. She started with Chet Grant of Kenosha who, she says, kept her in the League.

> The directors wanted to send me home in '48. "No," he says, "She's got a lot of spirit. I'm gonna keep her." It was Chet Grant that had me start catching rather than send me home.
>
> I worked hard for Chet, who was really no good at all as a manager; he had no background in baseball. I did my best for Chet. I did my best for Guy Bush [of the Battle Creek Belles] too, and I had no respect for him. And I tried to do good for Joe Cooper [who followed Bush in Battle Creek], who was knowledgeable about baseball.
>
> But Bill Allington was the best coach I played for. Bill was the one that was the teacher. He wasn't one to yell at you. But he worked you hard. If you didn't learn, it was your own fault. He was trying to teach you all the time. Sliding or bunting or hitting.
>
> Some girls were intimidated by Bill, but I never really was. If he said something that I knew would hurt my friend Boston, for instance, I'd probably say something back to him, and then he'd probably tell me it was none of my business. But I wasn't afraid to say what I thought.
>
> He never really ever got on me. Ever. Even when he told me that they were going to send me to Battle Creek, he was nice about it, and thanked me for the good years I'd played, and said he knew I'd played hard for him.
>
> But he wouldn't give me a chance to pitch. I used to throw batting practice, and one time he had to replace a pitcher. I asked to try out, but he said, "No, you have no wind-up." And I was already older than some of the kids that were comin' up.

Marilyn gave up trying to convince Allington, but her pitching aspirations did not die here; two years later, after Bill had traded her, she became a pitcher for the Battle Creek Belles.

◆◆◆

Although playing in the League was hard work, it was also a lot of fun.

There was pressure to do well, but it was fun too. Sometimes during the day we'd be able to go to the beach and have a picnic. We got to go to a lot of different places, like on the rookie tour.

The rookie tour was a player development and promotional tour that operated for two years, 1949 and 1950. The Colleens (for a brief time from Chicago) were pitted against the Sallies (also briefly from Springfield, Illinois), in exhibition games all over the country. In 1949, when Marilyn was part of the tour, thirty ballplayers, two chaperones, a business manager, a manager and the driver travelled by bus 90,000 miles through twenty-seven states. This experience was critical for some players subsequently incorporated into the League itself.

I asked Marilyn what she liked best about the League.

I liked meeting people from all different backgrounds. I liked most of the girls. There were some I didn't really care for, but they were few and far between. If you didn't like somebody, you just didn't socialize with them. You know, you had to play ball with them anyway.

I disliked people on the other teams more than the people on my team. Like they slid in hard or threw right at ya. Some of them played extremely hard. They played to win.

I asked Marilyn whether she thought women played baseball differently than men do.

Different? No. We played as hard, ran as hard, and slid as hard. We hit as good, and threw as good, and thought better!

No, I think we didn't play any different than what they play. Except we got a hell of a lot less money.

◆◆◆

A catcher plays one of the most physical positions in baseball, one with a high risk of bodily contact and injury. I asked Marilyn how she prepared for my favorite play, the collision at homeplate, where a runner is trying to score, the throw is on target, and the catcher is blocking the plate, waiting to make the tag. She told me, "You have to keep yourself in shape, for one thing. And, if you get the ball thrown to you in the right place, then you're not in any danger."

But baseball is a dangerous business. In fact any sport—played as often and as hard as professionals must—results in physical damage.

Marilyn held up her right hand so I could see all the misshapen fingers.

I broke fingers when I was learning how to catch. I think all of my fingers on this hand. [She counts them off, bending back each one with her other hand.] See, this is broken, this is broken, this is broken. And this one I did playing basketball. [The thumb is okay.]

She explains the proper technique to try to avoid such injuries.

When you're first learnin' to catch, you got both hands out there. You don't do that. Only the glove hand stays out. And you learn to keep your eye on the ball!

In '49 I had a splint on my throwing hand. You ever try to throw a ball with that? Otherwise I just had aches and so forth. And with aches you just played. If you hurt your arm not warming up properly, you played with that. And many of the ladies—not me, I never slid—they played with those strawberries [the large areas on a player's thighs, unprotected because of the uniform skirts, that were scraped raw when they slid into base]. Those were sick.

We had a lot of ladies that really played hard. I mean, I played hard, but those base-stealers, they were amazing.

We tried to take care of ourselves, because if you couldn't play, you were hurtin' yourself. And everybody else.

The League did have adequate insurance and took care of injuries players suffered on the job. But there's no compensating for the aches and pains that persist, as Marilyn readily admits.

My mother always said that when I got older, my joints were all gonna ache, and some of them do. It could be from having played ball. Of course, I'm sixty-five. My joints might ache if I had just knitted all my life!

The All-American style of baseball relied on running; base-stealing was a major offensive tactic. Catchers—with the help of fastball pitchers—were the only way defensive teams could put a stop to such larceny. Marilyn could throw out base-stealers.

I did good. I had a pretty good arm. I threw out some of the better runners. I was thrilled to throw out Jo Weaver, and I threw out Betty Weaver Foss, and they were good. And Wilma Briggs, who's from Rhode Island too, probably wouldn't admit it, but I threw her out too.

Of course it makes a difference who your pitcher is. If you got a pitcher that throws slow, you don't have a chance. Nobody was gonna steal against Lois Florreich and myself, because Lois fired the ball at you. She gave it to you so quick they weren't gonna steal. But when I had a chance, I did throw out some of the better runners.

Because Marilyn was a rookie, she mostly hung out with other rookies on the team. This division between rookies and veterans was one of the informal structural features of a team. Rookies often roomed, ate and went to the movies together, giving each other support. They idolized veterans, players who had preceded them and who had established reputations. Rookies were set far apart, especially in their own minds, from stars.

I just hung out with the younger people. I never really socialized with half of the team. You know, when we played ball, there wasn't much socializing. You'd go out to eat after the game, but you all were at different places. Unless a fan or someone got a picnic together, you didn't all go to the same place.

I always admired Kammie [Dottie Kamenshek]. If she ever spoke to me, Holy Cow, I'd really love it! She paid attention to slow rookies.

Marilyn's roommate was rookie rightfielder and later pitcher Marie "Boston" Mansfield, also from the East Coast. While Marilyn was stoic and worked hard, Boston was flamboyant and relaxed. She caught Allington's attention more than Marilyn did.

Boston was one that was underage, and Bill took a liking to her; he was on her more than on me. He was trying to ignite her, you know, to play better. She was tall, maybe 5 foot 10, and had this lackadaisical walk out to the mound, and big, dangling earrings, and long fingernails. But she was a good pitcher.

Bill had her take her jewelry off.

The All-Americans, by and large, dressed and looked natural, like girls with something other than appearance on their minds. Players like Boston were an exception. The League promulgated strict rules about dress and behavior, and went to great effort to teach the girls how to look "feminine." Though not the style of most of these girls, they went along with it so they could play baseball.

I have a picture of the whole team in their ball uniforms, and a similar picture of us all dressed up. We've been invited somewhere for lunch or dinner. We all had heels and dresses and everything, and you wouldn't even know we were the same girls!

I asked Marilyn if she could have worn her hair as short when she was playing as she did now.

Oh, probably not. When you were practicing, your hair was a mess. You practiced, and then you'd shower and go home, and then you'd shower again after the game. And you were always doin' something with your hair. It was nice to wear it just straight, with do-lollies [pigtails], they called 'em.

We talked about why management made such an issue of the players looking feminine.

I think the fans wouldn't come to see a bunch of girls that acted like boys. They wanted to see a bunch of girls that acted like girls, and looked like girls . . . and played like boys. The public thinks it's great if you've got a female-type person, and she can really play ball. They don't think it's so great if you're a tomboy anyway, and you look like a tomboy, and so what if you can play ball.

How many times have I watched somebody playing catch and said, "My God, they throw just like a girl!" Well, some of the girls I know, they really threw!

Players relegated to backup roles have particular challenges to face. It's hard to keep in shape and to keep your attention on the game when most of the time you won't be called on to perform. It may also be hard to keep your pride intact. I asked Marilyn how hard it was for her to play second-string and what she occupied herself with all those times she wasn't playing.

I'd sit on the bench and yell. And I'd coach our first base sometimes, and I'd warm up the pitchers when the catcher was puttin' on her equipment, and I'd catch battin' practice, and I'd pitch battin' practice. I was thin then. I can see why, because I worked hard.

It was never really hard for me to be second-string, because I was second-string to people that I knew were better than I. But had I thought I was better than them and then I was second-string, it might have been a different story.

I wondered how important winning was to Marilyn.

It wasn't as important as playing well. If we didn't lose because of some dumb thing, I wasn't concerned. If they beat us on base hits or something, well, that's how it goes. Of course, I wanted to win. And when we played in the playoffs, I really wanted to win, because that first team we played against was my old team, Kenosha.

◆◆◆

Though nervous to be catching at such a critical time in the 1950 season, Marilyn Jones played very well in Rockford's playoff victory over her former team. Jonesy played errorless ball behind the plate, delivered four hits in fifteen at-bats, one a double, for a .267 average, and batted in four runs, which tied her with her teammates Snookie Doyle and Charlene Barnett for the most Rockford RBIs. Perhaps she was inspired. Players who were traded relished triumphs over their previous teams. "They had let me go, in '48, you know, so when we beat them, I thought 'nyah 'nyah. Gotcha!"

Marilyn did not play as well against Fort Wayne in the championship series that followed, though she did contribute. Through five games she batted .286, four hits in fourteen at-bats. She beat out a bunt for one of those hits, simultaneously advancing Eleanor "Squirt" Callow to second. Both Callow and Jones subsequently scored. In the last two games she got only one hit in eight attempts, so she finished the series with an average average, .227.

Jonesy was credited with one run batted in, because in Game Two she was hit by a pitch with the bases loaded, forcing in a run. In the series she scored three runs and even stole a base.

She did have three errors, two of them resulting in Fort Wayne runs, but neither run affected the outcome of a game. I can't tell from the game accounts whether any of these were her nemesis, dropped pop-ups.

I asked Marilyn how she felt about that post-season series.

That was a thrill. That was a thrill. And I kept thinking, we're doing this with me catching, you know. But our team was good. We had some good pitching. And everybody knew I had to catch, and they all encouraged me.

I don't know if I played well, but I played adequate. I did my job, you know, that's all I can say.

Marilyn regards the playoffs and championship series as "the second best moment" of her career. Marilyn was traded from Rockford to the Battle Creek Belles in 1952 and her "best moment" was to come. I asked her first, though, if it felt bad to be traded.

Yeah, except that I was gonna get to play. You know, with the Peaches, I was always second-string to Richie. I did get to play in the playoffs, but then the next year I went right back to being backup. And I wasn't a very good hitter, so I wasn't going to get much chance to catch. [Players other than pitchers were expected to have a respectable batting average.]

But after Bill let me go from the Peaches, I went to Battle Creek, and I became a pitcher, and I was quite good.

Marilyn's best moment came very soon after she started to pitch for the Belles. She has her own laminated copy of the Battle Creek newspaper account. This is part of the *Rockford Morning Star*'s description of her triumph.

Former Peach Hurls No-Hit, No-Run Game
Rockford Blanked by Marilyn Jones

BATTLE CREEK. Marilyn Jones, rookie pitcher making her second 1952 start on the mound, presented her manager with a no-run, no-hit game and beat the Rockford Peaches, 1 to 0, here Thursday night before 1,300 fans.

There was no question of Jones's no-hitter, no Rockford batter getting anything that looked like a base blow. She walked five, but one Rockford runner was forced out at third and two others were eliminated by double plays. She struck out three.

The Peaches' only scoring chance came in the first inning when Alice Pollitt Deschaine led off with a walk. She stole second but was forced out at third by Ruth Richard's grounder. One other Peaches runner reached second during the game. After the first inning, Jones set the Rockford batters down in order in the third, fourth, fifth, sixth, seventh, and ninth innings.

Of course Marilyn savored the fact that her best game was against Bill Allington, the man who years before had refused to let her pitch.

He come right over to me after the game and congratulated me. I didn't like some of the things he did, and I probably told him about it, but I really admired him for that.

Any enterprise that has best moments has worst moments too. Some players have conveniently forgotten—or are unwilling to recount—their worst moments, but not Jonesy.

I pitched against South Bend's Jean Faut, one of the League's greatest pitchers. I walked fourteen batters and hit one and lost the game one to nothing. After I'd get the bases loaded, then I'd get 'em out. Not to win that game after enduring...[the memory renders her temporarily speechless]. I had done well, because I was matched against Jean Faut, but we just couldn't hit her. And my mother and my father and my sister were there. I really cried on the mound. Because I had lost.

Even in her worst moments, though, Marilyn's sense of humor persists.

We had a terrible umpire for that game, I remember. Our first catcher had already been thrown out for arguing. When the backup catcher came in I said, "Whatever you do, keep your mouth shut!" Because I didn't want to wind up catching my own game.

In 1954 Marilyn's relationship with Bill Allington came full circle. Allington had left Rockford after the 1952 season, and moved to manage the Fort Wayne team in 1953 and 1954. In 1954 Marilyn found herself traded again, this time to the Daisies. I asked her whether she thought Bill was happy to see her again. Characteristically understating her satisfaction with the situation Marilyn replied, "I think he had a choice. So I was kinda pleased."

◆◆◆

The end of the League came after this 1954 season. Marilyn took it like the realist she is. "Well, I was disappointed, you know, but there wasn't anything you could do." She got a job with the Michigan telephone company, and met Bud playing softball. They married many years later, in 1969 when Marilyn was forty-two years old. "We had a lot of the same interests. We used to go out of town for fast-pitch softball tournaments. Mine and his." They play golf and bowl. Sometimes Marilyn outdoes herself.

Yesterday I bowled two 200 games. I haven't done that well in five years. I was doing really good. Then I came back to earth and bowled

124 for the third game. I did really good, but I could have done so much better!

Bowling well doesn't really compare, though, to her ball-playing days. Marilyn regards her years with the All-American Girls Baseball League as "the highpoint of my career. It was much more exciting than my thirty-one years working!"

With her baseball career over, Marilyn settled down to a more conventional life—until recently. When the women of the League reconnected, Marilyn was among those who had kept in close enough touch with a couple of players to be found immediately.

I love the newsletters. I tell 'em where Bud and I are and what we've been doin'. We got to some of the reunions. But, you know, I'm not available to do the things those single gals can do.

I asked her how it felt to have everyone suddenly know about her because of the movie.

Well, that was a shock, you know. Now people come up and say, "This is one of the girls that played in that League that the movie's about." We didn't think we were anything when we were playing. It was just . . . it wasn't so big. [She pauses.] We were big to our fans.

"You were big to me," I said.

PICK the PEACHES

To Top Your Holiday Enjoyment!

WHOLESOME ENTERTAINMENT FOR THE WHOLE FAMILY!

3 Big Games

See Your Rockford Peaches Battle Fort Wayne's Pennant-Contenders in American Girls Base ball Windup

COLORFUL, EXCITING ACTION! NATION'S TOP PLAYERS!

SUNDAY
6 p.m.—Rockford's Keith Jewelers Ko-Eds vs. DeKalb Gau Oilers
Attendance Prizes—Valued up to $50 Each
8 P. M.—Peaches vs. Fort Wayne

MONDAY
7 p.m.—Big holiday doubleheader— Peaches' last regular game of '52 A.G.B.B. season.
Fans Association Presentation of Gifts to Peaches

PUT THE PEACHES OVER THE TOP!

Peaches have 52,000 season attendance to date . . . need 12,000 over Labor Day weekend to assure return to Rockford in '53.

Show your support . . . enjoy big league girls' baseball under the stars . . . make convenient, spacious Beyer stadium first on your holiday fun schedule!

Rockford's shortstop Dorothy "Snookie" Doyle tags second ready to complete a double play with the throw to first. Her eyes are on the runner.

EARLY
INNINGS

"I just loved to play ball." —Dottie Schroeder

The girls who became professional baseball players were tomboys, girls passionately involved in activities conventionally reserved for boys. Of course lots of girls are tomboys, but somewhere in adolescence they run up against our society's demands that proper men and women be very different from each other, in looks, thought, word and deed. Tomboys, who have been enjoying a temporary stay of these rigid rules, are at puberty supposed to forego their childish pursuits and turn their attention to becoming women. They are supposed to exchange their baseball mitts for white gloves.[16]

What is extraordinary about these girl ballplayers is not that they acquired their love of baseball so young, but that they remained true to it; they kept playing ball when they grew old enough to know better. Several important factors worked to protect them from society's more conventional pressures: the families who supported them, the working-class origins that made fewer "ladylike" demands upon them, and the extraordinary skills that brought them to the attention of coaches. There was also an intangible ingredient, these girls' love for baseball, a love that burned so strongly it could not be extinguished, even by the cold water of society's wake-up calls to womanhood.

Dottie Schroeder's beginnings are a blend of these elements. Dottie was Fort Wayne's shortstop in 1950,[17] and one of the most photographed girls in the League: pretty, exceptionally graceful in play, and capped with a signature look—her blond braids. Charlie Grimm, the manager of the Chicago Cubs at the time, said of Dottie, "If that girl were a man, she'd be worth $50,000 to me."

When I talked with her forty years later in the Champaign, Illinois home she shares with her twin brother, she looked like an identical, simply older version of her young self. She is in excellent physical shape, tan and healthy looking, wearing a single long grey-blond braid down her back.

Dottie was one of the first sixty players recruited for the All-American Girls Softball League (the original name of the League) in 1943, its first year of operation. At the time she was only fifteen years old—one of the youngest players ever to join the League. She came from a farm in central Illinois that had been in her family since her great-grandparents' generation. Her love of baseball began before she owned a real ball. "I remember out on the farm we didn't have a bat or a ball; we would play imaginary ball out in the cow pasture. You can imagine what we used for bases!"

Dottie had an older brother and a twin brother. The three of them had seen her dad and uncles and other men of the nearby small town play ball. So they had all the material they needed—the ballpark, the cheering fans, the crack of bat hitting ball—right in their heads.

Imagine the scene: Dusk is falling on the cultivated fields, chores are done, and the three kids have bolted their suppers to get outside before the light fails. They climb the fence into their baseball pasture, Dottie runs to her favorite fielding spot at shortstop, and twin brother Don winds up to fire at elder brother Walter. Walt tags the very first pitch for a sharp line drive deep in the hole at short. Dottie scampers to her right, scoops up the ball cleanly, whirls and fires to Don, now at first, for the out, a whisker's width ahead of the runner. There's a brief argument with Dottie, now the umpire, but Walter is clearly out.

The Schroeder family moved to Sadorus, Illinois, population three hundred, when Dottie was nine. Her father became the postmaster and manager of a fast-pitch softball team. Finally the kids had all the bats and balls they needed. Dottie began playing girls' softball for the Sadorus Pirates, and even she, practiced at flights of fancy, could not imagine what would happen next.

In 1943 my dad read in the *Chicago Tribune* that they were holding try-outs down in St. Louis for this new girls' professional softball league. So he and I boarded the train in our little home town and went down to St. Louis. There must have been sixty-five girls there that were trying out. Just two of us, Lois Florreich and myself, were selected to go to the Cubs' Wrigley Field in Chicago for the final try-outs.

My mother went with me on the train to Chicago. I tried out again and I was picked. I was so young it never occurred to me that I might not be picked to be on a team in the League. I never thought about if I was good or bad. I just loved playing ball.

◆◆◆

Dottie began playing imaginary ball with her brothers and graduated to an organized team only when her family moved from the farm into town. Other girls also cradled their love of the game somewhere deep within themselves. Many players told me stories of being content playing ball all by themselves, accompanied only by the rhythm of their bodies—throw, balance, prepare, eye on the ball, move, catch, throw again—in a repetitive, somehow comforting, almost sensual physical mantra.

Louise Erickson, a Rockford pitcher, played alone using her uncle's second-base glove, memorable to her as a talisman, the first real glove she ever played with.

I'd get a ball and throw it up in the air out in the yard, and catch it myself, just run around under it. His glove was so old it had holes in it, so old the horsehair it was padded with was comin' out. I'd stick rags in there so the ball wouldn't sting so bad.

When Marie Mansfield, a Rockford rightfielder and pitcher, was twelve years old she bounced the ball against the family garage or off the stairs. "I thought that was the greatest, all by myself. I didn't need another soul."

Dorothy "Snookie" Doyle, Rockford's shortstop, was already "throwing for accuracy," as she puts it, when she was just a child, alone in the yard.

> I used to get out with a tennis ball in front of my grandmother's house and throw at a square in the brick wall. I'd miss every once in awhile and hit her big bay window, and she'd yell, 'Snookie, you stop that right now!'

Of course the girls didn't play by themselves most of the time. All of them played with other kids in the neighborhood, mostly with boys. The boys greeted their participation with varying degrees of acceptance, the acceptance conditional on a combination of the girls' ability and their boyish air.

Helen "Sis" Waddell was a Rockford utility infielder who grew up the youngest in a family with five older brothers, her nickname a foregone conclusion. Sis recollects,

> All the kids in the street would get out and play baseball, girls and boys alike. I was such a tomboy, they didn't challenge me. They came to get me to play ball 'cause I was better'n most of the boys anyhow. [She pauses, thinking back, then laughs.] Well, I was. Better'n most of 'em. When you think about it.

I asked Marie "Boston" Mansfield, remembered for her glamour on the mound, whether her older brothers were okay playing with her even though she was a girl.

> Oh, sure. I was a tomboy. I liked to play boys' games. I liked to climb trees, throw snowballs in winter, rocks in summer [she chuckles]. And run! I liked to do most things little girls didn't do.

The players describe themselves almost universally as tomboys. Amy Irene "Lefty" Applegren, a Rockford pitcher, recounted for me the complex interweaving of social pressure, skill, self-fulfilling prophecy, parental support and spirit that kept her in the game.

Lefty talked with me in the kitchen of the home in Peoria, Illinois where her family has lived since 1937. The house is located in a working-class neighborhood, and is a bit down-at-the-heels, dark inside, decorated from an earlier era. It feels peaceful and well-lived-in. Amy Irene lives there with her eighty-eight-year-old mother, Amy Jane, who listened with interest to the interview, kept us in coffee and brownies, and spoke up.

Irene explains,

I played with boys when I was in grade school, the only girl. I got teased a little bit.

Her mom interjects, "She was left-handed and they liked her!" Irene continues,

I know they thought I was a tomboy...I knew I was a girl. I have a twin sister. And an older sister, which makes me the third girl. My twin was born just minutes before me, and when it came my time, the doc said, 'This one's sure to be a boy.'

Irene "Lefty" Applegren winds up to pitch an underhand fastball in the softball era of the All-American game. Applegren later became a hardball pitcher and played ten years in the League.

My twin tried out for a softball team here, but one of those big girls threw the ball so hard at her, it stung her hand, and that was it. But she played tennis and she bowls.

Mother: She's a good golfer.

Irene: My older sister isn't athletic at all. She had rheumatic fever when she was twelve years old and had to lay on her back for a whole year. It must have been hard for her watching us other kids play.

Mother: But she is a wonderful organist.

Susan: How come you kept playing baseball anyway, Irene?

Irene: Oh, because I loved to play ball.

The behavior and presence that made these girls tomboys was completely natural to them; they were just being themselves. I asked Boston Mansfield whether or not, at the time, she thought of the tomboy label as being a value judgment, either negative or positive.

I didn't even consider myself one at the time. After I grew up, my family would say, "She was a real tomboy when she was small." I never gave it a thought really. I just did what I felt like doing. If that was a tomboy, it didn't bother me at all.

Although all the women played primarily with boys when they were young, some found it a relief not to be the only girl. Louise Erickson felt the companionship of her one best girlfriend, who also played, was critical. "I don't know if I would have kept playing, being the only girl, you know."

This business of not wanting to be the only girl resurfaced for Lou in high school, where the baseball coach tried for two years to convince her to play on his boys' team; he wanted to be the first coach in the State of Wisconsin to have a girl play for him. Lou says,

Thank goodness I had brains enough to say no. After all these years he would say to me, "Lou, I'm still mad at you. You wouldn't play baseball for me." I didn't want to play, though, because I knew it was illegal. And I didn't want to make a fool of myself. It was too much attention. I'm not lookin' for that.

The All-Americans are, on the whole, a self-effacing group of women, just as they were a shy group of girls. The source of pleasure for them in their careers was actually playing the game they loved, not basking in the adulation that went with it. A few, of course, relished the limelight and played to the fans, but most simply wanted to get on with the game. They had to learn how to deal with whatever portion of stardom came their way, especially once they became professionals.

You can sense this about them when they talk about playing as young girls. All they wanted to think about was the game they loved. The fact that they were girls wanting to play a boys' game necessarily meant they stood out, especially as they got older. In order to play without undue self-consciousness, they developed a capacity for ignoring their own specialness, an attitude that expressed itself in a chronic understating of their accomplishments. That attitude of humility has followed them through their lives, so that now in their old age they are amazed and more than a bit uneasy to find themselves famous.

Very few players reported mortal struggles with family about their androgynous little-girlhoods. Those who did have to fight a family member or a teacher were the exceptions. Snookie Doyle remembers her particular struggle against a fifth-grade teacher and just how confusing the unstated message was.

> My teacher wanted to stop me from playing with the boys. She didn't think that was a good idea. She had it in her mind, I guess, that you're gonna grow up to be on the wrong side of the fence, as they say, if you're not involved more with the girls. But I see nothing wrong with playing with boys. Don't they really want you to mingle with boys? So I don't know what they're thinking.

But few report such experiences. Perhaps the battles were too subtle to be recalled, or have been forgotten because the girls won them so long ago. Perhaps the poor and working-class families these girls came from had too much on their minds in Depression-era America to be worrying about what their little girls were doing as long as they were safe and fed. I believe, though, that most of these girls were simply blessed while growing up with people who supported them in their natural bent toward being active and risk-taking. While their tales of discouragement are few, their stories of support are many and are gratefully remembered.

◆◆◆

Any enterprise develops its own mythology, a fertile combination of history, creative memory and everyone's desire to tell a good story. One of the myths of the All-American Girls Baseball League is that the girls were all like Dottie Schroeder, innocent young things from farms and small towns. Young they were, and mostly innocent, but not all came from the country. Half of the women I interviewed came from cities as big as or bigger than the middle-sized cities in which they played.[18] All the girls had to adjust to the daunting prospect of leaving home, but their trepidation had less to do with functioning in a big city than with moving outside the confines of their own families.

Of course, those who were from rural small towns faced a truly radical change of environment. Louise Erickson grew up in Arcadia in west central Wisconsin, population around 1,900 in 1950. She lives there now, at age 63, and as I drove up in search of her house, a sign announced the population forty-two years later to be 2,166. Lou was the oldest of seven kids, five of them boys. Her dad was a truck driver and a lab technician for the local creamery, her mom a sales-clerk at the hardware store. Lou was surrounded by support for her athletic interests by the males in her extended family. "I played catch with my dad. He was a very good pitcher for local teams, though I never got to see him play. He showed me how to throw a curveball."

Families were very important to the girls' experience of baseball as they were growing up. My stereotype of a baseball-playing girl was that she was a first-born child with a father who promoted her sports interests. As it turned out, this was a myth based solely, I came to understand, upon my own experience. Only two of the twenty-six players I interviewed are the oldest in their families. Lou Erickson was the oldest of seven children, and Betty Weaver Foss, Fort Wayne's power hitter, the oldest of five. Betty's dad set an example for all the kids.

> My father liked baseball and he played with us quite a bit. He was an avid fan who played country baseball in small towns all around our farm. On Sundays us kids followed him all over.

Mr. Weaver's three daughters all became professional baseball players in the All-American League. Two of them, Betty and Jo, dominated the batting statistics for the last five years of the League. Betty tells the story of one All-American game her father attended.

> My folks had come up to see me, and was sitting right behind the batter's box. We was tied into the 11th inning when I come up to bat. I heard my dad say, "Let's get this game over with, Bess!" and I walked up and hit a home run. That was one of the most wonderful moments in my career.

These fathers were influential in encouraging their first-born daughter's baseball activities. But fathers were critically important to many of the girls, not just the first-borns. Irene Applegren had an older and a twin sister plus two younger brothers. But her father paid attention to Irene's baseball, working on her pitching. Irene later set down League batters for nine years.

> My dad spent many hours out there in the back catchin' me. When I'd come home from school, why he'd have that ball and glove right there ready for me, whether I wanted to or not!

Dottie Collins, a Fort Wayne pitcher, was an only child. Her father too was involved in her young career.

> My dad started training me when I was just knee-high. Every night at 4:30 he came home from work and we were out in the neighbor's empty lot next door, practicing. I loved it. He was really training me; he wanted a pitcher.

Dottie spent six years in the League, was a successful pitcher in both the underhand and overhand eras, and finished with a lifetime 1.83 earned-run average.

Other males in the family were also important. An unusual number of these ballplayers (eighteen of twenty-six) had older brothers; they supported their baby sisters by letting them tag along.[19]

Helen Ketola, a Fort Wayne utility infielder, emulated her brother.

> I hero-worshipped him. I loved to tag behind him, and if he and his friends needed somebody, I was always sittin' on the bench, waitin.' They'd let me go out into right field or some such place.

Vivian Kellogg, Fort Wayne's first baseman, had three older sisters and three older brothers. Her mother died when Vivian was seventeen months old, and the brother nearest to her age took care of her.

> He more or less had to babysit for me. So when he'd go out to play ball, he had to take his baby sister with him. That's where I learned to play ball. They'd stick me in the outfield.

Many a baby sister had to put up with such banishment to the least crucial areas of the field. It is, of course, a wonderful irony that these tag-along little sisters grew up to play the game far beyond what their big brothers achieved.

While fathers and older brothers were major sources of support and example to the girls, mothers were equally powerful influences for some. A mother's support could take the simple form of telling a story that made a big impression on a daughter. Fran Janssen's mother and father were immigrants from Germany "who didn't know anything about baseball."

But mom always bragged about being able to throw the ball the farthest when she was in grade school. She'd talk about that. She still does, and she's ninety-three now!

Kay "Swish" Blumetta, a Fort Wayne pitcher, credits her mother with having kept her spirits up about her career choice. "My father wasn't interested in sports." And some other relatives were more than disinterested.

Some of my relatives would say "When is Kay going to stop playing baseball and get married?" [Swish never did marry.] They talked about baseball like it was a disease or something.

Rockford centerfielder Dottie Key's mom and dad were separated when Dottie was three, and her mom then raised her alone.

My mom worked at a dry-cleaning place at the front counter. We were poor. We couldn't afford bats and balls. Remember when parcels from the store were tied up with string? We saved all the string, and my ball was made from this hard ball of string. My mom and I varnished it. Somebody else made me a bat.

At the time Dottie was playing ball just for fun; her real sport was speedskating. A friend saw Dottie whizzing along the ice and suggested to her mom that she might "go places." Her mother moved herself and Dottie to the big city of Winnipeg to further her daughter's skating career. There Dottie began to play softball on the side, and that's how scouts discovered her.

Not every mother's support was completely benign. Over the course of the League's twelve-year history, eight Cuban girls were recruited to play. Isabel Alvarez, a pitcher who played for several teams including Fort Wayne in 1951 and 1954, experienced her mother as overpowering. "I didn't tell my mother I wanted to be a ballplayer; my mother told me I'm gonna be a ballplayer."

Although Isabel's father was a policeman for Cuba's dictator Batista, the family was not well off. "There was never enough food to go around. We were not poor poor, but the middle class didn't have nothing either." Although Isabel's baseball had been limited to street play, at age eleven her mother took her to see the manager of a Cuban girls' team that was forming. She introduced Isabel, "This is my daughter. She's a pitcher and outfielder." The manager took a liking to Isabel, and she joined the team.

Isabel Alvarez, one of eight Cuban girls recruited for the League, winds up to pitch for the Chicago Colleens. In 1947 the All-American players, managers and chaperones assembled for spring training in Havana, where the womens' contests outdrew the Brooklyn Dodgers' spring-training games.

I used to spend weekends out there training, and he fed us, and we stayed overnight. I was having a real good time because there were a whole bunch of girls, and we were eating good and everything, and playing ball. I loved it!

Isabel recounted many examples of her mother's controlling behavior, but looking back, she credits this difficult mother with pushing her into a "destiny" that has turned out okay. "Those Cuban people are having a rough time, and I'm doing very well here. (She still lives in Fort Wayne.) That was a gift to me. My mother had a vision."

A majority of the female ballplayers had some kind of family support for their activities. But several of the players had to find their support outside the family. They did so, and managed to flourish anyway.

Thelma "Tiby" Eisen, Fort Wayne's centerfielder, spent years playing softball, informally with other kids and later on fine women's teams, largely without attention from her family. Tiby had moved away from home to play baseball professionally when her father finally took enough notice to ask, "Just what do you do?" Tiby told him she was an outfielder. "What's an outfielder?" he replied.

◆◆◆

Baseball is historically a sport played by and for the working classes of this country. Though invented and first played by middle-class men of British ancestry, "by the end of the nineteenth century the Irish-Americans and the German-Americans had all but taken over."[20] These were people with immigrant backgrounds and not yet much money, who embraced baseball as a way of pledging allegiance to their new homeland. According to sports sociologist Allen Guttman, "Baseball was the national game. To know baseball was to be a real American." It was also a sport associated with the "lower classes." "Baseball, like soccer, began as the invention of the middle class and was taken over by society's less privileged members."

The great majority of the families of the twenty-six Peaches and Daisies I interviewed were working-class (thirteen families) or poorer (five families).[21] These hard-working families, single mothers and one single father also had to contend with the Depression, the poorest time for the most people in modern American history. In fact it was usually either the Depression or a marital separation or a death that moved a family from working-class into a more poverty-stricken situation.

The stock market crash of 1929 was the dramatic beginning of over a decade of the worst economic times the country has known. Blanche Wiesen Cook, Eleanor Roosevelt's recent biographer, describes the country in 1933, when the Depression was well under way.

> The United States credit structure was paralyzed. In state after state, banks closed and locked their doors. Fear mounted as the savings of millions of Americans—workers, farmers, small-business families—seemed to be locked behind iron gates. The savings of countless oth-

ers had simply evaporated as 85,000 businesses failed. Over 13 million Americans were unemployed, more than 25 per cent of the entire work force.[22]

All of the women except two that I talked with were born between 1922 and 1931. By 1933 most of the girls were between two and eleven years old. These children were easily old enough to experience the threatening possibilities and sobering realities facing themselves and their families.

Dottie Wiltse Collins' father worked for the Standard Oil Company as a welder and "lead burner," a job that went out of existence once the four or five men in the country so skilled had retired.

> He went to work there when he was fourteen years old, lied about his age. When the Depression hit, they gave him his notice, and he tore it up. He said there was no way they were gonna get rid of him, and they didn't. He worked all through the Depression.

Even so, the Wiltse family did not have any extra money.

> I can always remember, I wanted a bicycle for Christmas so bad. This was right in the middle of the Depression. And Christmas morning, I had my bicycle. But I didn't find out 'til years later that my Dad stole it. When he got off work one night, he stole a fellow worker's bicycle, brought it home, repainted it in the neighbor's garage. That was my Christmas present!

Norma Metrolis, like most of these women, saw her family's poverty as relative. Her dad was an auto mechanic and later an installer of gas equipment. "No," says Norma, "we weren't poor; everybody was poor then."

The fact that these girls grew up in working-class homes may have helped them in their efforts to be ballplayers. In the working-class family women are expected to work, often at physically demanding jobs, and girls see their mothers doing such work. The demands our society places on girls to become "feminine" runs counter to this experience of working-class females.

Looking and acting feminine means being decorative and frivolous, dependent and powerless, what Susan Brownmiller calls an "artful fragility." It is primarily middle-class people, aspiring to "borrow the affectations of upper-class status," who pay attention to their girls being "ladylike."[23] Working-class girls raised in the Depression escaped such ornamentations. Most of these girls' families did not have the time or the inclination to instruct them in how to act middle-class, in how to look and talk and act like ladies. They were free instead to play ball with the boys.

Sandlot and street corner baseball was the sport these girls could afford. The game was right at home, involved minimal equipment that could be fabricated from homemade materials (or simply imagined), and could be played anywhere with any number of kids. Looking back, the players are completely aware of the social and economic distance between themselves and girls who could afford other, more upper-class women's sports. They are also painfully aware of the economic benefits they might have enjoyed had they played a different game. Even Dottie Schroeder, who played ball with no purpose but pure enjoyment, can look back and imagine a more lucrative sports career.

> As much as I love baseball, as much as I love playing, for a lot of girls in our league, if we would've been brought up playing tennis or golf, we'd be making a lot more money than we do now. But we were born in that era when tennis and golf was a rich person's game.

At the time none of the girls could think of baseball as a potential job. And, by definition, there was no money in amateur softball. Tiby Eisen had already tried several unusual careers. At eighteen (and 5 feet 4 inches, 135 pounds) Tiby played fullback and linebacker in the first women's football league. The year was 1940.

> We played a few games here in L.A., and they stopped us. So we got two teams together and went to Mexico to play. We had a wonderful time, and thousands of people came out to watch us, but they didn't pay much, you know. By the time we were ready to come home, the United States' Embassy had to help us get back.

> Women weren't supposed to do those things. Women didn't play football. Women stayed home and, you know, got married and cooked and took care of the babies.

> People thought football was too rough for women. But we were well protected. We had foam-rubber pads around our breasts and shoulders. We really couldn't get hurt, unless somebody five hundred pounds bounced on you. But nobody weighed that much!

I asked Tiby where she thought she got her adventurous spirit. She remembers she was unique in her family.

I always had dreams of doing all these wonderful things, and some of them I did, and some of them I didn't. But I never dreamed of being a professional baseball player, because women didn't play baseball.

◆◆◆

Women did, however, play softball. Almost all the girls who became All-Americans played some form of organized softball before they joined the League. Helen Nicol "Nickie" Fox, a Rockford pitcher, benefited from Canada's fine system of softball leagues. It was while Nickie was competing in Regina, Saskatchewan, for the Western Canada playoffs, that a scout saw her pitch.

I get this wire from Chicago asking me if I'd consider comin' down to play ball in the United States for $85 per week. At the time I was making $12.50 a week clerking for the Army Navy Department Store. I must admit, I didn't believe them at first and had my coach check out whether the offer was for real or not.

Nickie joined the League in its first year, 1943, pitching for the Kenosha Comets.

The girls in California (Dottie Collins, Snookie Doyle and Tiby Eisen were California girls who played for either the Peaches or Daisies in 1950) were able to play in highly developed softball systems sponsored by the Los Angeles Parks Department; they could play all year as well. Dottie Collins remembers her first position in organized softball, bat girl.

We had great leagues out there. Great leagues. They always had men's and women's games together. The women play the first game, the men the second. So consequently you were all involved. This one team asked my Dad if I could be their bat girl. And that's how I got started. At nine years old that was real exciting, you know. I had a satin uniform to wear!

Our team was very good. We only carried one pitcher, and she was excellent, one of the best in the state. We were playing in the Southern California Championships at the old Wrigley Field in L.A., and she just went to pot. She never did that before in her life. She couldn't get the ball over the plate.

By this time we were down nine to nothin'. So, just for the hell of it, the manager put me in. It became just a fun thing, and the girls relaxed, and we won the damn ballgame. I was eleven years old . . . And there were 25,000 people in the grandstand!

Dottie went on to play women's softball for Bill Allington, and it was through Bill's contact with the All-Americans that she and six other California girls arrived to play in the Midwest in 1944.

Often players had met each other in battle before they joined the All-Americans. The level of excellence at which they played meant they would clash in championship softball competitions around the country.

Lefty Applegren was pitching for her team, the Caterpillar Tractor Company's "Dieseletes" when she encountered Connie Wisniew-ski's team in the National Softball Championships in Detroit in 1944. Although at age seventeen Applegren won both the games she pitched, her team lost to Wisniewski's.

Both Applegren and Wisniewski were recruited for the 1944 season by scouts at these National Championships. Wisniewski, playing for the Grand Rapids Chicks, went on to become the League's best pitcher in the early years when pitchers threw underhand. Her earned-run averages of 0.81 and 0.96 won her pitching honors for the years 1945 and 1946. Wisniewski tied with Joanne Winter in the 1946 season for most games ever won by an AAGBL pitcher, 33. Wisniewski's record was 33-9, Winter's 33-10.

Mary Rountree played girls' softball around the Miami area. She caught for her Miami Beach team in the National Softball Tournament in 1938 and in 1940 for a St. Petersburg team. Like Nickie Fox, Mary didn't believe the first offer from the All-Americans could be legitimate.

> I was working for the State Department in Washington, D.C., in 1944, and a stranger called the apartment. I don't even know how he got my name or number. So this gentleman identifies himself. "My name is Arthur Meyerhoff, and I'm the advertising manager for Phil K. Wrigley, who owns the Chicago Cubs. I need a catcher very badly in South Bend, Indiana, and I'd like you to seriously consider taking the job, and I'll arrange for your transportation tomorrow."
>
> Well, any girl with any common sense knows any Joe Blow can call you up and say, "meet me such and such a place," and that's the way a lot of girls get hurt. I didn't know if this man was who he said he was. And I'm just an ordinary little kid [Mary was twenty-two in 1944].

So I told him that I couldn't go, which was true, because I had three brothers in the service, and I had to keep myself available for any kind of emergencies at home, because there were no men to go down there to help tend to whatever problem might arise.

In 1945 my brothers came home, and by that time Max Carey, the President of the League, had called and said, "Mary, whenever you're ready, let us know, because we'd like you to come and play." Mr. Carey had come over to Flamingo Park and had seen us play. I didn't go to play until 1946.

By the time Helen Ketola joined the League in 1950, older players from the League itself were acting as recruiters. Helen was a young-ster in Quincy, Massachusetts when Mary Pratt, who had pitched from 1943 until 1947, became Helen's junior high school gym teacher.

I idolized her. I waited for her every morning at her office door. She was probably sick of seeing me there. It's what they call hero-worship. Later I've become her friend, and I always say, "Mary, if it wasn't for you, I wouldn't have been in sports." She should have been athletic director for the City of Quincy, no doubt about it. They gave it to a man.

Mary Pratt told four girls about the local try-outs in Medford, Mas-sachusetts. Two girls eventually made the League.

Three of the twenty-six Daisies and Peaches came to the League by way of men's baseball. Wilma Briggs, Fort Wayne's rightfielder, played for her father's team in East Greenwich, Rhode Island, the "Frenchtown Farmers." Betty Weaver Foss played for a men's team in Ledbetter, Kentucky. It sounds a bit rough, though Betty puts it delicately enough: "It was nerve-wracking. I was the first woman that'd ever played down there with them. They were just country people and didn't know the finer points of baseball."

Lou Erickson played nothing more organized than pick-up base-ball in her small Wisconsin town and now can compare herself with the more experienced players.

They played in fast-pitch leagues in their home towns on the coast, either coast, and in Canada and Cuba. I played on the back streets with the neighbor kids. At the time I didn't think about it. I really didn't. I just figured, well, I knew how to play ball.

A coach from a neighboring town sent Lou's name to the League office in 1946, though it took her until 1948 to make the circuit. Lou is still amazed that she was ever discovered, "How they found me, that's enough right there. From a little hole in the hill like this is . . . and to have it turn out like it did!"

◆◆◆

What did it take to be an All-American player? Many players had family support, some didn't. Many had organized leagues to help develop their talent, some didn't. Snookie Doyle's story may illustrate the most important characteristics of all: talent, tenacity and a love of baseball.

Snookie started out playing softball in school and with the boys in the street.

> I was a tomboy, as many girls are. I was the only child, with my mother, but she didn't bring me up to be a boy; she brought me up to be a person.
>
> My uncle had a catcher's glove that my grandmother hid behind her player piano. If my grandmother wasn't around I would sneak the mitt out and play catch with it. We used boards instead of bats. And we'd sew up our balls when they'd split and use them over and over again.
>
> My mother had gotten me a catcher's mitt and a baseball uniform when I was about five. My mother was a great baseball fan.
>
> There was only one other girl who played ball in elementary school. In fact, that girl was just six days younger than I was. Her mother and my mother had a race to see whose baby was going to be born first.
>
> My teacher wanted to stop me from playing with the boys. She didn't think that was a good idea. She stopped allowing me to play in fifth grade, but I'd go home and be playin' ball with the boys.
>
> We would play "burnout." They'd try to throw at me as hard as I could take it. Their mother would get upset with them because she thought they were being too hard on me, but I loved it! They were trying to get me to quit, is really what it was. They didn't want to be bothered with a little kid. I was maybe nine or ten, and they were five or six years older. But I had my own catcher's glove by that time.
>
> When they didn't want me to play with them that day they'd say, "Well, Snookie, let's play 'left-out' today." I'll never forget that. And it was my ball!

This feeling of being left out was one all the girls had to struggle with. It was the nature of these youngsters who would grow up to be All-Americans to want to do things uncharacteristic of their sex, to be more active and risk-taking and free. As a result, they were left out, unwilling to join with other girls in girl-type activities, and sometimes unwelcome in their attempts to do boy-type things. They were also isolated because they performed at a level of skill unusual for either sex. Not until professional baseball became available to them did they find others who could match their skill, determination, courage and competitive spirit.

Snookie remembers, "I used to be so sad because we never did have a girls' league. My aunt said to me one time, 'Someday, Snookie, they're gonna have a league, a girls' league, and then you're gonna be able to play.'"

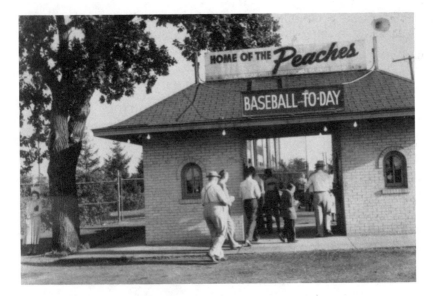

The ticket gate at Rockford's Beyer Stadium, home of the Peaches.

The 1950 Fort Wayne Daisies outside their team bus. Left to right: Manager Max Carey, Dottie Collins, Doris Tetzlaff (coach chaperone), Wilma Briggs, Vivian Kellogg, Helen Ketola, Mary Rountree and Ruth Matlock.

GAME TWO

Monday, September 11, 1950

Rockford's 3-1 defeat of Fort Wayne in the opening game was unexpected, not because Rockford was unaccustomed to winning, but because they did so with such ferocity at the plate. Normally the Peaches won through excellent pitching, consistent defense, and a trick or two. In Game One they pounded premier Daisies pitcher Maxine Kline for fifteen hits. The Daisies, a power-hitting team, managed only four hits against Nickie Fox.

With all that hitting, however, the Peaches scored only three runs. They left eleven runners stranded, surely a cause for concern for Manager Allington.

As they approached Game Two, the visiting Daisies would have worked with special fervor, hoping to win on Rockford's home turf, thus splitting the first two games and establishing their own home-field advantage for the remaining five games, three to be played in Fort Wayne, the last two in Rockford.

When the Peaches and Daisies took the field for the second game of their championship series, both teams had plenty of woman-power to do the job of winning. Rockford's and Fort Wayne's contending championship teams sparkled with sixteen players named to the 1950 All-Star team.

After the regular season ended, thirty-seven players from eight teams were honored for their excellence by the sports editors of League city newspapers. Selection to the first team meant the editors felt this player was the best in the League at the particular position. The Peaches had been awarded nine All-Star spots—more than any other team—with five on the first team. The Daisies placed seven girls, two on the first team.

The thirteen-member first team was led off by Dottie Kamenshek, Rockford's first baseman, the only player to receive ninety votes—a unanimous choice by the editors. Dottie eventually played ten years in the League and was selected to the All-Star team seven of those years. In 1950 she ended the season second in batting with a .334 average. Kamenshek's defensive play was typically consistent during the championship series and her bat and fielding led the Rockford team. In Game One, for instance, Kammie hit 3-for-4, scored one of Rockford's three runs, and made ten put-outs.

Dottie was joined on the first All-Star team by four other Rockford players. Snookie Doyle was chosen at shortstop and received the third-highest number of votes of any player, seventy-five out of a possible ninety.[24] Doyle played an excellent Game Two in the championship series. In the field she made a spectacular throw to beat one of Fort Wayne's fastest runners, Tiby Eisen, ran down another experienced baserunner, Willie Briggs, between third and home to prevent a run scoring, and had a total of two put-outs and four assists. At the plate she had two hits in five at-bats, batted in one run and scored another.

Lois Florreich, a twenty-game winner for the Peaches in the 1950 season, was chosen a first-team All-Star pitcher. Lois finished 1950 with a 20-8 won-lost record (a .714 winning percentage) and was the undisputed strikeout queen, fanning 171 batters, fifty-three more than her closest rival. Lois had a reputation of being intimidating to batters, her incredible speed sometimes coupled with an alarming lack of control.[25] Florreich will get her chance to pitch for the Peaches in Game Three of the championship series.

Jackie Kelley, a utility player named to the first team, was a major factor in Rockford's championship series because she replaced the injured Alice Pollitt at third base. Pollitt had torn ankle ligaments earlier in the season and had to watch the series from the bench.

Rockford's fifth first-team All-Star choice, catcher Ruth Richard, was another casualty of the regular season. Ruth broke her ankle in the last game and joined Al Pollitt in a banged-up cheering section.

Fort Wayne placed two players on the All-Star first team. Evie Wawryshyn, their second baseman enjoying her best year in the AAGBL, finished the season third in the batting race with a .311 average. Evie had the series of her life at the plate during the 1950 championship.

The other Fort Wayne first-team All-Star was Maxine Kline, who won more games (twenty-three wins to nine losses) and had the best winning percentage (.742) of all League pitchers. Max got pummelled by the Peaches in the first game of this series, but this was unlikely to happen again.

The second-team All-Stars named from Fort Wayne were Wilma Briggs, Betty Foss and Naomi "Sally" Meier. Briggs was Fort Wayne's rightfielder and a successful individual performer in Game Two. She scored both Fort Wayne runs, had one hit in three at-bats, and made two put-outs. Betty Weaver Foss, Fort Wayne's powerful third baseman, was the only rookie in the League to capture an All-Star position. Tall, strong and fast, Betty captured the League batting crown, her final average of .346 beating out both Kamenshek and teammate Wawryshyn.

Sally Meier was acquired by Fort Wayne in mid-season to be their regular leftfielder and performed well both in the field and at the plate during the regular season and in the championship series.

Rockford's sole representative on the second-string All-Star team was Dottie Key, the centerfielder, known for her speed on the bases and in the field. Dottie found many ways to get on base, even if that meant not quite getting out of the way of an errant pitch.

Fort Wayne placed two players on the All-Star third team, shortstop Dottie Schroeder and centerfielder Tiby Eisen. Rockford's three third-team All-Stars were Eleanor Callow in left field, Al Pollitt at third base, and pitcher Lou Erickson.

Erickson's 1950 regular season record of sixteen wins and ten losses won her the starting role in the second game of the championship series. She faced Millie Deegan, Fort Wayne's choice for Game Two starter with a record just a hair better than Erickson's: sixteen wins and nine losses. Rain on Sunday had forced postponement of Game Two; both teams had to wait an extra anxious day to resume their confrontation.

Peaches Take 2nd Straight from Daisies
Erickson Pitches 7 - 2 Victory

Staff sportswriter
Rockford Morning Star, September 12, 1950

One big inning, the second, when the Peaches scored seven runs, gave the league pennant winners a 2-0 edge over Fort Wayne as the Peaches defeated the Daisies, 7-2 here Monday night.

The two teams move on to Fort Wayne tonight, where the next three games are scheduled to be played. Manager Bill Allington of the Peaches announced that Lois Florreich, his ace hurler, will take the mound tonight in an effort to make it three straight over Fort Wayne. Manager Max Carey said Dottie Collins would try to stop the Peaches in tonight's game.

The game was started in a fine mist that cleared up after a couple of innings had been played. The Daisies jumped away to a one-run lead in the first inning. After one was out Wilma Briggs hit an easy grounder to Erickson, who tossed the ball high over Dottie Kamenshek's head, Briggs going to second. She went to third on Evelyn Wawryshyn's infield out and scored on Betty Foss' single.

Deegan is Wild

Millie Deegan gave evidence that her control wasn't the best when she walked Kamenshek in the last of the first inning. In attempting to bunt, Snookie Doyle popped out to Dottie Schroeder who doubled Kamenshek at first.

The last half of the second inning was a different story. Rose Gacioch started the Peaches rally with a single. Charlene Barnett beat out a bunt and then Deegan blew up. She walked Eleanor Callow to load the bases and then hit Marilyn Jones with a pitched ball to force in Gacioch. She walked Erickson to force in Barnett, and then threw four wide ones to force in Callow.

Kamenshek grounded to Kellogg, who threw Jones out at the plate. Fran Janssen had relieved Deegan before Kamenshek grounded into the force play at the plate. Snookie Doyle singled to score Erickson, Jackie Kelley singled to score Key and Kamenshek, and Gacioch drove out her second hit of the inning to score Doyle. The Peaches were held runless by Janssen the rest of the way.

The Daisies scored their second run in the third inning when Briggs singled and scored on Wawryshyn's double, her first of two two-base hits. Erickson was in trouble in the first of the eighth when she walked Briggs. Wawryshyn hit a ground rule double, Briggs stopping at third. Foss grounded to Kelley and Briggs was tagged out by Doyle in the run down between third and home. Sally Meier struck out and Schroeder flied out to Doyle to end the threat.

Two Spectacular Plays

Doyle made a great play on Thelma Eisen's grounder in the third, going back of third to field the ball and throwing Eisen out at first. In the fourth Meier hit a line drive over Barnett's head that appeared to be ticketed for extra bases. Barnett leaped into the air, spearing the ball one-handed.

A collection was taken among the fans for Catcher Ruth Richard, who broke her ankle in the last game of the regular season. The total collected was $602. Ruth will have to wear a cast on her leg for eight more weeks.

Summary

Runs - Briggs 2, Kamenshek, Doyle, Gacioch, Barnett, Callow, Erickson, Key. Errors - Meier, Kellogg, Erickson. Runs batted in - Wawryshyn, Foss, Doyle, Kelley 2, Gacioch, Jones, Erickson, Key. Doubles - Wawryshyn 2, Foss. Double plays - Schroeder to Kellogg, Schroeder to Foss. Left on base - Fort Wayne, 7, Rockford, 8. Base on balls - Off Deegan 4, Janssen 2, Erickson 3. Strike outs - Erickson 3. Hit by pitch - Jones (Deegan), Erickson (Janssen). Winning pitcher - Erickson. Losing pitcher - Deegan. Time - 1:45. Attendance - 2,397.

Rightfielder Wilma Briggs was Fort Wayne's ideal team player, batting second and sacrificing teammate Tiby Eisen along the bases.

Wilma Briggs waiting her turn at bat during an exhibition ball game played by former All-Americans at their 1986 reunion.

WILMA "WILLIE" BRIGGS

Fort Wayne, Right Fielder

Statistics: Born: 1930. Home town: East Greenwich, Rhode Island. Height: 5 feet 4-½ inches. Playing weight: 138 pounds. Bats: Left. Throws: Right. Entered League:1948 at age 17. Teams: Fort Wayne, 1948-1953; South Bend, 1954. Lifetime totals: Batting average: .258. Fielding percentage: in right field, .962; at first base, .970.

Wilma Briggs gave Game Two of the championship her all, but one player having a good day does not a win make. Willie would be the first person to agree, because throughout her career she was the consummate team player.

A winning spirit means that everybody's working with one another, helping one another, talking to one another, sharing with one another. You know—whatever you did was for the team, not for yourself.

Wilma, batting second, and Tiby Eisen, leading off, had perfected an interdependence of skill, knowledge and intuition that makes the game of baseball complex, subtle and intense. The twosome also accounted for a lot of Daisies runs. Playing the Peaches just raised the stakes higher.

We used to love to play Rockford and beat 'em, because they were the New York Yankees of the League. And Max [Carey] wanted to beat Bill [Allington] so bad!

The most exciting play for me—it wouldn't be exciting for anybody but me—was when, with Tiby at first, Max would say, "Bluff the bunt, and find out who's covering second. Then hit through that hole." Well naturally Snookie, Rockford's shortstop, would be covering, because I was left-handed and therefore more likely to hit between first and second. When Tiby runs, Snookie's gonna take the throw for a forceout, because the second basemen has to stay put to field my hit.

So we bluff the bunt, Tiby's gone—actually it was a run and hit, not the hit and run—and poor old Snookie . . . She takes one step toward second, so right away I know for sure what I figured anyway, that she's gonna cover. Snookie's almost to the bag and I hit just right through that hole where she was. I mean, that was so perfect!

And Max is over in the coach's box jumpin' up and down! I thought he was gonna stand on his hands, you know, 'cause he loved to do something like that against Rockford. That was exciting for me.

◆◆◆

I interviewed Wilma Briggs during a lull in the activities of the 1992 mini-reunion of the All-American Girls Professional Baseball League Players' Association, an organization formed in 1987 by ex-players to facilitate socializing, look out for each others' welfare, and promote recognition of the League. We were in Fort Wayne, Wilma's home for six of her seven playing years.

Willie is sixty-one years old now, tan, freckled and in excellent shape. Ten years ago she led her local softball league in batting. "I was ten years older than the oldest, and at least twice the age of most of them." She retired from the game only last year, having played softball for thirty-seven years *after* her baseball career. She is talkative and earnest, with a clipped Rhode Island accent, and energetic even when sitting for an interview, often gesturing and jumping up to demonstrate a point.

Growing up, Wilma always played baseball.

I never played softball. My father had a baseball team, and I had seven brothers—and four sisters—but all the boys and I played baseball. I was born in the middle of my brothers.

My father was never quite good enough to make anybody's team, so he said, "I'll have my own team." He was a dairy farmer, so our team became the Frenchtown [a section of East Greenwich] Farmers. He always put me in the game, first in right field, pretty soon at first base. He said, "You won't get hurt there because all you have to do is catch the ball."

East Greenwich, Rhode Island, where Wilma was born and now lives, had a population of three thousand when she was growing up. Now maybe twelve thousand people call it home. Her mom worked on the farm and raised twelve children.

Nick, the pitcher on her father's team, coached high-school baseball, basketball, football and gym. The summer before Wilma's senior year his first baseman had gone to Sea Scout camp, and he asked Wilma to play first base for him.

I said, "Boy, fine!" At the end of the summer he said, "Why don't you go out for the high school team next spring?" I became the only female high school baseball player in the state. After I went out for this team, two other girls in Rhode Island tried out and made high school teams, but they were never in a game.

If I had it to do over, I probably wouldn't do it. Because Nick didn't wind up coaching the team. And I really felt like the new coach was a little prejudiced. He treated me all right, and I did play, I played the outfield. But he never played me on first base, and I was really a better hitter than the regular first baseman. He just stuck me in now and then.

I went to Nick and said, "You know, probably I shouldn't be playing." But the school had gotten so much publicity he said, "Can you stick it out?" Well, sure.

I didn't ride on the bus with the rest of the team. I rode with my father. He went to all the games anyway, but I had that feeling. It was uncomfortable when you got to the ballpark, and the whole team went in the locker room where I never went. It was an experience, to say the least.

I remember we played one team and there must have been two or three hundred people in the stands. Usually high school games didn't draw that many fans. And soon as I batted, they all left! They only came to see me. That was kind of embarrassing too.

A local sportwriter contacted the League on Wilma's behalf, and just after high school graduation in 1948, she made the trip all the way to Fort Wayne for a try-out.

I was so petrified that by the time I had my try-out and they said "You made it," I was ready to go home. So Max Carey [then League President] said, "Well, offer her more money." Well, money had nothing to do with it. I was scared. I had never stayed away from home before. So, instead of starting at the rookie pay, $55 a week, I started at $60. I should have cried a little bit more!

The competition for making a team in the only professional baseball league available to women was fierce. Only about twenty percent of the aspiring players actually made the League.[26] Every year many prospects failed to get beyond their local try-outs. If they succeeded at that level, they advanced to spring training, a pre-season period of a few weeks when all the League players congregated at one place to get in shape and show their stuff for League management, team owners and managers. Rookies could fail to make a team during spring training or even later, after they'd been assigned to a team. They went home, maybe to try again another year, usually to settle for the traditional jobs and lives that awaited them.

Rookies were not, however, the only vulnerable players. Veterans had to prove themselves anew each year, and they scrutinized the incoming crop of rookies with caution. This was the natural reaction of Vivian Kellogg, Fort Wayne's veteran first baseman, when seventeen-year-old Wilma appeared.

> Kelly has since told me how she felt when I showed up for my try-out. "I saw this rookie comin' with this red cap on and a first baseman's glove. Boy I hated you as soon as I saw that glove!" Then she found out we were both born on November 6th. I wasn't so bad then.
>
> When the Fort Wayne team got to Chicago [the Chicago Colleens existed briefly in1948 and became a travelling team the following year], they had me pinch hit. I'm still petrified, right? I fouled off two or three or four—I used to hit a lot of foul balls—and one of them, I really ripped it. It was foul, but it would have been out of there. So then Max Carey wanted me to stay in Chicago, but Fort Wayne's coach, Dick Bass said, "No, we want to keep her. We don't have any left-handed batters." So I stayed with Fort Wayne.
>
> They didn't really need me to catch or play first base. Fort Wayne had Kelly and Mary Rountree. But they did need left-handed batters, so really, that's why I got in.
>
> I played right field. I think I was there less than two weeks and I was playing right field in a regular position. Then I got charley horses.[27] The muscles just knot up, and these knobs form and crawl up and down your legs. It's much worse than cramps, which you

could just rub out. Where I lived I was crawling up and down stairs, and my landlady would say, "You should tell somebody." I said, "No way. If I tell them, they'll take me out, and I may never get back in." That's how much everybody wanted to play! "Don't take me out of the line-up. I'm all right!"

Finally they found out about them, and Millie Deegan [a Fort Wayne pitcher] said, "I'll fix those." She put extra-strong Musterole, the worst, mustiest-smelling salve, and hot, wet towels on me. I had blisters like a sunburn peeling, but after two days they were gone. It was incredible.

My father's team had only played once a week, and here I was playing every day. After that I got in shape in spring training.

All the girls who made a team in the All-American League were by definition good ballplayers, but few knew much about the strategy of playing winning baseball. The calibre of coaching enjoyed by both the Peaches and the Daisies meant players could learn the subtleties of the game. Willie told me, "As much as I had played baseball, I had no idea all of the strategies that were part of the game." She explained, for example, how to distinguish between two subtly different plays, the hit and run and the run and hit. The latter was the play Tiby and she had worked with such good effect against Snookie Doyle.

In the hit and run, the runner goes, and your job at the plate is to protect that runner. So you've gotta try to hit the ball on the ground no matter what the pitch is. The runner's gone, she's dead if you don't do your part. That's on a hit and run.

On a run and hit, it's the runner's responsibility not to get caught if you hit a line drive or a fly ball, something that can be caught. So she's gonna start, and then hesitate enough to find out what you do with the ball. If it's on the ground, she can go ahead.

In the one play you *have* to get the ball on the ground. The other you try to, but if you don't, that's her responsibility. Well, I'd never heard of either one before the All-American League.

I'd never heard of the delayed steal. Suppose you got runners on first and third. If you're the runner on first, you take off like you're really goin' to second. Now, the poor catcher says, "Holy cow! She's goin' to second." And you stop. But the catcher still throws to second, and the runner scores on the throw.

You're hoping the runner is on the ball and is taking a good lead, 'cause a smart catcher will fake the throw to second, turn and throw to third, and the runner's dead. But it took catchers a long time to learn that, so that was a good play.

Now the Peaches' Bill Allington, they didn't call him the Silver Fox for nothing. He had another play. You've got a runner on third and one at first with nobody out, and a pop fly's hit to the catcher. It's a foul ball. Allington would have the runners tag up, and the one at first heads for second after the catch. [A foul ball that is caught is in play.] The catcher throws to second for an easy second out, but in the meantime the runner on third tags up and scores.

There were a lot of things like that—the element of surprise. You couldn't always do it, the circumstances had to be right. But boy, when it worked, wow!

What every player wanted was good coaching, someone who knew these skills and strategies and could teach them.

Max came to coach Fort Wayne in 1950 and 1951. He was a great base stealer [Carey led the National League in stolen bases for ten seasons.], so he had everyone running. I stole twenty-nine or thirty bases in 1950, and I don't think I stole two the year before. [According to her baseball card, Wilma stole two bases in 1948, fifteen in 1949, twenty-nine in 1950, and thirty-two in 1951.]

I played for him for two years. He taught me to bunt and how to fake a bunt. "Don't give it away," he'd say. When you bunt as a sacrifice, just to move the runner along, you turn around and give yourself help connecting with the ball. But when you're bunting for a base hit, you don't want anybody in the ballpark to know you're gonna bunt. So you stand up there like you're really gonna go for it. Of course, you've got to deaden the ball so it doesn't roll a mile. I'd be four steps out of there, and my bat is just hitting the ball!

I loved bunting behind Eisen. If I was out, it was a sacrifice. If I was safe, it was a hit. I couldn't lose.

I don't know how he had the patience. He spent hours and hours with me. In batting practice, everybody else would hit five, bunt two. I'd bunt five and hit two until I learned to do it. So you can see why I liked Max Carey.

When I went home I taught my brothers how to do it. My left-handed brother Jerry was a good little ballplayer, and became the best bunter in his softball league. He'd say, "My sister taught me!"

Since I was left-handed, Max taught me to block the catcher out. With a runner on first, a left-handed batter could get in the way just enough so the catcher didn't know when the runner was stealing. You go after the ball, and then you just kind of turn and back up. The catcher has to step a little bit to the side to see around you. But you have to do it on every single pitch; it has to become part of your natural move. Otherwise the umpire's gonna say you're obstructing. If it's part of your natural movement, and the catcher hits you, that's her problem; you're not obstructing. Little things like that give you the edge.

Wilma Briggs is never happier than when she's talking about baseball. Unless, of course, she's playing baseball. She described more of the routines she and Tiby developed to keep the opposing team off-balance. The point of all of them was to move Tiby—the batter ahead of Wilma—ever closer to home plate and a score.

Max kinda had a system with us. If Tiby's on first, my job batting behind her is to get her to second. She was supposed to steal, because Max didn't want me wasting a hit to move her to second.

I could also protect her if she didn't steal. I could place the ball pretty well and keep her from being forced out. He wasn't depending on my power; he was depending on me to move her over to the next base, one way or another, for the power behind me [Evie Wawry-shyn, Betty Foss] to bring her in.

So Tiby and I had our own signal. She'd just go down her skirt and touch the hem, and that meant this is her pitch, she's gonna go on this one. So I don't swing. When she'd get to second by stealing, now I could either drop a bunt or gloss [fake] a bunt. When I bunt, I'm bunting to beat it out, not for a sacrifice. Suppose I look like I'm gonna bunt, but I hold the bat back and they call it a ball. Now the third baseman's coming in, sometimes Tiby could steal behind the third baseman.

So now Max says, "Maybe if the third baseman's playing back, drop the bunt. If she's playing in on the end of your bat, gloss the bunt." So we had another thing, just look at the third baseman and let her position tell us what to do next.

Now here's this runner that was on first is now on third. 'Course I probably got two strikes on me by now. But I've moved her two bases. And although she's done the running, I did my job too. I helped her by what I did and didn't do at the plate. It didn't matter if I then grounded out, or popped out, or struck out on the next pitch. I got two batters behind me that can bring her in. To do what you were supposed to do. You cannot imagine how exciting that was to me!

I made a lot of sacrifices by batting second. My job wasn't to get hits. A good hitter is very selective, she waits for a pitch she really likes. Well, I couldn't do that. My pitch was always gone before I had a chance to swing! But if we win, who cares?

So then Max said, "You need to learn to hit down the third-base line," which I could never do being a left-handed batter. Well, he taught me that. Now, I'm left-handed, right? And I had a very closed stance [feet lined up parallel to the plate]. [Willie has jumped to her feet now and has assumed her batting stance next to the easy chair in my hotel room. Her hands are together on the imaginary bat, holding it high, cocking it a little, keeping loose for the incoming pitch.] Now most of the time I'd come around like this and really pull the ball. [She swings from her heels, hitting the imaginary ball just a little ahead of the plate.] Max said, "Stand the same way, but now you're gonna hit the ball after it's come back even with you, almost by you." He taught me how to do that. And that was really exciting. Third basemen like Al Pollitt and Jackie Kelley would be out there, off balance, rockin' back and forth, "We never knew if you were gonna bunt or not. If we moved in, you hit it by us. We never knew what to do with you."

Less able managers could destroy a good thing, an established relationship between two players that felt right and worked well for the team. Sometimes the players let their coach know what might work better.

Jimmy Foxx [a Hall of Fame big leaguer who coached Fort Wayne in 1952] had me batting fourth, he had me third, he had me fifth, and I wasn't doing anything. Finally one night he asked us, and we said, "If Tiby and I got first and second. . . ." We went out that night like old times. It was so refreshing!

The relationship between Eisen and Briggs extended into their defensive play too, because they were outfielders together.

I played with Tiby, both sides of her, right field and sometimes left field to her center field. We never had a collision. Max taught us. If the ball is hit in the air between you, so that neither one can call it, you just decide ahead of time what you're gonna do. Otherwise you're gonna kill each other out there. We decided she would get it. I would back up. So if we didn't hear a call it was automatic: it's yours, Tiby. Dive after it, do what you want to because you know I'm gonna be behind you.

If the ball went between us on the ground, are we both gonna run and both try to pick it up? No, one of us is gonna stop. We know which one's gonna get there first by where it's hit, so the other one stops, turns around, finds the play, and then tells her where she's gonna throw it before she ever picks it up.

This kind of relationship is priceless. It's acquired through knowledge, experience and endless practice, but also depends on something more psychic: "We just knew what each other was gonna do." It's what team play is all about.

Other teammates could also help a player out. In fact, an observant player could be helped even by opponents. Rose Gacioch, Rockford's rightfielder, held the League record for assists from right field to first base.[28] Wilma recalls:

> The thought had never occurred to me that from right field you could throw a runner out at first base. Well, suppose you have a right-handed hitter up, so you're playing a little shallower than you would for a leftie. Dottie Schroeder, our shortstop, says to me, "When you get a line drive on one hop, and you're charging after it, just keep going. Throw the ball to first base and throw 'em out." She says, "You know, Rose Gacioch does that."
>
> So every time a line drive would come at me Dottie would scream, "Throw 'em out at first, Gacioch!" The first time she scared me. She wanted to make sure I was alive, awake to do it.
>
> The most devastating time, Schroeder screams, I come charging in, boy I go after that ball . . . and I missed it. It just kept right on goin'. I bet whoever that batter was ended up with a triple. Well, Dottie and I roomed together, so when we got home she says, "Didn't throw her out, did you, Rosie?"
>
> Dottie tells everybody about my worst play, the worst play I was ever in. I was the runner on third base, Betty Foss was on second, there's one out or nobody out. The batter just hit a little routine ground ball back to the pitcher. The pitcher picks it up, looks at me— I'm not gonna go anywhere—and Betty comes charging around third base and passed right by me. This thing goes by me like . . . I'm glad she didn't hit me, they'd still be picking up the pieces. She was out from here to the wall (gestures five feet from us).
>
> Oh, that was funny. I mean, it was funny, but it wasn't funny.

◆◆◆

Two more incidents stand out in Wilma's memory, both associated with her family and her father's wry sense of humor.

My father would try to come out once every year. This happened the first time he ever saw me play professional baseball. I knew somebody from the family was there because I'd seen the car, but I couldn't spot them in the stands. Then the game began and I forgot about it. During the game I made a shoestring catch. It was lucky, but nonetheless, it was a good catch! So when the game is over my father doesn't say "Hello" or "That was a great catch!" he says "Lucky catch."

The last time he ever saw me play I hit a grand-slam home run in South Bend. It not only went over the fence and out of the ballpark but over the parked cars behind the fence. I knew where he was sitting at that game, behind third base, and my mother was there too. When I circled the bases and was coming from second to third I was looking right at him. He takes off his hat, throws it down on the ground, and shakes his head like, "I can't believe this." When the game is over he doesn't say "Nice hit," he says to me, "Lucky hit!" It was really exciting for them, so I was glad.

◆◆◆

Playing in the League was not just a matter of natural ability, technical skill and strategy. The girls were also expected to project an image of decorum and femininity. Willie thinks that image was critical to the success of the All-American League.

I don't think there'll ever be another women's baseball league because they won't be able to enforce any rules and regulations. I just don't think they'd be able to find enough women that will say, "We'll do just what you want us to do in the public's eye."

Now I'm not saying that today we would make the players play in skirts. They'd be out of place today. But there are other things, like not drinking too much, you don't smoke in public, you dress for the occasion.

I think the point of those rules was to make sure the public saw us as girls and not men. They wanted us to be a class act. They wanted us to be women but play like men.

I wondered if Wilma thought that girls who were good-looking were more likely to get hired to play. "Well, they hired me," she replied with asperity. "I'm certainly not very feminine. I think by the time they got to overhand pitching, they were looking for ballplayers."

♦♦♦

As the years wore on, women who had been major players gradually left the League.

> You saw it change. Especially when Tiby left [after the 1952 season]
> and Kelly [after 1950], those that I was in awe of when I joined the
> League, as they disappeared, everything changed.
> These younger kids, they had a cocky air about 'em. Bill Allington
> [who moved from the Peaches to the Daisies in 1953 and 1954] liked
> new kids that he could work with and develop, and he felt I'd been
> around long enough, that I should go. So I went. I didn't like it, but I
> could understand it.
> I wasn't gonna go. We had taken a cut in pay to keep the League
> going that last year, and South Bend gave it back to me, so I went to
> play for them. But I felt like an outsider. A bunch of us went that year,
> and we weren't sure they accepted us. I dunno. It just wasn't the
> same. If you're on the same team that many years, it's a drastic
> change. When I was first assigned to South Bend I'd read the paper,
> whose score did I look for? Fort Wayne! I still consider myself a Daisy.
> I think if I'd been in South Bend two or three years, I think I would
> have enjoyed it. I know I would have. Because I liked to play.

When the League ended, Wilma went back home to Rhode Island. She'd briefly considered getting married during her playing
days—to the catcher on her father's team—but,

> I wasn't giving up my career! The implication was there. He'd say,
> "Well, I'm in the Air Force, so we can live here and there." I'm saying,
> "Oh, I'm not sure I want to do that. Let's just wait a little longer and
> see what happens." So I decided he really wasn't in love with me. So I
> didn't do it.
> And I'm glad now. I met him in Florida, we're still good friends,
> but he is so dull! He doesn't do anything. And he's meticulous. Even
> his wife made a few comments, and I thought, "Oh boy, better you
> than me!" And he was a pretty fair ballplayer.
> I've never been sorry.

Wilma worked a foot press for a knife company for twelve years,
and in 1965, at age thirty-five, went to college.

> The League was the most important influence in my life. I was a
> very shy person. I got the confidence playing in the League to want to

go to college. I commuted about 110 miles round trip a day. But I couldn't both work and go to college, so I quit my job. The family said, "Where you gonna get enough money to go to school?" I didn't know. Then an uncle died unexpectedly, and I had enough money for the first year. I really felt led to go to college. I felt, "If God really wants me to go to college, He'll provide my needs." And He did.

Then I taught elementary school for twenty-three years. I just retired. I taught all the subjects, so that was kind of fun.

During recess Wilma played baseball with sixty-five youngsters to "stay in shape." She was, of course, playing softball too, for teams like Allie's Donuts, and the Charlestown Mini-Super team. Her young teammates valued her skill and experience. In 1982 a local newspaper article quoted teammate Vicki, "I just stand there in awe of her. The knowledge she has you just don't have unless you've played for years and years. She's quite an incredible person."

Wilma enjoyed the attention the movie and the Hall of Fame exhibit brought the League. Once again she is being asked by fans for her autograph.

I consider it an honor and a privilege to give my autograph to somebody. I did a little autograph session, and this guy comes up with a gorgeous Lucite case, and inside is this beautiful autographed bat. He takes out the bat, and asks me if I'll autograph it. I'm looking at the bat and I see the name of all these major leaguers and Hall of Famers, Willie Mays and Carl Yastrzemski, Jim Lonborg and Enos Slaughter, and I asked, "You sure you want me to autograph this bat?" And he said, "Yes I do." I asked him two or three times, but he said, "My father almost didn't go to his slow-pitch softball tournament clear across the country because he wanted to get your autograph. So I'm getting it now to surprise him."

Can you imagine autographing a bat with those names? Then he put HOF 11-5-88 on it, which is when they opened the display about us in Cooperstown. Talk about excitement! That's gotta be one of the most exciting moments in my whole sports career.

Of course Cooperstown itself was the ultimate. The movie gave us public recognition, now everybody in the country knows about the League. But Cooperstown, to be recognized by the ultimate in baseball, that has to be the greatest thing.

I hope it stays as a tribute to the League. I just don't think there should be any individuals' names there. How could you possibly compare a player from 1943 with a player in 1954? The game changed; it was like two different games. The exhibit honors the League, and that's the way it should be. That's the pinnacle. But signing the bat was close!

I told Wilma how thrilled I was that the players and the League had been rediscovered.

Well, we rediscovered each other. That's the best thing. I had kept in touch with Dottie Schroeder and Maxine Kline and Ruby Heafner. But that reunion in 1982 in Chicago, let me tell ya. We didn't even recognize each other. Now, everybody knows everybody; it's like it was yesterday.

I remember when I was a rookie, I just sat and listened to all those veterans. We rookies would get in a team meeting and be quiet as mice.

I still listen. When those stars get together now, like Al Pollitt and Kammie and Tiby and Kelly, Pepper Paire, Doris Sams, Audrey Wagner, Jean Faut. They were great ballplayers. I never felt like I measured up to them. I was just trying to play as hard as I could. But I always admired and respected them. And I still do to this day. When I sit in a group with Snookie and Kammie and Kelly, like I did this morning at the reunion breakfast, I feel like the rookie still. [She pauses.] I wish the league had kept going. I was just learning the game.

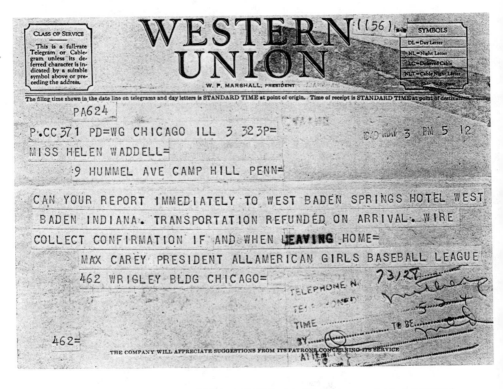

WESTERN ((56)
UNION

W. P. MARSHALL, PRESIDENT

The filing time shown in the date line on telegrams and day letters is STANDARD TIME at point of origin. Time of receipt is STANDARD TIME at point of destination

PA624

P.CC 371 PD=WG CHICAGO ILL 3 323P=

MISS HELEN WADDELL=

9 HUMMEL AVE CAMP HILL PENN=

CAN YOUR REPORT IMMEDIATELY TO WEST BADEN SPRINGS HOTEL WEST BADEN INDIANA. TRANSPORTATION REFUNDED ON ARRIVAL. WIRE COLLECT CONFIRMATION IF AND WHEN LEAVING HOME=

MAX CAREY PRESIDENT ALL AMERICAN GIRLS BASEBALL LEAGUE 462 WRIGLEY BLDG CHICAGO=

73129

TELEPHONE N.

TIME

462=

Helen "Sis" Waddell's telegram from president of the League Max Carey asking her to report for spring training in 1949. Waddell travelled with a player development team in 1949 and became a Rockford Peach in 1950.

PLAYING
TO WIN

"It's like breathing, winnin' was."

—**Mary Rountree**

By definition, there is no sport without competition. Usually we think of the contest taking place on the field of play, but it begins long before, in the minds and hearts of the players. Like many of us, the women who hoped to play baseball had to battle their own inner fears before they could take on an opposing team.

By May 1943, Wrigley scouts had culled two hundred eighty girls from the thousands who showed up for local try-outs. These able few were sent to Chicago for spring training. Based on their performance at the Cubs' Wrigley Field, sixty were chosen to inaugurate the All-American's first season. Dottie Schroeder, only fifteen years old, was among them. She told me how stark was the moment of decision.

> Then it came time for my mother to go home, and I was homesick. I'd never been away from home before. She said, "Well, I'll leave it up to you. You can come home, which will be all right, or you can stay." I thought, "But if I go home I can't play ball."

I could have played softball, but not in the League. And once you taste the big time, you know. . . .

So I decided to stay, and my mother boarded the train and came on home. I was just really almost sick I was so homesick. But the girls took me under their wing and the feeling left, just like that, after several days. But it was a terrible feeling.

The players had confidence in their abilities. Playing ball was second nature to all of them, and many of the girls already had experience winning. Helen Waddell, who tried out in 1950, recalls, "I didn't have sense enough to be scared! I liked to play ball, so I was playin' ball." What intimidated the girls most and gave them second thoughts was the big city and the Big-League setting.

Helen remembers how frightened she was contemplating her tryout in Chicago. "You don't go to Chicago. That's like the end of the world." Nickie Fox's father agreed. From the relative safety of Calgary, Alberta, he envisioned disaster for his twenty-three-year-old child. "No daughter of mine is going to Chicago!" Nickie and her mother prevailed upon him.

I told my father that my trip down would be paid for, as well as all my expenses. And if I didn't make the cut, I had an all-expenses-paid trip back to Calgary. If nothing else, it would be like a vacation.

Financial arrangements like these gave the message to daughters and parents alike that the League was a legitimate, professional organization that would take care of its charges. Players remember with appreciation their "first-class" treatment from League management. Wrigley organizers went out of their way to reassure families by closely supervising their daughters. They met the trains bringing girls from all over the country, and escorted them to the hotel where they stayed. Taxis or buses took the girls from the hotel to Wrigley Field and brought them home after their workout. Later, the girls who made the League were accompanied to Charm School. No girl was going to get lost or have a bad experience in the big city.

I asked Irene Applegren's mother if it was hard for the family to let their seventeen-year-old daughter go. She responded with a definitive "No," and her daughter explained,

They weren't nervous, I was! In fact I would've rather stayed home. I went because my dad thought it would be a wonderful opportunity for me. They offered $75 a week, and back then that was pretty good money.

Then I got there and I really liked it.

A player not only had to battle her own fears and shyness; she had to consider her other choices. Some girls let a contract pass them by because the alternatives were too compelling. A catcher friend of Irene's tried out but opted to stay home and keep her good job. She continued to play softball for the company team and at age forty-eight retired after thirty years of work, with full pension and health benefits. She comes to AAGPBL reunions as Irene's guest.

Helen Waddell remembers two sisters who were prevented by other considerations from going on to spring training even after they'd made the cut in local try-outs. "They decided not to go. One was scared to leave home. The other was married and had two kids. They were good ballplayers. But they didn't go."

Those who did go had to make sacrifices. Vivian Kellogg recalls the attitude of the State of Michigan.

The first year I came back home from playing, I went to work for the prison here in Jackson. The next spring, when I told them I was quitting, they said I would never have another job from the State of Michigan because I was quitting for a job that they didn't feel was as important as the civil service job I had.

Most of the women, however, were more than willing to sacrifice secure conventional jobs in order to play baseball for money. But personal demons remained to be battled before the competition on the field could begin. The fear of failure was the worst of these, and this fear could be daunting. Dottie Key, Rockford's centerfielder, refers to try-outs as "the trying days." Her double meaning conveys the painful blend of striving and anxiety that some girls felt.

A lot stayed and a lot went home. It would have been hard for me to take, having to go home. Because I wanted to play ball. I don't know what else I would have done. I really don't. I was determined. I think I would have been ashamed to go home.

I asked her who she would have been ashamed to face—her mom? Her friends?

No, myself. Nobody else. It was just myself. Well, I'm going to tell you, I never worked so hard or kept my eyes and ears so open, because I was not goin' home!

Dottie signed a contract with the Peaches for $75 a week in 1945. At the time she was working in a warehouse for between $18 and $20 a week. Though few girls considered only the financial benefits of playing ball, the management of the All-American League had established a pay scale that would compete very favorably with the other jobs available to them. Rockford's Nickie Fox joined the League in 1943 as an $85-a-week pitcher. She'd been clerking for $12.50 a week. In general, salaries ranged from $45 to $85 per week in 1943, from $55 to $125 by 1950, plus money for meals and all other expenses on the road. In 1952, pitcher Irene Applegren made a total of $1,325 for a four-month season, an average of $80 to $85 a week.[29] There were bonuses for making the playoffs and championship series. In 1949, a player for the Grand Rapids Chicks made an extra $167.82 for having beaten Fort Wayne and Muskegon in the playoffs before losing to Rockford in the four-game championship series.

Well-paid veterans are still secretive about how much money they did in fact make; those who made less are more likely to share the details. But at the time everyone was pleased with the pay. These were girls raised in the Depression, and, as Dottie Collins, now the Players' Association treasurer reminds us, "In a lot of cases, the girls were making more money than their fathers. It definitely was more money than a woman could make in an office someplace. We were very well-paid and very, very happy about the whole situation."[30]

Dottie Schroeder can cite the astonishing particulars, "Not too many years before1943 my father was the postmaster of Sadorus, Illinois, making $20 a week, and here I was, fifteen, and a girl, being paid $55, to play baseball!"

◆◆◆

Dottie Schroeder was indeed only fifteen years old when she joined the League in 1943. Rose Gacioch was considered an old lady when she joined in 1944 at age twenty-eight. The average age at which these twenty-six Peaches and Daisies joined the League was twenty. They had been recruited from throughout the country, eleven from the East, nine from the Midwest, three from Los Angeles and three from Canada.

As each new season started, the girls were asked to play a different brand of baseball. Both the physical parameters of play and the rules of the All-American League changed continuously over its twelve-year history. The ball shrank, the basepaths and distance from pitcher to home plate expanded, and new rules were concocted to increase fan appeal, maintain parity among teams, and develop new players. League management wanted to create a distinctive, exciting game of baseball for the women to play. What emerged was a women's professional hardball league.

By 1950 the pitchers were hurling overhand a ten-inch ball from a mound fifty-five feet from the plate, the base paths measured seventy-two feet, and the new "rookie rule" required a manager to have one rookie on the field at all times.[31]

The AAGBL started with a 12-inch ball in 1943 (far left). In 1950 they played with a 10-inch ball (second from left) and by 1954 they were playing with a 9¼-inch official men's sized ball.

As spring training began, Bill Allington looked forward to the smaller ball. "It looks as if there's going to be a lot of hitting. The new ten-inch ball is extra good, and it looks as if it's going to improve play in the League." He made his remarks after the Peaches' opening exhibition game in Quincy, Illinois. It hadn't been easy getting there. Sportswriter Dick Day reported the difficulties.

> First of the Peaches to hit a home run this year was Snookie Doyle, who connected Sunday against Peoria in the opening game of the spring tour at Quincy. Snookie probably was mad at the time. The Peaches' bus broke down twice and tempers were short when they reached Quincy an hour-and-a-half late. After the game, they had to hop right back on the bus and head for Keokuk [Iowa] where they started another game immediately upon arrival.[32]

After two more games on the road, the Rockford and Peoria teams were headed for Dwight Reformatory for Women where they played a game inside the prison walls. By the next day the two teams had played eight games in seven days. Allington was happy: "What really counts is the amount of work the players get." The pre-season was off to its usual frenetic start.

More than forty years later, some players remember vividly their very first game, whether a try-out, pre-season or regular-season game. Louise Erickson pitched batting practice and relief for the Racine Belles in 1948, when she was nineteen years old. With only a little help from a carefully preserved newspaper clipping she recounted the details for me.

> The Belles were behind 5 to 0 after the first inning. I started the second inning and pitched until there was only one out to get in the sixth inning. By that time Racine had scored four runs in the third inning, four in the fourth, and one in the fifth. Eventually the Belles won 12 to 7. My entire record for the year 1948 was one win and no losses. This was the win.

Sis Waddell's memory of her first game is more painful and funny.

> I was just so shy and so scared. I remember the first game I played. Al Pollitt, the regular third baseman, got hurt, so Bill stuck me in at third. Of course the first thing, they hit one to me. I grabbed that thing, froze up, and one-bounced it to Kammie at first. I was scared to death.
>
> So we got the outs, come back in, and Kammie says, "Sis, don't worry about it. Fire it. If it's anywhere around me, I'll catch it. Now just let it fly."
>
> We went back out in the field, they hit me another, I grabbed that sucker and threw it over the bleachers on the first-base side. Kammie looked at me, shook her head, and back in the dugout said, "Sis, I know I told you to fire it. I know I told you I'd catch most anything you throw at me. But that's just a little high."
>
> That kind of calmed me down and we went on to play a pretty good game, but for a while I had gotten too much of the old adrenalin pumping.

Catcher Mary Rountree played her first year with the newly-formed Peoria Redwings. She remembers opening night, the first game Peoria played before its home-town fans.

> We were playing the Racine Belles who had been in the League since it began; they were pros, wonderfully trained. We had only a few veteran players and were a brand new team. In the very first in-

ning they get a runner on first, who moves to third with only one out. Their coach puts on the squeeze sign. Of course at that time I wasn't trained to pick up the signs. I just knew with a player on third and one out in only the first inning, that's what he's gonna do.

So the batter bunts the ball down the third-base line. I flipped off the mask, ran down the line, picked up the ball, tagged the girl that was coming in from third, then turned around and threw the ball as hard as I could to first base. The runner was just one step away from the bag, but I got the ball there in time. It was a double play that ended the inning as well.

Well, for the fans this was unreal, to see girls break up a squeeze play. As I walked back to pick up the mask, there were six or seven thousand people on their feet, clappin' and screamin' and hollerin'. It was a tremendous ovation, not just for me, but for the fact that every kid was in place. The second baseman had covered first base. The first baseman had come in to field the bunt in case it was on the first-base side. The third-base girl was in along her line. It was beautiful.

They beat us, but it was somethin' like three to two or four to three, and we fought like little tigers. And even though we lost, we won all the fans.

I had learned that pleasing the fans was satisfying to Mary, but I also wanted to know how important it was to her to win. Her response was immediate and unequivocal.

It's like breathing, winnin' was. It was everything.

The women who played professional baseball were competitors. They played well, they played hard, and they played to win. I asked Tiby Eisen what she thought was the key to having a team that works together. Her first criterion: "You've got to have people that want to win."

Winning was so important to Dottie Key that the alternative never occurred to her. She told me, "I never thought of losing. Always had to win. No matter what, any sport, playing cards, doing anything, I'm out to win. So there you have it."

Sis Waddell felt the same way. Winning was a habit and a good one at that. She put it this way, "I never knew any different. I didn't know what a loser was. I don't like second. That's a loser. If you have a winning attitude, you do better."

Dottie Collins believed that a winning attitude not only got results, but could compensate for other shortcomings.

I don't have the ability that a lot of other people have. But I'm a competitor. And that is very important. If you put me in a tough situation, I'll beat you nine times out of ten.

You've got to have the desire. Most people are just out there for a good time. To go into the pros, that's a big difference. If you had me in a ball game, with three on base and nobody out, that was a challenge. I could get out of that real easy.

That aggressive desire to win was, of course, encouraged by the All-American managers. Isabel Alvarez wasn't very aggressive or outgoing, and as a result sometimes felt inadequate to the task. "I wish I would have been more outgoing. I could even have been a better ballplayer if I could have been aggressive. I wasn't aggressive enough."

Sometimes players who were extremely shy suffered for it. Norma Metrolis played for four different teams during her five years in the League. She was usually a backup catcher, riding the bench. She told me she thought her personality had something to do with her position.

I'm not a real outward person. I'm kinda shy, and I had asked one manager about playing, and he told me I wasn't outgoin' enough. I couldn't figure out what that had to do with playin' ball.

A competitive spirit bolsters self-confidence, intensifies focus, justifies hard work, increases the chances that an individual will in fact win, and—in sports—guarantees approval from the coach. But there are drawbacks. For women for whom winning was so critical, losing posed a problem: it was upsetting, it was depressing, it was hard even to conceive. Losing was such a foreign concept to Dottie Collins that she and I had the following non-communication. She had told me how horrible it was to get beat, and I asked what she did after she lost a game.

Dottie replied, "Well, just try to forget it, really. It's still only a game, you know."

But I wanted to know more and probed, "It must be hard to have the kind of competitive spirit that you have, and yet lose and have to just let it go."

Dottie didn't reason based on losing scenarios and so asked, "What do you mean, lose?" I clarified myself, "Well, I mean, if you lose."

Dottie now figured out the basic silliness of my hypothetical case, and humored me with a reply, "Oh, if you lose. Well, yeah, I didn't win everything. It hurt to lose, there was no doubt about it."

Competitiveness showed itself in the way these women felt about winning against players who represented a personal challenge of some kind. Rockford pitcher Irene Applegren cherished her recollections of beating Dottie Collins.

Dorothy "Dottie" Wiltse Collins was a fierce competitor in both the underhand and overhand eras of the League. She once pitched—and won— both games of a doubleheader.

One of my favorite memories must have been when I beat Dottie Collins. I beat her four to three, I think. In Fort Wayne. I never could beat her.

She was one of my idols. I can remember Dottie when she was

pitching underhand. She could throw a curve underhand, the only one I ever seen pitchin' softball that could throw a curve. That was quite a challenge for me to beat her.

I liked to win. I felt terrible when I lost.

I wanted to know how the rest of the team reacted to a player's temporary failure, what happened for instance if Irene wasn't pitching well and Bill took her out. I asked, "Would anybody on the team say anything to you, or would they leave you alone?"

"Just ignore me. Don't talk about it! was how I preferred it," she replied.

I persisted, "Was that how most of the players felt? Like if they made an error or something, just leave me alone?"

"Yeah. You wouldn't say anything to 'em."

The image I was left with was a stark contrast: Winning brought clapping and cheering and hollering. Losing brought silence.

It can be exhausting, maintaining the level of intensity that such competition demands. With hindsight, Applegren believes she could have relaxed a bit, relied on the defense behind her.

I really tried too hard out there on the mound, many times, and walked them. I could have just lobbed the ball in there, because the other players would have gotten it. Now that I think about it, I didn't need to try that hard. I'd be tired at the end of the season. And I finally quit I think because I was tired.

I went to the Chicago [softball] league, but softball was a lot easier; it wasn't near as strenuous as baseball.

Some of the players, while liking to win, valued other parts of their game as much as victory. As Fran Janssen observed, "Losing bothered some more than others." Dottie Schroeder always wanted to win and took the game seriously, but what was most important to her was "playing the game and doing your best. Then if you won, that was just topping on the cake."

Fort Wayne catcher Kate Vonderau didn't feel that winning was that important to her. In fact when she became a college coach after baseball she felt that "participation was more important than winning or losing. When it got to the point where you had to win or else, I stopped coaching. So winning wasn't one of my high priorities."

Rose Gacioch, one of the oldest women to play professional baseball in the League, knew that you play a lot of games over a long time and thus, she told me,

> Winning wasn't really that important to me, because you're not that good that you're gonna win all the games. You might as well make up your mind there'll only be some you win.

> You want to win, especially if you're pitchin'. And you help other people out to try to win, because I know how they feel. But it wasn't real important for me. I loved the game of baseball, and I'd do anything I could to win, but I wouldn't go break my neck.

◆◆◆

While Rose wouldn't gratuitously "break her neck," injury is simply an occupational hazard of a physical sport like baseball. Extremes of competitiveness can add to the risk. Mary Rountree, who was playing ball to save enough money for medical school and was thus especially sensitive to the physical mayhem around her, is adamant that her will to win didn't go so far as to endanger other players.

> I will never accept trying to hurt somebody to win a game. If you want to fight, get out there and fight, but the idea is to have athletic skill. So, winning was everything, but not to the point of hurting somebody.

On the other hand, Mary wasn't beyond a little physical retaliation. During her rookie season as Fort Wayne's catcher, a veteran baserunner sent Mary sprawling in a collison at home plate. Mary not only held onto the ball after making the tag, but held onto the incident in her mind so she could reply later. Mary recounted her tale of sweet revenge forty-two years later to a *Miami Herald* reporter.

> The runner had gone out of her way to give me a real blow, and I thought to myself, "OK, well, let's see how we play this game." When the opportunity came later in the season, and that girl came at me again, I caught her in mid-stride, gave her a nice little shove.

The reporter noted, "a small grin crawls across a genteel face as Rountree, now 69, reclaims her dream."[33]

Because sports involve competitive physical skills, the body is the tool of confrontation. The women who played professional baseball were not unusually big, however. Ruth Richard, the All-Star catcher, was only 5 feet 4 inches and 134 pounds. Nickie Fox, whose pitching lead the league in 1943 and 1944, was even smaller, 5 feet 3-½ inches and 130 pounds. Betty Foss, at 5 feet 10-½ inches and 180 pounds, was the biggest girl of the two teams in the 1950 championship series, Fran Janssen at 5 feet 11-½ the tallest. The average size of the girls was just that, average, about 5 feet 6 inches and 140 pounds.

The women were rugged, though: hardy and strong and physically unafraid. I remember as a kid shortstop flinching when I tried to field grounders, pulling up and back just a little for fear the ball would bounce in my face. I asked shortstop Snookie Doyle if she had had to conquer this fear. Was she ever afraid of the ball?

No, I wasn't. I learned to rollerskate when I was three. When my godchild was born I had him rollerskating when he was three. But his mother was afraid for him. So it can depend on the parents. I think if you're fearful of becoming injured, you'll be more apt to be injured.

Dottie Key said a prayer before each game while the National Anthem was playing. Each prayer began, "Give me strength." Dottie needed the strength because sometimes the play got just as rough as these women were tough. Key remembers being decked by a bullet throw from Dottie Schroeder.

We were playing in Fort Wayne. I'd gotten on first base, and the ball was hit directly back to second. Now I'm running to second, Dottie picks up that ball, and suddenly it was coming right at me. I went down. She would've killed me.

Key was used to having the ball thrown at her, but only when she was batting. She made a career of getting on first by being hit by pitched balls.

I wasn't a hitter. But in my leading off I knew how to work the pitcher. I could always work the count to three and two. I stood right on the line and crouched, so they had to bring that ball in. I led the league in being hit by pitches.

"But weren't you afraid to get hit?" I wondered aloud.

No. Because you're standing up like this. [She gets out of her chair at the dining room table where we're talking, crouches in her customary stance, poised for the imaginary pitch; I remember her younger, thinner self looking just like this, game after game.] I'm in my batter's box. [She points to the floor, outlining the edge of the box just grazing her toes.] But if they come in close and they're gonna hit me, I roll with the ball [left shoulder leading her body away, but not too far away, from the ball]. Some of the balls hurt, yeah. They weren't throwing them easy. But I was on.

At a reunion a couple of years ago South Bend's pitcher Jean Faut says to me, "Dottie, I'll never understand why the devil you didn't stand up at the plate there. You could have hit that ball a mile." "Well, Jeannie, why should I?" I said. "I can get up there and work you and you can put me on first base. It's much easier."

In ten years of play, Dottie was never injured by a pitch.

Sometimes, however, aggressiveness crossed the border of legitimate competitiveness into what players regarded as excessive violence. They would retaliate in kind.

Sis Waddell remembers her teammates protecting her.

One time I was playin' second base and a girl slid into the base with her spikes high, intending to get me. She cut up my arm and leg a little bit. When we went back into the dugout, all the veterans came over to me and said, "Okay, Sis, we'll take care of it."

Well, this girl was herself a second basemen, and when we got up to bat, Kammie, and Snookie and Al, all of them, went into second spikes-high. This girl got the message. She was a good ballplayer, but she thought she could do this and get away with it. She didn't. Not with us anyhow.

These physical confrontations, where one team is punishing another for perceived violations, can take a whole game or perhaps a whole series—even a whole season if memories are long—to reach their conclusion. Sometimes the clash is much more immediate. Snookie Doyle and Vivian "Kelly" Kellogg remember the fight they had at first base that got them both thrown out of the game. Snookie tells her version of events.

I had a base hit and was rounding the bag to go to second. I didn't realize she was standing there in the way, which I understand she used to do quite often.

I guess I bumped her with my hip, and she went flying. Her hat flew off and she came back, madder than a hornet, and took a swing at me, barely grazed my chin. I grabbed her around the neck. I started it, I went after her, and they had to break it up. We were both put out of the game. But we've been very good friends ever since.

Kelly's story differs slightly, of course.

> I remember we got into it, and then we turned out to be the best of friends, even though we were on opposite teams. She claims I swung first, but if I had swung first, I sure would have hit her!

Both players were fined ten dollars.

Emil Pietrangeli, an experienced umpire who worked for the All-American League during the 1950 and 1951 seasons, found the women players intense to say the least. At age seventy-four, he recalled that umpiring in the League was "tougher than anything else I've done. I had to ignore a lot and walk away." He found that with his imposing size, 6 feet 1 inch and 225 pounds, he could glare at male players "and they'd shut up. If I looked at those young women like that, they'd give me a glare twice as bad. And they could make you feel pretty bad with their words." But, he hastens to add, "After the game, they forgave and forgot, like all good ballplayers."[34]

♦♦♦

Injuries play a significant role in any sport. Even in a technically non-contact sport like baseball, minor injuries happen to everyone; major injuries are every player's greatest fear. They can affect the outcome of a team's entire season, as they threatened to do the Peaches in 1950. And, more seriously, they can interrupt or prematurely end the career of an individual player.

The women often remembered their worst moments on the field as the times they got injured. Somehow the memory of the injury is auditory; the break, the tear, the wrench lingers in the ear as much as in the damaged body part.

Norma Metrolis was Fort Wayne's third-string backup catcher in 1950. Earlier, in 1948, she'd worked her way into a regular catching job with South Bend. She only had a chance to play twelve games before an injury took her out.

> I was playin' regular, and then I tore the cartilage in my knee. I can still hear it crack in my mind, if I think about it. Then every time I played it'd go out, so they finally operated on it. But still I had to be careful with it. They told me not to go after bunts, let the infielders do it, but when a bunt is laid down, you don't think about it, you just automatically go. That's part of the job. So consequently, every time I did, it went out again. You learn to live with it. It isn't that bad.

This stoic attitude characterized all the All-Americans. Norma, like all backup players waiting for their chance, knew all too well the durability of the regulars.

You were on teams where they had old standbys who had been there a long time. They were first string and had to be dead before you got to play.

Ruth Richard, Rockford's catcher, got her spike caught sliding into second in the last game of the 1950 regular season and broke her ankle. She was used to Manager Allington treating injuries on the spot.

He always used to grab somebody's finger or leg and twist it and pull it and carry on. I yelled at him, "Don't you dare touch it!" 'cause I heard it crack when I went in.

Richard's injury sent her to the hospital where the evidence was inescapable that she was cast in a different mold from other women of her era.

I was just there overnight. I was in a room with four other women, and they all had miscarriages but me!

Then the newspaper came down and took pictures of me laying there with Snookie and Rosie Gacioch visiting, and I guess these other women thought, "What the heck's goin' on here? Nobody's comin' and takin' pictures of me with my miscarriage!" I got a chuckle out of that.

When serious injuries occurred, the League took responsible care of players, paying for all medical expenses. But the vast majority of injuries Richards and others played right through.

A lot of my fingers were broken but never taken care of because you didn't dare have anything wrong with you. Because you had to play ball. One time I had a broken finger, but we had to go on a road trip that night. That finger hurt, and Bill said, "Put a lemon on it." All night long I had a lemon on this finger. It hurt somethin' fierce. It was the throwing hand. I could bat okay.

Then he just taped two fingers together and that was it. Very seldom did you have an injury x-rayed or anything.

When I got hit on my toe with a foul ball, my nail got all black and blue and really hurt, but you couldn't not play, so I cut a hole in my shoe to play in.

There was one chronic source of injury for any baserunner who regularly slid, the much-feared and painfully-remembered "strawberry." The All-Americans played in one-piece tunic-style dresses, with short skirts and shorts underneath, the uniform designed to express a complicated melange of feminine propriety and display. Whatever the skirt did for management and fans, it failed to protect the players who needed to execute one of baseball's fundamental plays, the slide.

Snookie Doyle describes her second baseman, Charlene Barnett.

> She was tough, really. She wasn't tough as a person, but she would get injured and you wouldn't even know it. One time she had been scraped all the way down her shin, from sliding into the base. It was a mess, a terrible injury to have. And she didn't complain about it at all. I just thought she was great. It was really fun playing with her. You do better when the person next to you is good.

Players' exposed thighs were most vulnerable to strawberries, and they tried a variety of protective gear. Dottie Key remembers one strawberry vividly.

> It was this mammoth scrape, kinda oozing. My husband Don's mother was watching the game, and she got so upset. The chaperone cleaned it, and laid a "doughnut" [a protective circle of rolled-up surgical dressings or towels] around it which she taped in place. The next day I'm walkin' around with this big doughnut on my side under my uniform.
>
> Don's mom said to me, "Well, if you get on first, how you gonna steal? You can't slide."
>
> Well, I get on first, and down I go to second, and I slid on the other side. She didn't see me because she had covered her eyes!

Sometimes the women insisted on playing on with conditions that alarmed their teammates. Dottie Collins was four months pregnant before she decided the time had come, in midseason 1948, to relinquish the pitcher's mound. Dottie took 1949 off but was back in1950.

I asked Dottie how it was to be pregnant and still that active.

> It was very easy for me. The doctor recommended that I continue to be active. I knew when to quit, it was just a feeling I had. I was goin' up to the clubhouse after a game, and I said to Dick Bass, our coach, "Dick, I think that's it." He was much relieved. Of course he had been

a nervous wreck for months. So then they made an announcement over the loudspeaker, that I had just retired. And they said the reason too. I got congratulations from all the players.

Dottie told me only she and her manager knew she was pregnant. Apparently her secret wasn't as well kept as she thought. Mary Rountree, her catcher, remembers the situation clearly.

> We knew she was pregnant! I was always tryin' my best to make sure that nobody hit somethin' too hard back at her. I'm behind the plate just prayin' to the good Lord. But she made it, and we all lived through it.

Kate Vonderau, Fort Wayne's backup catcher, sustained a finger injury serious enough to end her career.

> I caught a foul tip on the index finger of my right hand. It damaged the joint capsule, and I had to have surgery on it several times, but they couldn't really repair it too well. I thought, "Well, that's enough of that."
>
> Now it's just a crooked finger. I have good use of it, but I can't bend it at that joint.

Sometimes a combination of long-tolerated injuries, aging, and the appearance of a fresh, robust rookie meant the end of a career. Vivian Kellogg retired from her successful seven-year career with the Daisies and their predecessor, the Minneapolis Millerettes, after the 1950 season even though that year she had knocked in a career-high forty-nine runs batted in.

> I kinda lost interest, and I had had surgery on my knee for torn cartilage and wasn't able to participate like I wanted to, and I wasn't gettin' any younger.

The 1950 batting champion and rookie of the year, Betty Foss, took over Vivian's position at first base the following year. Her sister Jo claimed an outfield spot, and sister Jean became the Daisies' third baseman. The era of the Weaver sisters had begun.

I asked Betty if she thought her presence ushered in Vivian Kellogg's retirement.

> Well, I don't know, honey. Maybe that was it. 'Cause they wouldn't take me out of the line-up, and my other sister Jo was comin' in, and they wanted her bat in there, and my middle sister Jean, she was an

infielder, and she swung a pretty good bat, so they wanted to make room for her. So I think Kelly just gave it up, you know.

Betty herself was not immune from the assaults of the young. She won the League batting championship in 1950 and 1951 with averages of .346 and .368. By 1952, however, her sister Jo had deposed her and went on to win the title the last three seasons of the League's existence, with averages of .344, .346, and—the best average ever turned in by an All-American—.429 in 1954. Betty smiles ruefully and says, "I always told Jo someday she'd catch me, and she did."

When talents like the Weaver sisters emerge, the competitive nature of baseball means other players have to make room. Helen Ketola learned this at the beginning rather than the end of her career. "I started the season there at third base, and then it was my unfortunate luck to have Betty Foss come into the League! Needless to say, I became a utility infielder then."

Helen played only one year in the League, a total of thirty-one games, in her rookie season of 1950. But her competitive nature was unaffected by a shortened professional career. At age sixty-one she talks just like the veterans of many years.

> I liked to win. I still like to win. I've been competitive all my life, basketball, baseball, bowling, golf. It's just something an athlete has; they like to do well and they love to compete.

◆◆◆

The women of the All-American Girls Baseball League were, with few exceptions, comfortable in their bodies and sure of their physical skills. They were strong, tough, undeterred by pain, and courageous in the face of probable injury. They were unafraid of physical confrontation. And they were highly competitive; they simply loved to win. This is the reality of the women who played professional baseball.

There is a contrary image of women, however, that is used to discourage us from being self-confident and active in our world. We are taught to distrust our bodies and to hold back from using them. We are told we are weak, timid and afraid of being hurt. We are encouraged to be so uncomfortable with winning that we would rather lose. And, because of our "tender natures," we are reminded that we need to be protected from engaging in the rigors of adult life, one of which is sports.

It is one of the tragedies of women's existence that many of us believe this damaged view of women, live it out in our own lives, and teach it to our daughters. Of course it is not true. Women can be powerful, combative, fierce, relentless, sure of their own capabilities, and focused on the prize. They can be rough, they can be tough, they can fight to be best. In other words, they can play hardball.

Tiby Eisen reminds us,

> We played baseball just like the big boys. I broke up double plays with spikes held high and we stole bases in our skirts. We did whatever it took to win.

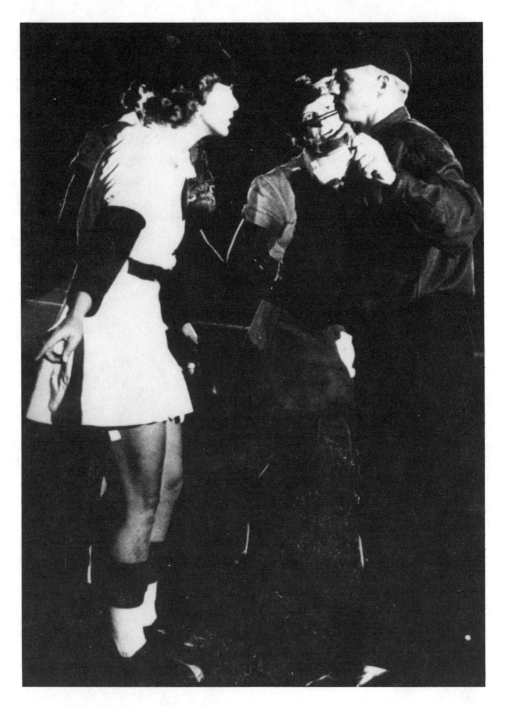

All-Americans were competitive and played to win. Here Rockford pitcher Lois Florreich and catcher Ruth Richard argue with an umpire (unidentified).

GAME THREE

The first two games of the 1950 championship series were played in Rockford, home of the Peaches since the League began in 1943. With the third game, the contest moved to Fort Wayne.

The Daisies had first fielded a team in 1945. Their first incarnation, the Minneapolis Millerettes, had lasted just one year, 1944; girls' baseball did not fare well in big stadiums in big cities. League President Ken Sells thought that men's baseball parks were "too large for intimate fan participation." In 1945 the Millerettes moved to Fort Wayne, were renamed the Daisies, and found a permanent home.

In 1950 Fort Wayne was a city with a population of 133,607, the second-largest city in Indiana, located about 160 miles southeast of the League's supervisors in Chicago. Fort Wayne was named after an 1816 military garrison located at the confluence of three rivers. It was variously called the "City of Churches" and the "Summit City," because it commands the highest elevation in northern Indiana, a breathtaking 791 feet.

Like the other All-American cities, Fort Wayne was an industrial center situated in flat or rolling farm land on a body of water, either Lake Michigan itself or a navigable river emptying into the Lake or the Mississippi River. International Harvester made farm equipment there, and General Electric, Magnavox, Phelps-Dodge and Essex Wire formed an industrial base that was quickly converted to supplying war materiel for both World War II and the Korean War.

Fort Wayne was a sports-minded city, home to an excellent men's fast-pitch softball team, an ice hockey team, and the original home of the Pistons, a founding team of the National Basketball Association. When the Daisies came to town, experienced sports fans welcomed them with enthusiasm. By 1950 Fort Wayne led the League's eight cities at the gate with a total attendance of 91,000, the highest of any sports team in the city's history.

In the other seven cities, however, attendance was falling off by 1950. 1948 had been the League's most successful season, when 910,000 fans watched games in ten cities. In 1949 Rockford had drawn 91,634, nearly as many fans as the city's entire 1950 population of 92,503. In 1950, however, this figure was down to 78,000. Falling attendance was, of course, a mortal threat to the League's existence.

Rockford, located eighty miles west of Chicago was, like Fort Wayne, an industrial center, known for its furniture and machine tool industries, the latter a significant contributor to the war effort. Rockford's thousands of oak and elm trees spread out east and west from the winding Rock River, giving shade and a sense of calm to an otherwise hard-working city. Just beyond, perfectly flat farm lands, planted in alfalfa and corn and soybeans, stretched at least as far as the next All-American city.

There was, however, growing evidence of post-war urbanization. Eight months earlier Rockford had installed its first thousand parking meters. The first commercial airliner connecting the city to the rest of the country took off in September 1950. Newspapers and radio were clearly the dominant media; there were no television listings in the Rockford paper. Instead, the daily Radio Log guided the listener to "Young Widder Brown" and "When a Girl Marries," or, for kids like me, "Challenge of the Yukon" that recounted the adventures of Royal Canadian Mounted Police Sergeant Preston and his wonder dog Yukon King.

Women in Rockford and Fort Wayne were still the exception in professional occupations. Out of 186 physicians in Rockford in 1950, six were women. There was one woman dentist. Women were expected, instead, to be nurses. A recruiting pitch in a 1950 Rockford paper read, "The initials R.N., meaning registered nurse, after a girl's name can be an open sesame to a world of travel, adventure and service to humanity."

The Marine Corps, however, was just beginning to accept women. Women had been actively recruited into war-related factory work. And some women's sports figures, like Olympic track and field star Mildred "Babe" Didrickson Zaharias, received some attention from the press.

Cities like Fort Wayne and Rockford were politically conservative, but World War II had created a climate that encouraged women to work and excel outside their homes. The women who played for the Daisies and the Peaches were the beneficiaries of this liberalized era, as were the fans who saw them play.

◆◆◆

The Peaches travelled by bus the 250 miles to Fort Wayne to resume the Championship Series. Rain in Rockford had caused the postponement of Sunday's Game Two to Monday. While the players looked forward to better playing conditions in Indiana for Game Three, the month of September1950 was wet throughout the Midwest. Players remember this Championship series as "the one we played in all the rain."

Daisies Turn on Rockford, 7-3

by Bob Reed
Fort Wayne Journal-Gazette, September 13, 1950

The Daisies beat the rain and the Rockford Peaches last night, 7-3, to get back in the running in the final play-off series in the All-American Girls Baseball League.

It was officially a seven-inning contest, being called with the Peaches at bat and two out in the eighth inning. The game reverted to the even inning, wiping out a base hit for Snookie Doyle and a double play for the Daisies. The result left the series standing two to one for Rockford with the fourth game here tonight at 8:15.

The Daisies, who couldn't do much with Nickie Fox or Louise Erickson, two of the comparatively lesser lights of Rockford's strong pitching staff in the two games at Rockford, took some liberties with Lois Florreich, their ace and 20-game winner.

They scored six runs and made six hits off Florreich during the five innings she pitched, topping the attack with four runs in the fourth, when Florreich walked two and yielded three hits, including two doubles.

Vivian Kellogg and Kate Vonderau each delivered a timely double during the big round. Kellogg slashed a bounder just inside the first base line with the bases filled as a result of a single by Evie Wawryshyn and passes to Betty Foss and Dottie Schroeder. With two still on base, Vonderau poked a double into right field that scored Schroeder and Kellogg.

The Daisies had scored an initial run in the second on two perfect bunts by Sally Meier and Schroeder after Foss had walked and stolen.

This five-run lead was whittled away fast in the fifth, when Dottie Collins, who had pitched beautifully for four innings, found the plate swinging. She walked three straight batters and gave up a double to Florreich and a single to Dottie Key without retiring a batter, and with two on and none out, Millie Deegan came in and shut off the scoring aided by a beautiful double play, Schroeder to Kellogg to Vonderau.

The Daisies scored a sixth run off Florreich in the fifth on some daring and desperate base running by Wawryshyn. She beat out a bunt along the third base line. She stole second off Marilyn Jones, who had no success at all in stopping Fort Wayne base runners and then purloined third, to which Jones made a wide throw. Wawryshyn picked herself up and dashed for the plate, sliding safely in ahead of the throw.

The seventh run, off Applegren, was aided by the catcher's error on a dropped throw to the plate, with Dottie Kamenshek attempting to nip Wilma Briggs on Foss' bounder.

Tonight the Daisies seek to even it up at two apiece and Manager Max Carey is likely to come back with Maxine Kline, who pitched most of Saturday's game at Rockford.

Summary

Runs - Foss 2, Wawryshyn 2, Schroeder, Kellogg, Briggs, Barnett, Callow, Jones. Errors - Jones 2, Briggs. Runs batted in - Kellogg 2, Vonderau 2, Schroeder, Florreich 2, Key. Two-base hits - Kellogg 2, Vonderau, Florreich. Stolen bases - Kelley, Eisen, Briggs, Wawryshyn 2, Foss, Meier. Sacrifices - Meier, Schroeder. Double plays - Doyle to Kamenshek, Schroeder to Kellogg to Vonderau, Applegren to Barnett. Bases on balls - Collins 3, Deegan 1, Applegren 1. Strikeouts - Florreich 3. Hits off - Collins 3 in 4 innings, Florreich 6 in 5. Hit by pitcher - by Applegren (Vonderau). Winning pitcher - Collins. Losing pitcher - Florreich. Left on bases - Rockford 4, Fort Wayne 4. Time - 1:50. Attendance - Not reported.

Alice "Al" Pollitt poses for her official 1950 promotional photo. Rockford's veteran third baseman has autographed the picture "To Larry," a nephew who idolized her.

Alice Pollitt Deschaine in 1992 shows off her cap, ball and glove. Her hair, she admits, is no longer regulation length.

ALICE "AL" POLLITT
Rockford, Third Baseman

Statistics: Born: 1929. Home town: Lansing, Michigan. Height: 5 feet 3 inches. Playing weight: 150 pounds. Bats: Right. Throws: Right. Entered League: 1947 at age 17. Teams: Rockford, 1947-53. Lifetime totals: Batting average: .255. Fielding percentage: .914.

with memories of

Jackie "Babe" Kelley Rockford, Utility Player

Statistics: Born: 1926. Home town: Lansing, Michigan. Height: 5 feet 7-½ inches. Playing weight: 140 pounds. Bats: Right. Throws: Right. Entered League: 1947 at age 21. Teams: South Bend, 1947; Chicago travelling team, 1948; Peoria, 15 games in 1949; Rockford, 1949-1953. Lifetime totals: Batting average: .207. Fielding percentage (all positions combined): .912; as a pitcher, earned-run average: 3.45.

Under normal circumstances Alice Pollitt would have spent the 1950 championship series crouched at her regular third-base post, poised to spear line drives, swoop up hard-hit grounders and fire the ball to Kammie at first. Alice was Rockford's mainstay at third, a player who frustrated batters around the League. The Fort Wayne *News-Sentinel,* for instance, applauded her fine defense in a Daisies-Peaches game played August 13, 1950: "The game was loaded with spectacular fielding, especially by Alice (In Wonderland) Pollitt, the Rockford third baseman. She took hits away from Schroeder, Kellogg, and Wawryshyn with gaudy stops."

Only a few days later, Pollitt tore ankle ligaments sliding into second. As a result, when the Peaches made the championship series a month later, Alice was sitting on the bench.

I had the cast taken off when we were going into the playoffs. I tried to run, but I couldn't. No push-off. Bill let me try and bat and I just couldn't do that either. You want to play so bad.

I dressed though, I dressed in my uniform every day and sat on the bench.

Jackie Kelley, Rockford's veteran utility player, took over at third. She and Alice had been friends since their softball days together. Their careers became intertwined, and their friendship lifelong. Jackie died of lung cancer in 1988, and Alice can tell us something of Jackie's story as well as her own.

Kelley was a good player. She just didn't get a break, get a regular position. But she hustled. And she could play anywhere. She could play any position there was.

◆◆◆

Alice Pollitt Deschaine lives alone in the lake cabin in northern Michigan that she shared with her husband Glen until his death in 1991. Her son and daughter live nearby. I had made the long drive north from Fort Wayne through blazing autumn reds, oranges and yellows. The sky was clear, the air crisp, and that feeling of fall melancholy was in the air. It was early October 1992, forty-two years and a few weeks after the championship events of 1950.

We sat at Alice's kitchen table, drinking coffee, looking out at the lake and remembering. Alice now has hair shorter than the League would have allowed, and at sixty-three, while not in playing shape anymore, has a fine memory for her baseball past.

Alice came from a poor Michigan family ("My folks had nothing, but we were all happy, I think.") Her dad, a painter and decorator, had been a professional soccer player in England. He was forty when Alice, the youngest of four children, was born.

I remember him running. Lots of running. He would run with me to get in shape before I went to spring training because running is the best thing when you're young. Not when you're older; it's bad on your knees, and I have bad knees, 'cause of playing ball I think.

I remember once coming back to elementary school from eating lunch at home. The boys were out there playing workup, where each time there's an out you work your way up to bat. But if you catch a fly ball you go up right then.

I just naturally went out there, everybody making fun of me, you know. I had a skirt on, but no glove. I caught a fly ball, went up to bat, and hit the ball. Those boys were amazed.

I've since had men come up to me, introduce themselves as boys from my class, and say, "I remember you playin' ball with us. You were better than some of the boys."

Alice tagged along after her older sister Maxine, a softball player in a sports-minded family. Maxine got her baby sister on a team when Alice was twelve, playing shortstop. A few years later Alice joined another softball league where she met Jackie Kelley.

Both infielders, Jackie and Alice were always on opposing teams, but a coach encouraged them to try out together for the All-Americans.

One day he came to me and said, "How would you like to play ball for money?" "Well, yeah," I said. So then he talked to Kelley, and we both went together. I'm not gonna say we were the best hitters then, but we were outstanding in the plays we made.

So they sent us down to try out at spring training in Cuba. I was scared to death. You just try your darnedest. I ran after the ball no matter where it was. And we both made it.

Jackie and Alice made the League in 1947, but Alice's career proved more stable and secure than Jackie's. Alice joined the Peaches her rookie season, made the starting line-up, and stayed with Rockford throughout her seven-year career. Jackie played for South Bend in 1947, for the Chicago Colleens travelling team in 1948, and for a time with Peoria the following year. Finally, later in the 1949 season, she joined her friend Alice in Rockford.

Kelley played for the Peaches for the remaining five years of her career, but never captured a full-time starting position. Her value to the club lay in her versatility. Kelley's baseball card reports lifetime statistics at six different positions: 20 games at first base, 21 at shortstop, 43 at second base, 52 catching, 58 at third base, and 8 in the outfield. By 1950 she was even pitching, delivering the ball in 53 games from 1950 to 1953. She posted a 12 wins-11 losses record in 1952, her best season.

Alice liked Jackie's turning up in Rockford, especially since they'd maintained their friendship while playing for different teams for nearly three years.

Pollitt confirms what the other Peaches remember about coach Bill Allington, both his strictness and his ability to teach the game. But things were different in 1947, her first year, when Allington was gone for a year.

> We had Eddie Ainsmith as a manager, and he was an alcoholic. He and the players were drinking on the bus, and I didn't go for this. Well, they got found out in Rockford, and it hit the headlines, and Eddie got fired. I thought, if it's gonna be like this, I don't know if I want a part of it.
>
> But I come back the next year, and Bill was there, and that made a world of difference. Now Rockford had practice every day we were at home. How long it lasted depended on whether we'd won or lost the game the night before, longer, of course, if we'd lost. When we were on the road we had quizzes every day.
>
> You played for Bill. And he taught you. I'm gonna say he was one of the greatest managers in the League. If you had baseball in you, he brought it out.
>
> Bill wouldn't let us sleep in. Then Sunday he'd say, "Okay, you can go to a movie today." Of course we all got into playing poker on the road too, just for nickels you know.

I told Alice that the naughtiness of the players' social lives sounded very tame, very innocent by today's standards. I wondered if this was how it seemed to her too, looking back.

> Yeah. It wasn't bad back then. Today what we did would be nothing.
>
> Of course if they said, "You can't do this," we went out and did it. For instance, we weren't supposed to play golf—Bill thought it ruined your baseball swing—so of course we did. And there was a bar that served food and had a piano player. They banned that, so we'd try to sneak out there. If we got caught, we got fined. We'd get fined $5 if we were caught wearing jeans, which we all tried I think.
>
> I'm gonna say, though, that our team was the strictest. Bill was strict, and our chaperone Dottie Green was too. Now when we see Dottie Green we ask, "Did you know we did all these things?" She said, "I played ball once myself, you know."

"But it still doesn't sound very serious," I pursued. "Nobody was on drugs, nobody was having sex with anybody, right?"

"Well, some people went out. I went out. Everybody went out.

But we . . . it's hard to say." Alice was struggling, trying to get across just what was going on without being too graphic.

"When you say you went out, do you mean you were being sexual with people?" I pursued, intent on understanding what was being said within the pauses.

"Oh no, no. Not me. No," Alice was quick to reassure me. She continued,

> I don't know if anybody else was or not. This was something we didn't talk about. Even with our good friends. You just went out and had a good time. You didn't even think about sex.
>
> And there was a lot of them didn't go with men, either. You know. They didn't have men friends. But a lot did go out on dates.
>
> I remember after I got married, in 1951, Joanie Berger, the Peaches' second baseman by then, went with my husband and me to the Amvets hall. This guy who asked Joanie to dance said, "My goodness, you have calluses on your hands!" She's never forgotten that. She reminds me of it every time we get together. She'll say, "I've still got calluses on my hands!" But we were normal people, you know.

I asked Alice if she had worried about being too masculine?

> I was always masculine, from when I was young. It was just natural for me, I guess. My sister was just the opposite. She'd trip over a piece of paper. She wasn't graceful. She couldn't run or anything, even though she did play ball. I will say, though, that I was a little more athletic than she was.

Like all the women I talked to, Alice believes the League had a good idea when it tried to ensure that its players looked and acted feminine. Some of the attempts, though, seemed more hopeless than others, especially Charm School, to which Alice was subjected in 1948.

> You had to walk with a book on your head, and learn to sit. I know I was terribly pigeon-toed walking. But you're not gonna change our walk! I don't know what they were thinking of there; they just wasted their money. We just laughed about Charm School, you know, like we knew it all anyway. Of course, the truth is we didn't know it all.
>
> We had to go to dinners with the Kiwanis Club or the Lions Club. We had to dress up. In heels. We sat at round tables and always had chicken, it seemed, and just as you'd get something in your mouth,

they'd ask you a question. Once in a while they'd have every one of you stand up and tell where you was from, and tell about yourself. We hated to go to those.

They tried to bring out the feminine in us. I'm sure we're all tomboys. I'm sure we are. Without their rules we would probably have worn men's shirts. We did wear men's jeans 'cause they didn't make good women's jeans then. And we probably would have worn men's shoes. We would have looked like a man.

I think when they come out with the skirts and the uniforms, I think it was a good idea. I really do. Although my legs were raw all the time. I used to get strawberries. I got the scars to prove it. But it didn't bother me to slide. Bill taught us. And I'd rather slide than run in there and risk a collision. Of course I never went in head first. You can get killed that way!

"Do you remember a wonderful play that you made, a great moment on the field?" I asked.

"Yes. It was with Betty Foss. I broke her leg," Alice replied with some relish.

This talk of high heels at polite dinner parties juxtaposed with broken legs on the field lends a certain surrealistic quality to the accounts players give of their experiences with the All-Americans. The image projected by the League and the reality of life on the field are so at odds as to seem the product of a split personality. The players, however, had little trouble with the scene. The clash between image and reality was just a condition of their work. To them it was simple: they were tomboys, who had to look like girls, and sometimes like women, so they could play baseball like men.

Alice went blithely on to describe her wonderful moment confronting Betty Foss who, because of her size, strength and speed, was one of the League's most intimidating players. Alice was covering third, with baserunner Foss bearing down on her.

I had the ball and was gonna tag her, and she went to run me down. Bill taught us never to block 'em, roll with 'em instead. So I rolled with her. She did knock me down, but I hung onto that ball, and she was out. She went flyin' and somehow broke her leg.

But I'm a friend with her, so she don't hold that against me today!

I also remember a horrible time. We'd played nineteen innings against the Muskegon Lassies, both teams playing shutout ball. Doris Sams was pitching for them and Lois Florreich for us. It must have been 1950. There had to be a runner on third, and the ball come to me. I knocked it down, but by the time I picked it up and threw it to first, it wasn't in time. [She pauses, a pained expression flickering across her face.] It wasn't in time. It was an error, the runner scored and we lost the game one to nothing.

Lois wasn't mad at me, and Bill never said a word. Not that time. Things like that just happen. But I really felt bad.

Alice likes to remember the routines Bill would teach everyone in practice. She described Rockford's infamous squeeze play, and then another Allington favorite.

If there was a runner on third, and you got walked, you'd trot down to first and as soon as you got there, you'd take off. The pitcher turns toward the runner, sets to throw, and while she's distracted, the third-base runner comes in.

First Bill would teach us all these plays, and then teach us how to break them up if anyone tried them on us. If we were in a game, and the other team had runners on first and third, for instance, Bill would signal or yell, "Heads up."

You were thinking all the time, "If I get the ball, what am I gonna do with it?"

Number 9 Al Pollitt, her foot blocking the bag, stretches to take the throw ahead of Tiby Eisen sliding into third base.

Third base is a dangerous position. You're very close to right-handed batters pulling the ball down the third-base line. You risk being hit by a line drive that comes at you too fast to get your glove up for either the play or simple self protection. Third basemen get hit in the chest.

You had to be quick. I played in really close. Kammie did too. Bill taught us that. And you can't be afraid of the ball. You're gonna get hit. You always had marks on your legs.

I asked if she had any special protection, like special bras.

No. Nothing. In fact I didn't even wear a bra back then. I didn't have any breasts back then, too young. I got hit there once really badly, though, I remember that.

I never took a position behind the bag. I was usually way in. In fact I asked the groundskeeper at home to cut out the dirt of the infield in front of third base so I could move in closer yet without being on the infield grass.

When I batted I always pulled the ball down that third-base line. And Bill said, "If I played against you, I'd put my whole outfield toward left field." In 1953 Bill moved to coach the Fort Wayne team. When I come up to bat against him, he did it, everybody come over here to my left. And I hit it to right! He couldn't believe it. "Now why didn't you do that when I was managing you?" he says.

I was never a home-run hitter. I hit one home run in seven years, and I hit it on the ground. It went out to left field, before they had any fences up, and just rolled and rolled, so I had to run all the way around those bases.

I did hit a lot of doubles and triples. And I was a bad-ball hitter, I could hit pitches that were high out of the strike zone. Bill would get upset with everybody swinging at bad pitches and say, "I don't want anybody swinging at bad balls except Alice."

Periodically Alice returned to thoughts of her friend Jackie Kelley.

Jackie was a loner. She was a moody person. You left her alone, she left you alone. She would get up early in the morning and take off somewhere. We never knew where Kelley was. On the road was the same way.

She typed for Bill. And they were good friends, Kelley and Bill. They always sat together on the bus. Always.

She was a comic book fiend.

Kelley was practical too. In 1949 we got a bonus of $707 after the play-offs, which was quite a sum back then. I bought myself a car, but Kelley put a down-payment on a house. Her husband still has that house, and my car's long gone!

Kelley was good-hearted. She'd give you the shirt off her back. Literally. I used to get so dirty 'cause I always slid and was always wipin' my hands on my shirt or skirt. I could wear Kelley's uniform back then, so when both mine would be too dirty, I'd be Kelley sometimes, Number 15!

Jacquelyn "Jackie" Kelley, Rockford's versatile utility infielder, in her 1950 photo. The author picked this up at a fan picnic, got Kelley's autograph and has kept it for more than forty years.

◆◆◆

Alice Pollitt married Glen Deschaine, a Rockford boy and a fan, in 1951.

Glen watched the Peaches before I even played for them. He never told me not to play once we got married. He said, "You're gonna quit on your own. I'll never tell ya to quit ball." Of course he enjoyed it as much as I did.

Without quite intending to, however, Alice became pregnant. Her last season for the Peaches was 1953.

> I don't think I'd ever get married again. When Joanie Berger comes to visit, she brings her husband, and we talk, if we had it to do over, would we really get married again? We both said, "No, we don't think we would," but then we like our kids, too!

Jackie Kelley also left the Peaches after the 1953 season. She joined the Marines where she met her husband. She then began a difficult marriage. Perhaps it was the influence of the autumn afternoon, or the fact that Alice was recently widowed, or maybe simply Alice's excellent memory for her teammates, but the talk had taken a somber turn.

> Jackie had a rough life. She married a man who was an alcoholic, and stayed with him. Finally he took the cure. But it was too late in life when he took it, you know. He was good to her at the end, though. They had vacations together, which they'd never had. I don't think Kelley knew what a vacation was because, hey, she just had a hard time.
>
> I quit smoking a while ago and I could light up again today. But I won't. I've seen too many people go through that. And I wasn't a heavy smoker. But Kelley was one, she smoked three or four packs a day. They told her to quit or she was gonna die. Well, that was too late. She already had cancer in both lungs.

Jackie Kelley died of lung cancer in 1988. She lived long enough to enjoy the players finding each other again and to witness the formation of the Players' Association. She was able to attend the 1986 reunion. She died before the All-Americans were honored at the Baseball Hall of Fame. Her husband and children made the trip to Cooperstown without her.

Kelley's baseball card reads in part, "We knew Jackie would want to be on a baseball card as well as in the hearts of her friends. We salute Jackie Kelley Savage for her talent and her courage. Our thanks to teammate Alice Pollitt Deschaine for the loan of the photo."

◆◆◆

Many All-Americans began smoking during their League days, Alice among them. Beer or Coca-Cola were the drinks of choice. At the time there was no consciousness about smoking or nutrition and very little about alcohol or even exercise. No one was lifting weights or cross training or "eating to win."

On the road we'd just eat anything cheap, hamburgers, hot dogs, malts. At home we'd go out to eat after the game, spaghetti or steak, and then go home to bed.

Of course bodies were young then and more forgiving of abuse. Now those bodies are getting older. I was curious whether Alice thought people who've been athletes take any better physical care of themselves than anyone else.

"No," she said somewhat ruefully. "Look at me."

Alice is in comparatively good health, but is overweight. She quit smoking ten years ago. She has had a bout with breast cancer, and has arthritis and bad knees. Alice considers herself fairly lucky, actually, but nonetheless, "It's terrible to get old, you know. They tell you about the golden years, but they're not very good on some people."

Her baseball-playing days are definitely over.

I have broken both of my Achilles tendons. I did one bowling and the last I did thirteen years ago, when I was fifty years old, helping my daughter play softball. My husband said, "Now, don't play. Don't you play!" And I said, "No, I just want to help 'em, you know." I thought, "I can play as good as these girls. I'll show 'em some fundamentals of the game."

Well, I could run back then, I could still throw a ball, and I could hit it out there. Wouldn't you know when I hit the ball I hit a home run. I was rounding third and when I hit the bag I heard the tendon pop. I went right down, they got the ball and tagged me out. So that was my final out.

Alice had told me about Glen's nephew Larry Larson who was ten years old when Alice would take him to practice with her.

Every day he'd go with me. He was just amazed by me. He and his little boyfriend would come over to my apartment, stand outside my big window, and just watch. He idolized me.

Alice has lost track of Larry, though, and wondered what he was doing today. "He must be about your age," she said to me.

I could assure her that, if Larry was anything like me and the other Peaches fans, whatever he's doing today, he still idolizes her. The heroes of our youth never have their final out.

Sometimes the skirts-in-public rule was interpreted too rigidly. When their team bus broke down, the Daisies were required to change jeans and shorts for skirts and dresses to hike back to town.

At a 1952 promotional event in Rockford, former stars and chaperones gathered at Beyer Stadium to celebrate the Peaches' tenth year in the League.

LIFE OFF
THE FIELD

"I entered a strange world with people I didn't even know." —Maxine Kline

The All-American girls were without question and almost without exception committed individual competitors who liked to play baseball more than anything else in the world. But much of what would prove important to them happened off the field. It was here they learned something about life outside the confines of their traditional working-class families. They learned most from each other, but they also learned from the expectations placed upon them and the day-to-day constraints within which they lived.

The women remember themselves as innocent young girls. They had to help each other learn some of the basics. Marie Mansfield came to the 1950 Peaches at age nineteen, from a working-class section of Boston.

> I wasn't worldly-wise. I wanted to use Tampax 'cause everybody was usin' 'em, but I didn't have the foggiest idea where to put it! So they told me. Oh my gosh, I was green about everything.

Irene Applegren at age seventeen was very nervous about leaving her Peoria family.

I guess I was scared of just being out on my own. I think we players were pretty well taken care of. We lived in private homes, and my houseparents were like my second mother and dad. They watched over us. So I wasn't scared of that part. But when I traveled, staying in hotels and worrying whether somebody's gonna come in, you kinda had to watch yourself and be careful who you'd meet.

And I was always forgetting things. One time I had to get off the train we were on bound for Racine, and catch a cab back to the station where I'd left my luggage. Then I had to catch another train by myself. I was plenty scared.

I did send money home to the folks. But another girl, Jo Leonard and I, we'd go shopping and buy not one blouse but five or six. Jo was my roommate too. She kinda took care of me. She's still a good friend.

I liked Snookie and Kammie, they were real good to me. I can't remember any of the Rockford girls being standoffish, ignoring me, you know. They were older and used to tease me because I'd forget my uniform, my shoes, my glove.

The All-American League saw to it that Irene and the other girls were taken care of. The League developed a structure and a set of rules that acted in loco parentis for the girls. Central to this structure was the chaperone. Each team hired a woman, often an ex-player only a few years older than the girls themselves, to handle all the house-keeping arrangements, to enforce the standards of feminine appearance and behavior, to administer first-aid in the event of injury, and to be the girls' confidante and counselor. The chaperone, in a word, was the team mom who, according to her contract, was to "keep her club as a family unit." It is a measure of the flexibility of the chaperones and the basic good nature of the players that anyone could be found capable of fulfilling these potentially conflicting job requirements. In fact, players appreciated, depended upon, and were often close to their chaperones.

Norma Metrolis, who played with at least four different chaperones, felt a chaperone was a "buddy."

She was somebody you could talk to if you had a problem. If you were hurt, she was the first-aider. She made all the arrangements every place, doled out the meal money, and tried to keep everybody in line.

Evie Wawryshyn appreciated her chaperones too, among them Doris Tetzlaff, who was the Daisies' chaperone for four years that included the 1950 season.

> You kinda felt happy that there was someone there that gave you a sense of security. It felt good to have them, as a sounding block, for instance, if you were in trouble, or if you got hurt. They seemed to look after everything, and all you had to do was play ball. You didn't have to worry about other things. Everything they did was for your benefit, you know. I admired these girls.
> I think you had to be a certain type of person to be able to be in charge of a group of girls and still have the camaraderie.

Dottie Green was the Peaches' chaperone for the 1948 and 1950-1953 seasons. She had been a catcher for the original 1943 Peaches. Millie Lundahl, who preceded Green as the Peaches' chaperone in 1946 and 1947, remembers Dottie's career-ending injury. "I was with her when she tore the ligaments in her knee that ended her baseball career. And then I talked her into being chaperone. That was quite a come-down for her, to be told, 'You can't play anymore.'"

Green's 1948 contract with the League agrees to pay her $75 a week for duties extending from spring training until the conclusion of any post-season play in which her team may be involved. A list of twenty-three duties follow, from: "The Chaperone is reponsible for the appearance, conduct and behavior of the members of the Club over which she is appointed. She will be accessible to the girls at all times" to "No player may change her residence without permission of the Chaperone" and "Any violations of rules and regulations for Players that are not reported to the Manager of the Club or the League by the Chaperone will make the Chaperone subject to the same fine as the Player."[35]

The chaperone was the go-between, conveying and interpreting the manager to the players and vice versa, about any off-the-field matters. The chaperone's immediate superior was the manager, and while she had considerable discretion, his was the final word when resolving conflicts or meting out sanctions.

Sanctions came in the form of fines, or, most drastically, banishment from the League. It was this latter power that most intimidated the players, who had no union to protect them, no formal appeals structure, and nowhere else to play women's baseball. Fines, on the other hand, were an occupational hazard, something to be avoided, of course, but not punitive in the extreme. The amounts of fines varied considerably: 25 cents for forgetting part of one's equipment or removing your shoes before termination of the game, five dollars for the first and ten dollars for the second offense of smoking in the hotel lobby or appearing in non-feminine attire. For the Rockford team, the fine for a first and non-repeated offense was refunded at the end of the season.

While Millie Lundahl handled myriad problems in her two years as the Peaches' chaperone, nothing bothered her as much as knowing when a player was going to be released.

> They never told a girl she was through until after the game. The manager did it, but he always asked me to be with him. I hated watching them play what I knew was going to be their last game. When they were told, they'd cry, and I would cry right along with 'em!

The manager's authority was critical, both to the chaperone in being able to do her job, and to the cohesiveness of the team. But the chaperone had powers of her own. In 1947 Bill Allington left the Peaches for a year, and Millie worked with two other coaches. Eddie Ainsmith was particularly difficult.

> He did not know how to handle girls. He didn't want them punished for things, and I said, "But those are the rules!" He'd let them go in a bar and get a drink in their uniforms, and just say, "Oh, it doesn't hurt anything." After one road trip I called the Board of Directors and tried to resign. "I want you to get somebody else in my job; I'm not doing one thing. Eddie says they can do it, and I say they can't."
>
> The next day the President of the Board and three Directors told Eddie he was through.

When Bill the disciplinarian was there, of course, everything worked smoothly. "Allington was marvelous. He knew everything about the girls, and he used good psychology in getting them to do things, and he was a teacher as well as a coach."

The players accepted the authority of manager and chaperone and League officials almost without question. They simply followed most of the rules most of the time. Dottie Schroeder explained,

I was brought up to respect authority. Maybe you questioned it in your own mind occasionally, but you didn't say so in those days. You respected your elders because they were over you, and that was reflected in how you felt when you went out into the world.

Alice Pollitt put it bluntly, "Bill told us what to do. And you did it or else you didn't stay on that team."

◆◆◆

Players had little free time given their daily games and practices. Here Daisies Vivian Kellogg and Kay Blumetta warm up before a game.

The players didn't have a lot of spare time to get in trouble. Allington maintained a schedule for the Peaches, for instance, that accounted for almost all their available hours. If they were at home in Rockford, they had to be up, dressed, breakfasted and at the ballpark by 9 a.m. for a couple of hours of practice. They'd shower around 11 a.m., and only then have a few hours to themselves. They'd catch up on personal tasks like doing laundry or writing letters home, or they'd nap, or play cards, or go to the movies.

Around 5 p.m. they were due again at the ballpark for infield and batting practice before the game. The games started at 7:30 p.m. and lasted until perhaps 9 p.m. The girls showered again and went out to eat their big meal of the day. Rules specified that they had to be home again within two hours of the close of the game. The chaperone sometimes drove around Rockford, making spot checks of players' parked cars to see if they were really at home.

On the road, morning practice was replaced by Allington's daily meetings. The previous night's game was discussed, plans for that night's strategy were made and players took written quizzes about the rules of baseball. Allington issued a set of baseball rules to every new player, and she was expected to know them, down to the most obscure. Marilyn Jones kept a copy of one of these review quizzes. It includes Allington's ten typed questions and Marilyn's answers written in longhand. For example,

> Question 9: In a run down play, the runner's progress is impeded by a defensive player without the ball. Ruling?
> Answer: Umpire calls "Obstruction." Runner is entitled to the base she's trying to reach at the time.
> Question 10: When does the runner leave base on a juggled and then caught fly ball?
> Answer: The instant the first fielder touches the ball.

After the meeting the players were again free until late afternoon practice. The girls liked to spend their few free hours playing poker or, best of all, going to the movies. On June 4, 1950, the Rockford girls could have gone to see Johnny Weismuller and Brenda Joyce in "Tarzan and the Mermaids," Joel McCrea and Arlene Dahl in "The Outrider," or any of perhaps a dozen other films playing in neighborhood theatres scattered throughout the city. The newest movie in town was "Captain Carey, U.S.A." starring Alan Ladd, "the blazing story of an ex-OSS officer who returns to Italy to find the man who betrayed his outfit during the war and caused the death of the girl he loved."

Marie Mansfield remembers how narrow her choices for relaxation were, given the tight schedule.

> We used to love to go swimmin' up to Lake Louise. 'Course we had to get permission. You had to get permission for everything you did. Other than that, we had practices every day, so there wasn't a heck of a lot you could do.

Marilyn Jones describes how players were somewhat isolated from each other in their rare free time: "You know, when we played ball, there wasn't much socializing. You'd go out to eat after the game, but you all were at different places."

The lack of time for players to socialize created a paradox. Looking back the players report valuing the friends they made, but these friendships were not intimate by today's standards. If a woman had a personal problem—like unhappiness in her family at home or boyfriend troubles or difficulties with a teammate—she was more likely to discuss it with her chaperone than with a fellow player. Most likely of all, she kept it to herself.

These girls played baseball decades before our society accepted and promoted expressiveness and the ready verbalizing of problems, emotional or otherwise. Their era and their class taught them stoicism, an ability to endure difficulty without complaint, to shut up and—with good grace and good nature—get on with the job. Ruth Richard is aware of a big difference between the women she played ball with and the women she now works with in a Pennsylvania gauge factory.

I got along real good with the ballplayers compared to some of these women I work with now. They're always complainin', one's freezin' or one's hot or one's this or one's that, and they have to go tell the boss. I don't know if they're miserable doing what they're doing or what.

And they can't make a joke about it. A lot of times if you can joke about something it'll go over better than if you're gonna just be miserable and complain. When we played ball there was no bickerin' or carrying on. I enjoyed playin' with those girls. They were a special breed, I'll tell ya.

Acceptance without complaint is a virtue that allowed the All-Americans to get on with the game. It is significant, of course, that they loved the game, while it is more than likely that Richie's sister workers do not love the gauge factory. But the players' predilection toward being silent about problems does not make for shared confidences. I asked Irene Applegren why fellow pitcher Lois Florreich quit baseball after her very successful 1950 season.

I don't know, I never thought about that. Unless there was some reason she had to be at home. She never talked about it. Most of the girls were that way. They just never discussed so many things.

Now the constraints of time have changed; although the future is foreshortened because these women are aging, they can at least get together without the pressure of preparing for a ballgame that night. Vivian Kellogg says, "I'm really getting more acquainted with the girls now, after all these years, than I did when I played ball."

◆◆◆

Teams naturally divided into friendship groups. Girls who lived together in the same home in Fort Wayne or Rockford would, of course, see more of each other than the rest of the team. Girls sometimes lived alone, but more usually in groups of two, three or four.

Younger players were more likely to stick together and regard veterans from an awestruck distance. Tiby Eisen, one of Fort Wayne's team leaders, acknowledges,

> There were a lot of youngsters that came in, like Wilma Briggs and Maxine Kline. They kind of looked up to me because I had been in the League a few years.

Wilma remembers the feeling vividly.

> Tiby definitely was a leader. All the younger players looked up to her. Maxine Kline and I, we'd get in a team meeting and we just sat and listened. I always admired and respected her and the other veterans. I'd just sit there watching them.

The same was true on the Peaches team. Dottie Kamenshek and Snookie Doyle were the acknowledged leaders. Marie Mansfield was a rookie.

> As a rookie I wasn't goin' out with Kammie or Snookie. I was more with the other rookies, Sis Waddell and my roommate Marilyn Jones. The rookies were separate from the veteran stars. You just have to wait til you earn your way there.

Rookies were subjected to mild hazing from veterans. Marie explains,

> They'd put Limburger cheese in your glove, or hide your uniform or tie your clothes together. Things like that.
>
> It never really bothered me too much. And if it did, you certainly didn't let them know it.
>
> Of course once you were no longer a rookie, then you started doin' it to a new rookie. The torch got passed, you know.

These divisions within a team, while natural, could cause trouble unless they were intentionally counteracted. It turns out that, while the rookies were regarding the veterans with awe, the veterans were trying to reach out to younger players. Dottie Kamenshek believes one of the reasons the Peaches won on the field was because the team stuck together off the field.

You helped another player out if she was blue or down or she didn't have her family there. You cheered 'em up. You also included everyone when you did things. You'd say, "You eating with anyone tonight? Would you like to come along with us?" Especially the rookies, the younger ones, to have them become a part of your team.

◆◆◆

Most of the players kept their friendship activities to cards and movies, the occasional swim and a quick dinner together after the game. If players were going to get in trouble, it usually involved being out too late, not making the two-hour post-game curfew. Eating out after the game would—perhaps with the help of a few beers— turn out to be longer than planned. There are many stories of players creeping down hotel hallways, hoping to avoid the watchful eyes of chaperones. When they were discovered, which they nearly always were it seems, a warning usually sufficed.

Dottie Schroeder remembers, rather fondly,

We were young, and went out, and stayed out longer than the two hours, but you didn't put anything over on the chaperone or the manager. Because they'd been through this themselves; they knew all the excuses.

You would go to extreme lengths to get into the hotel without being caught. It never worked. You'd go up the back stairs, or pull the outside fire escape down and go up, take your shoes off and tiptoe down the hall. You'd round the corner and sittin' there by your door would be either the chaperone or the manager waitin' on you!

I don't ever remember being fined though. They'd say, "We'll see you in the morning." Then you'd be quaking in your boots all night, and then they'd say, "Well, let's watch this," or "You've got to get your rest." Just warnings, you know. We were never doing anything malicious, of course, we were just young.

Too much beer and too little sleep could, of course, mean not being in shape to play when, all too soon, the next day rolled around. This could hurt team performance. Snookie Doyle remembered a Peaches game in the 1940s, lost because a player was drunk during the game and made three errors. Snookie herself had had a beer before the game.

I booted one and I really felt it was because I had that beer and it relaxed me too much. I have to be more intense to play well. I had it four hours before game time, but still, with me, it did not work.

I just think you shouldn't do it. I'd also try to make sure I had the amount of sleep I needed. I used to get upset if I knew somebody had been keeping improper hours and I noticed that they played badly. I did attempt to set a good example, really.

◆◆◆

There were potentially difficult sources of division that every team had to deal with. The players who came from California were regarded with suspicion by some. They were thought to be cocky and rowdier than anyone else, and besides they had an unfair advantage: they could practice their skills all year round playing softball. Sis Waddell had never met a Canadian before, and Nickie Fox remembers having to explain that not all Canadians were French Canadians. Cuban Isabel Alvarez felt isolated, her ethnic difference from the other girls heightened by a language barrier. Isabel pitched for five years, but still felt set apart, lonely in her fear. "I just didn't fit in the League. I felt a lot of pressure to perform. I was very scared all the time. I was glad when it was over."

African-American girls were never introduced into the League. Author Lois Browne reports that two African-American players tried out with South Bend in 1951. Their arrival was met by—in the carefully chosen words of the keeper of the League minutes—"various views from different cities."[36] Marilyn Jones has a vague memory of African-Americans once trying out for the touring teams, and Dottie Schroeder remembers several African-Americans trying out at an exhibition game in Lafayette, Louisiana. Nothing came of any of these brief contacts; no African-Americans ever appeared on an AAGBL roster.

Apparently the All-American Girls Baseball League came too early for African-American girls. Black women's softball leagues existed, and excellent black women players could have been recruited from these had All-American League organizers wanted to do so.[37] But the League's time in history and the racism that characterized that time kept them from doing so. The Brooklyn Dodgers had shocked the country, after all, by introducing Jackie Robinson to major league baseball as late as 1947.

Barbara Gregorich speculates about one form racism may have taken that is special to a women's league.

> The men in charge believed that only a certain kind of woman should be recruited, one who met society's standards of "feminine beauty". . . . Social mores of the time excluded black women from the standards of "feminine beauty" (being set for the white players in the League).[38]

Sis Waddell struggled without success to remember any association between softball or baseball and African-American women.

> I'm sure there were some black players as good as there were white. I don't even know if they had a league. I don't even know that they played ball.
>
> But look what the fans did to Jackie Robinson. What would they have done to some woman tryin' to play ball? It just was never talked about.

◆◆◆

The few players who chose to marry during their years playing baseball created another special situation. Sometimes a player quit once she married, like Sis Waddell did after two years with the Peaches.

> My husband didn't want me to keep playing after we got married. So I didn't. In those days you did what your husband wanted you to do.

Sometimes such a withdrawal from the game was strategically timed as well. Sis' husband Neil believes—and third baseman Alice Pollitt confirms—that Sis would have had a difficult time making the team once infielder Joanie Berger arrived in 1952. Retiring to married life was perhaps forced by both a new husband and a new rookie.

Dottie Key and Snookie Doyle both married after the 1949 season and both returned to play for many seasons thereafter. Dottie remembers having her priorities firmly in mind.

> I knew what I wanted. Don kept saying, "Let's get married now." In 1946, 1947, 1948. "Nope," I said, and "Nope" and "Nope. I'm going back to play ball." Then in 1949 I said, "Okay, but I'm still going to play ball." That was fine with him. He was my number one fan.

The husbands of players who stayed in the game were, indeed, their best fans and became integrated into the team as significant supporters. In 1945, in the underhand days of the League, Dottie Wiltse had pitched and won both games of a doubleheader against Rockford. Later the same day Dottie met Harvey Collins and married him the following year.

Being married changed her off-the-field time with the team. She went home to eat while they went out after the game. During spring training she worked out in Fort Wayne while the rest of the team was down south; she'd join them moving north for the exhibition season. Management was very flexible about letting this established pitcher make whatever arrangements she needed to keep playing.

Dottie Wiltse Collins feels her marital status had no effect on how she played or how the team felt about her. Having a baby was a different story. Dottie stayed out for the 1949 season and made her comeback in 1950. But things had changed.

> I just decided this is not the life I wanted to lead. I had a great mother-in-law who took care of the baby. And Harvey was one of those guys who was always for my playing. But I think I'd had enough; I had been playing ball since I was seven or eight years old. And I wasn't being a part of my baby growing up. After spring training that year Harvey and his mother brought the baby to an exhibition game, and I couldn't even recognize her, she had grown that much.

Dottie retired for good after the 1950 season.

◆◆◆

Perhaps the most potentially divisive issue the All-Americans dealt with was the girls' knowledge of and for some, participation in lesbian activities and relationships. It is a tribute to both players and management that the issue was contained by using the tools of discretion and tolerance.

The 1940s and 1950s were a time of complete silence about the topic of homosexuality; homosexual behavior was so stigmatized that no one even spoke of it. This allowed some of the girl ballplayers to grow up ignorant of such things. One player told me she was asked at the time how many lesbians there were in the League. "Here I'm this dumb seventeen-year-old rookie. I didn't answer him because I didn't even know what he was talking about." Other girls knew what a lesbian was because they themselves were experimenting with being one. They, of course, were silent in the face of society's disapproval. As one player put it, "they were very careful."

To this day no player wants to talk openly about the existence or impact of lesbians in the League. Under these circumstances it is irresponsible to speculate about how many All-Americans were lesbians. There is no question that some players were lesbians at the time. I heard estimates running all the way from "eighty percent of the girls on my team" to "no one on my team." Surely the truth lies somewhere in between.

Life for the girls who were lesbians was undoubtedly difficult. They were supervised so closely and lived under conditions of so little privacy that it must have been a nearly impossible task to develop any kind of sustained relationship. Furthermore, the League did what it could to discourage lesbian behavior. Chaperones used their power to assign rooms on the road to try to discourage budding romances; they separated players they'd heard rumors about. Players might even be traded away to break up a relationship. And, of course, management had available to it the ultimate penalty: being openly lesbian was unofficial grounds for being kicked out of the League, and several players told me of individuals who had been let go for this reason.

It seems, however, that such sanctions were rarely used. Players and others reported to me that, on the whole, the League was accepting of lesbian behavior as long as the girls themselves were discreet. A manager told me about a team meeting he had to hold because a couple of rookies had been approached by older players.

If I had said to the girls on my team "Don't be gay," they could all have quit and gone home, leaving me stranded there! So I said, "I'm not going to pry into your private affairs. But if you put your private affairs onto me and the chaperone, then I'm going to take action. It could be that some of you might have to go home."

That was the trend of my thought. I talked maybe ten minutes. Long enough, since they got the idea.

The unspoken understanding seemed to be that discreet lesbian contacts were tolerated as long as youngsters coming into the League were not approached by their more experienced elders. With this unwritten rule strictly observed, players learned to be tolerant of each other's sexual orientation.

This attitude of basic tolerance is a notable achievement of the girls who played professional baseball. I held the following conversation with one particular player, but many others shared similar thoughts with me.

Player: It was a black mark on you then, if you were thought of as gay. Wrigley didn't want those kind of people. He wanted the League feminine.

Susan: You mean he didn't want those kind of people playing, or he didn't want people to think those kind of people were playing?

Player: Other people to think they were playing. Because anywhere you get a bunch of men or women together, it's just a fact of life you're gonna have gay people. I don't care where you go or who you're with.

Susan: Was there a split on the team between the women who were gay and the women who weren't?

Player: No. We all just ran around together. I didn't think anything about it. I was too green to know much about it. They didn't bother you with it and you didn't bother them. I just let 'em do their own thing, and I did my own thing. I mean, everybody's got their own lifestyle. That's what they want? Do it. You know? We can still be friends.

Some of the women who played professional baseball married during their careers and some married later. Some were lesbians at the time and some became lesbians later. Some were young and celibate and maintained their disinterest in sexual relationships as they grew older.

Looking back from our sexually explicit era, it is sometimes difficult to remember that these women grew up in a culture that kept daughters innocent and sexual matters private. The girls' participation in the League exposed them to different kinds of women and different lifestyles. But my guess is that at the time they were playing ball, the majority of girls were too young and too well-protected to be concerned with sex at all. Most of them were satisfied to pursue single-mindedly their greatest passion: baseball.

◆◆◆

From the League's inception in 1943 until teams became independent entities in 1951, players signed contracts with the League itself, not with the individual team for which they played. After each season teams would have the opportunity to protect a certain number of players from reallocation, perhaps ten or so of their total roster of seventeen. The others would go into a pool available for reassignment to teams that League management felt needed help to compete on an equal basis. This principle of maintaining parity among teams did result in teams relatively equal in skill and thus competitive with each other the following season. For the players, however, parity plus normal trades during the season created a situation of considerable insecurity. Unless you were a star with your team—and even then sometimes—you could expect sooner or later to be reallocated or traded.

Most of the girls who played professional baseball were traded at least once in their career. Of the twenty-five 1950 Peaches and Daisies who played more than one season, ten players were never traded, Dottie Kamenshek, Dottie Key, Snookie Doyle, Marie Mansfield, Louise Erickson, Sis Waddell and Alice Pollitt for the Peaches, and Dottie Collins, Vivian Kellogg, and Betty Weaver Foss for the Daisies. The rest had to deal with the disruption to lives and relationships that being traded produced.

Fran Janssen, a Daisies' pitcher in 1950, played for five different teams in the course of her five-year career. She tried to put a good face on the experience.

> I got traded a lot! You had to find a new place to live, and you're kinda disappointed if you get traded because usually it meant I wasn't doing as well as I should have. I really would have liked to have stayed with Fort Wayne, but I didn't get to do that either.
>
> The manager would tell you, and they were usually nice about it. They didn't like it either. They hated to hurt anybody's feelings, I think.
>
> But there were so many players that got traded and reallocated, that I don't think it was a big deal. Because I knew everybody on all the teams, it didn't matter too much.

By 1951 Betty Weaver Foss had been joined on the Daisies by her two sisters, Jo and Jean. Jo proved to be an even more spectacular player than Betty, which is saying a lot, but Jean was always a more average player. Fort Wayne attempted to trade Jean away, and Betty remembers this threat as the worst time of her career.

> I just spoke up. I said, "If you trade one of us, just trade us all three. We come together and we're gonna leave together."

Sister solidarity worked and management withdrew the idea, but later Fort Wayne was adamant to trade Jean. By this time she had cut a couple of toes off in a farming accident, lost her mobility at third base, and become a pitcher. Rather than leave the team and her sisters, Jean retired.

Even Dottie Schroeder, without doubt a quality shortstop and a star, experienced three trades in her career, the last after six years with the Daisies.

> I bawled my eyes out. I had been with Fort Wayne the longest time in my baseball career, and at the time you're crushed. I didn't want to leave my teammates. But all these things are for a purpose. I think it helped make me a better player, because you try a little bit harder against the team that traded you.

Dottie Schroeder tried harder against Fort Wayne once the Daisies had traded her to Kalamazoo. Marilyn Jones played with extra energy for Rockford in the 1950 playoffs against her former team, Kenosha, and later especially enjoyed pitching her no-hitter for Battle Creek against Bill Allington. Players uniformly reported high motivation to beat their previous teams. Although a trade or reallocation was always difficult to accept, playing against former teammates was a challenge to these women's competitive natures.

The League was apparently afraid, however, that players would not put out their best effort against friends or former teammates and thus promulgated the nonfraternization rule, the most unpopular rule with which players had to cope. "Fraternizing with players on other clubs is the worst enemy of discipline and cuts down the spirit of rivalry and competition on the field.[39] (Thus,) fraternizing on and off the field is prohibited, except by express permission from the chaperone."[40]

Kate Vonderau, the Daisies' 1950 back-up catcher who played for three teams in her eight-year career, is very clear about the difficulties occasioned by this rule.

> I felt the nonfraternization rule was kind of useless really, because there was so much trading going on around the League. Everybody at some time or other probably played with everybody else, so we were all pretty good friends, no matter which team we played on. It had absolutely nothing to do with winning or losing.
>
> So I thought it was a useless rule, and if I violated any rules it was probably that one, because I had good friends on other teams. They

tried to enforce it, but there were always ways to get around it, because we would go someplace out of the city and meet people. So they wouldn't know what we were doing.

I don't really know why the rule existed unless it was for the fans. If they saw people from different teams associating, maybe they would think there wasn't enough competition. It seems to me a lot of things were more for the fans than they were for the players.

In fact, players enjoyed competing not only against ex-teammate friends but against friends from home who wound up on opposing teams.

Snookie Doyle remembers triumphs against fellow Californians.

I just remember things against my friends from home, like Tiby Eisen. One time she hit what should have been a double, but as she was rounding first I kind of faked her out so she didn't know the throw was coming in from right field. I got the ball and tagged her out! She laughed and said, "That's a nice play, Snookie." You really are thrilled when you can fool one of your own friends.

Helen Ketola, a Fort Wayne rookie, didn't feel too inhibited by the nonfraternization rule because she felt it wasn't rigorously enforced.

I don't think they were strict with it at all. When we'd go to Kenosha I'd have supper with my friend from home, Jean Buckley. So they said I was to report the next morning because I'd been fraternizing. But it turns out they were just kidding me because I was a rookie. We wouldn't fraternize on or around the ballfield, just when you went out afterwards.

My thought is, if I had a chance to wipe out Jean Buckley at second base, I'd do it just as hard or harder than against somebody else, 'cause you want to do well against somebody you know.

An unpopular and oft-violated rule is always an occasion for selective enforcement. Ruth Richard remembers Bill Allington strictly enforcing this rule, just as he did all the others. "I don't know if a lot of them enforced it like Rockford did. I think our rules were enforced more than some of the other teams." But even on the same team players have a different recollection of how seriously the rule was taken. Marilyn Jones lists her leisure activities: "You might go to a movie, or you might play cards, or you might read or you might sneak out and fraternize!"

The problem with this rule, of course, was that it was attempting to solve a problem that didn't exist with a measure that went against the natural instincts of the players. The nonfraternization rule both insulted their competitive spirit and inhibited their sociability. It was doomed to relative failure among a group of women who had a dual allegiance; they were committed to winning, but also to friendship.

Nickie Fox and Irene Applegren, Rockford
Peaches pitchers, autograph baseballs with
Bob Feller, for eighteen years (1936-1956) a
Cleveland Indians fast-ball pitcher. Like many
other major leaguers, Feller missed the 1942-
1944 seasons due to World War II. He was
inducted into the Hall of Fame in 1962. Fox
pitched for the All-Americans for all twelve
years of the League, home games only in 1953
and 1954, and led the League in earned-run
average in 1943 and 1944. "Lefty" Applegren
also enjoyed a long career, 1944-1953.

Daisy players relax in the dugout. Left to right: Betty Foss, Evelyn Wawryshyn, Maxine Kline, Dottie Schroeder, Mary Rountree and Sally Meier.

GAME FOUR

Wednesday, September 13, 1950

The home field had agreed with both teams through the first three games of the 1950 championship series. The Peaches won the first two games in Rockford, and the Daisies took the third game once they got home to Fort Wayne.

Home-field advantage is a complex mix of concrete benefits and intangibles. Manager Bill Allington would direct Rockford grounds-keepers to mow the grass or keep it long, depending on his assessment of the visiting team's tendency to hit grounders. He designed the basepaths so he could position his infielders to greatest advantage. In 1950 Fort Wayne recognized the potential power of long-ball-hitting Betty Foss by erecting for the first time home-run fences, "expected to add punch and zest to Daisy games," as sports writer Phil Olofson put it.[41] As we know, Betty proceeded to punch her way to the League batting title, knocking out five home runs in the process.[42]

Home-field advantage also reflects the fact that the home players are more comfortable than the visitors. Unless it's the first game of a home stand, they haven't spent all night in a bus, travelling to the away city. They're at home in their own apartments or rooming houses, with familiar beds and food and entertainments. They can sleep and eat better than on the road and maintain a familiar routine.

Once they take the field their fans are there, roaring their support while greeting the exploits of visitors with stoney silence. Hometown players can get energy from their fans and can play beyond themselves. On the road it is a disciplined team that can consistently play well, faced with neutrality or even hostility from its audience.

The practical effect of fan support plus the other home-field advantages is easily documented: teams in all sports typically win a higher percentage of their games at home than they do on the road.

To be successful a team needs to win, both on the field and at the gate. Winning at the gate helps them win on the field, while winning on the field is necessary to attract fans to the gate.

Fort Wayne played its best season in the history of the franchise in 1950 and entertained more fans than any other team in the League. Some of this success is attributable to the congenial ballpark the Daisies called home. The team played most of its games at Memorial Park, a ballfield set within one of Fort Wayne's municipal parks. The field itself was surrounded by beautifully groomed expanses of grass, low rolling hills and curving roads. Middle-class homes lined the streets at the park's boundaries.

◆◆◆

Good baseball wasn't all that went on at the All-American ballparks. Admission cost about seventy-five cents for adults and a quarter for kids, leaving a little money left over for some treats, perhaps candy for ten cents, or for adults a pack of cigarettes at twenty-five cents.

A variety of promotions was devised to attract fans. On August 3, 1950, the Daisies-Peoria Redwings game was "preceded by the annual Track and Field Meet, which featured running, throwing and batting contests involving girls from both teams." Perhaps less related to baseball, on August 11 the Daisies treated fans to a pre-game program presented by the Fort Wayne Dog Obedience and Training Club. And of course there was Max Carey Night in August when the Daisies manager received a new automobile presented by Daisies fans, players and management "as a reward for his managerial prowess this season."[43]

The Rockford team created similarly entertaining events to supplement their games at Beyer Stadium, called, naturally, "the Peach Orchard." On opening day, May 24, 1950, for instance, "In keeping with baseball tradition, Mayor C. Henry Bloom will pitch the first ball and City Clerk Elmer O. Strand will be on the receiving end. The club will have an organist at the park, Mildred Peters, to play during and after the game."

Before opening day Beyer Stadium had undergone some needed repairs. "Several improvements have been carried out at the playing field. For one thing, the Peaches and the school board have replaced the old, coal-burning water heater with a new gas heater. The old heater was used to prepare water for players' showers, and frequently, when the wind was right, customers in some sections of the stands have been showered too—with particles of soot."[44]

In one week in August 1950, Rockford fans were treated to a fashion show, a pre-game contest between two men's softball league teams, a night honoring first baseman Dottie Kamenshek at which Rockford's 1949 League pennant was flown for the first time, Out of Town Night where the fan travelling the farthest won a prize, and the Fire Department's exhibition of their new hook-and-ladder truck.

For some, the promotions were more significant than the game. My little sister—six years younger—cannot remember anything about any Peaches games, but she does remember the family winning a free bag of groceries. Though I pride myself on being a serious fan, I admit to remembering the groceries too, the only time in my life I've won a raffle.

All the promotions were fun: they gave the community something to do and entertained little sisters. But what really kept the fans coming back was good baseball. For instance, on July 11, 1950, Memorial Park was host to 3,259 Fort Wayne fans who were treated to a spectacular game and at the same time boosted Daisies attendance to 15,300 for seven consecutive nights of baseball. On July 19 the newspaper reported convincing evidence of home-field advantage; the team had chalked up its eighth consecutive victory and 22nd triumph in 28 games at home.[45]

There was one problem with Memorial Field, however. If it rained too much, the "skin" infield of fine dirt became a sea of gritty mud. This forced the Daisies to play Game Four at another field. Regardless of setting, the Daisies desperately needed to win this game to even the series.

Maxine Kline, treated rudely by the Peaches in Game One, went to the mound for Fort Wayne. Nickie Fox, Rockford's winning pitcher in Game One, opened for the Peaches.

Daisies Square Rockford Series, 5-3; Fifth Game Tonight

by Phil Olofson
Fort Wayne News-Sentinel, September 14, 1950

The crucial fifth—and pivotal—game of the AAGBL championship series between the rejuvenated Daisies and the Rockford Peaches will be played at Zollner Stadium tonight, starting at 8:15 p.m.

The Daisies squared the series at two victories apiece by rallying to defeat the defending champions, 5-3, at the softball palace Wednesday night.

Maxine Kline authored one of her best performances of the season Wednesday night, holding the Peaches to six hits, two of which were tainted.

Rockford's leadoff punch, Dottie Kamenshek and Snookie Doyle, rocked her for a single and a double and a run in the first inning, but she settled down and retired the next 12 batters in order.

Callow Starts Trouble

Eleanor Callow singled to start the fifth. Then errors of omission on the part of Vivian Kellogg, Evelyn Wawryshyn and Betty Foss turned two bunts into hits and a run. The Peaches' third run scored on Kamenshek's fly to left field.

The Daisies had passed up one scoring opportunity in the first inning, when Sally Meier struck out and Dottie Schroeder popped out with the bases loaded.

In the sixth they caught up with Helen (Nickie) Fox, the Rockford pitcher. Foss doubled and scored when Schroeder duplicated the feat. Schroeder scored when Fox, covering third, let the throw from the outfield get away from her.

That made it 3-2 and set the stage for the seventh inning heriocs. Thelma Eisen, who has been hitting the ball hard all through the two playoff series, started the rally with a sharp single to left. Wilma Briggs collected her third hit of the night by grounding one into center field. Wawryshyn sacrificed the two along one base, a piece of strategy that was immediately questioned because Foss, coming to bat with two out and first base empty, was intentionally passed.

Sally Meier Doubles

Meier, who had flopped in three previous trips, each time with runners in scoring position, made Carey look like Solomon with a slashing drive down the third base line that emptied the bases and won for the Daisies, 5-3.

Kline retired the next six Rockford batters and the Daisies started looking down the throats of the Peaches.

A victory for the Daisies tonight would put them in a position where they could win either of the next two at Rockford and take the title.

Summary

Runs - Kamenshek, Callow, Jones, Foss 2, Schroeder, Eisen, Briggs. Errors - Fox. Runs batted in - Kamenshek, Doyle, Key, Meier 3, Schroeder. Two-base hits - Doyle, Wawryshyn, Foss, Schroeder, Meier. Sacrifice hits - Kamenshek, Jones, Wawryshyn. Stolen bases - Jones. Double plays - Kline to Schroder to Kellogg. Base on balls - off Fox 2, Kline 1. Strikeouts - by Fox 3, Kline 4. Left on base - Rockford 3, Fort Wayne 9. Winning pitcher - Kline. Losing pitcher - Fox. Time - 1:28. Attendance - 1200.

▲ Maxine "Max" Kline was Fort Wayne's ace pitcher for the seven years of her All-American career. Here she winds up, her eyes intent on the target.

▶ Maxine Kline Randall studies the pitcher while she waits her turn at bat at a 1984 reunion game.

MAXINE "MAX" KLINE

Fort Wayne, Pitcher

Statistics: Born: 1929. Home town: Addison, Michigan. Height: 5 feet 7 inches. Playing weight: 120 pounds. Bats: Right. Throws: Right. Entered League: 1948 at age 19. Teams: Fort Wayne 1948-54. Lifetime totals: Pitching statistics: Games won, 116; Games lost, 65. Winning percentage: .641. Earned-run average: 2.34. Batting average: .194. Fielding percentage: .970.

Fort Wayne's Maxine Kline was one of the three premier pitchers in the All-American Girls Baseball League in 1950. During the regular season Maxine compiled a record to be proud of, winning twenty-three games, more than any other pitcher. Only two others won twenty or more games, South Bend's Jean Faut (twenty-one) and Rockford's Lois Florreich (an even twenty). Among pitchers who worked at least 100 innings, Kline's .719 winning percentage was second only to Grand Rapids' Alma Zeigler's .731. Florreich was third at .714, Faut fourth at .700.

Kline was a tough, consistent pitcher, a critical ingredient for a team that hoped to be playing strong into the playoffs. "I was willing and I was durable," is how she puts it. Maxine started thirty-three games and completed twenty-eight of them. Jean Faut completed the most games, twenty-nine. Lois Florreich also completed twenty-eight games. Kline was second in number of innings pitched in the 1950 season, another measure of durability, with 266. Faut led with 290, and Florreich was third with 252.

Her earned-run average—an important pitching statistic that expresses how many runs, not attributable to fielding errors, opposing teams score against a pitcher in nine innings—was higher than her two principal rivals, but still low. Her 2.44 placed her thirteenth among the League's pitchers. Faut finished number one with an ERA of 1.12; Florreich was second with 1.18.

Maxine was named to the League All-Star team five of her seven seasons.

I asked Maxine to what she attributed the dramatic turnaround in the Daisies' fortunes in 1950. She responded with the humility typical of All-Americans, where teammates are credited first, oneself last—if at all.

> I think because of Foss, with her hitting and base-stealing. And of course Vivian was there. Dottie Collins was a good pitcher. And I had a good year that year. Maybe it was me too. I had to be doin' something right, or they got me a lot of runs, or something, to win twenty-three games.

A manager will start his ace pitcher as soon and as many times as possible in a crucial series like the 1950 championship. Maxine started Game One and was battered by the Peaches for fifteen hits. When I showed her a newspaper account of that game forty-two years later, she wasn't any too happy about the reminder: "They got 15 hits! Why, good God! You would have to show me that, wouldn't you!"

The damage sounds worse than it was. Maxine gave up only three runs (Rockford left eleven runners on base), but her Daisy teammates could put together only four hits and one run. Pitchers can rarely win with so little support at the plate. Maxine's account in her scrapbook reads, "Although blasted for 15 hits, Maxine Kline hurled good ball for the Daisies, being especially tough with runners on the bases."

She kept reading, reminding herself of the unpleasant particulars, commenting as she went. "Well, look at this. Dottie Kamenshek got three hits, and ol' Rose Gacioch got three, and Dottie Key got a crucial hit. Goddamn them!" I asked whether Max had ever hit Key with a pitch, given how the Rockford batter used to hug the plate. "No, but I'd like to! I'd love to hit her right between the eyes!"

Maxine is full of such fighting words, but I found they contrast with her behavior off the field, at least now. When I first asked to visit her for an interview she was adamant that she wouldn't talk to anyone who had been a Peaches fan. She was kidding, but I was a little intimidated nonetheless. "We didn't like those Peaches," she informed me. "They were the team to beat. I used to love to beat up on 'em." She also couldn't imagine why I would want to talk to her, an insignificant player with nothing interesting to say.

She finally relented, and once I got to her home, she was both hospitable and forthcoming. She fed me coffee and doughnuts, got out all her scrapbooks and other mementoes, and talked with me for three hours. She continued, though, to punctuate our talk with disclaimers. "You know," she reminded me, "I don't like sittin' here talkin' to you. It's somethin' we did way back then; I want to leave it. I don't know whether people would approve of it now."

Game Four of the championship series holds happier memories for Maxine than did Game One. She contained the Peaches, allowing only six hits and, though Rockford again got three runs, her own team supported her with five runs; Max was rewarded with her first win of the series. She struck out four and walked only one batter, achieving "one of her best performances of the season," as Fort Wayne sports writer Olofson put it. The Daisies and Peaches were now tied in the series at two games apiece.

◆◆◆

Maxine Kline grew up in the small town of Addison, Michigan, population less than five hundred, where she played a little softball but no organized baseball. Her father was a farmer, and her mother helped on the farm and raised ten children, eight girls and two boys. Maxine was next to the youngest.

> I practiced a lot throwing through a rubber tire. I could hit it. And I'd throw a rubber ball up against the barn, make it fly back to me, run like the devil to catch it. All by myself. My older brothers and sisters were much older and married, and my younger sister was into horses.
>
> My mother didn't know the first thing about ball. But my dad, he just ate it right up. He never played himself, but he always listened to the Detroit Tigers' games. And at the County Fair he'd go all week long just to watch the ballgames. There was nobody else in the family that played sports except me and my younger sister. The game around here was basketball, and she and I both played.

Maxine averaged more than twenty-three points a game for the area high school's girls' basketball team, leading them to three straight undefeated seasons. Her basketball coach must have recognized an accomplished athlete regardless of the sport, because he took her the hundred miles southwest to Fort Wayne for a try-out with the Daisies. She was offered a contract and reported after high school graduation in1948.

Kline's strong arm meant she was playing the outfield at first, but one night in Kenosha all Fort Wayne's pitchers were exhausted or injured.

> The manager, Dick Bass, took me out along the sidelines, showed me how to hold a runner on, and I pitched that night. Well, I was scared. I'd never been away from home or nothin'. I was with complete strangers. And I'd never pitched before, not even in softball. But we won.
>
> Bass had used me to pitch batting practice, so he might've saw something that he liked there.

Maxine's second victory came at home. She showed me the clipping. "Rookie Hurls One-Hitter," rejoices the headline.

> Coming up with two well-pitched games, the Daisies beat the Kenosha Comets twice last night 4 to 1 and 1 to 0, moving up a half game on the Grand Rapids Chicks. The star of the evening's double victory was rookie Maxine Kline, who graduated just two weeks ago from North Adams, Michigan, High School.
>
> She held the Comets to one hit in the nine-inning nightcap, and performed like a veteran, walking only one and seldom getting behind on a hitter. She retired the first 19 batters to face her and faced but 29 during the entire nine innings.

Maxine was a Fort Wayne pitcher from then on, amassing lifetime statistics of 116 wins and 65 losses, a.641 winning percentage, over the seven years of her career.

Displaying to me the reports of her early achievements made her nervous, though. "That's just when I started. Put them scrapbooks away!" I relented, knowing by now that the interview would cycle back to Maxine's playing days once we'd had a little respite.

What made Maxine so self-conscious was her awareness of how unconventional it was for women to play ball, even if baseball was a joy to her.

> A woman was supposed to be in the house, cookin' and like that. It was unheard of, a woman going out to play ball, why that was ter-

rible. That's a man's work and doing! But here us girls was doing it. It was somethin' I liked to do, and I got paid for it, and I just enjoyed it!

She attended the abbreviated version of Charm School to which the girls were subjected in 1948.

When we took our first road trip into Chicago that year, we had to go to that Charm School. We had to go up and down steps with a book on our heads, and learn how to set. I hated it! I hated to go down there. To have one of those ladies come up and tell ya how to put make-up on and how to comb your hair. Boy, I was so glad to get out of that place! 'Course, we giggled and laughed and made fun. You know how girls are.

But it helped me; it has stuck by me to this day. When I get ready to go out to a wedding or something like that, I gotta ask my husband, "Do I look all right?" And even if I was to go to town this morning in the jeans and polo shirt I've got on, I wouldn't feel right in doing it. It's not that I got that many clothes or anything, but I'm wonderin' if it's right, if it looks decent.

Wrigley had us playing in skirts. He didn't want us to look boyish. I felt real exposed, playing in a skirt. But you got used to it. Then after a while it was just like an honor to put that old uniform on.

I asked Maxine what her best pitch had been.

My fastball. I had good control. If I hadn't had good control, I wouldn't have lasted in the League. But wherever my catcher had her glove, I could hit it.

As much experience as I had in pitching, I would not call my own game. I made the catcher call it, whether they wanted a fastball, or a change-up, or a curve. I just thought they knew the batters. 'Course I knew the batters well too, but I thought, let them do it.

I very seldom shook 'em off, refused to pitch what they called. Very seldom. If that's what they wanted, that's what they got. I relied on hittin' the target.

Back then I didn't look like this [she refers to her rather thick figure]. I'll bet I didn't weigh a hundred and twenty pounds. When we was in Cooperstown at the exhibit, Wilma Briggs said to me, "My gosh, Max, if we could play now, and with the weight you've got, you could really throw that ball."

'Course she didn't let me forget that I hit a home run in the All-Star Game. Naturally, when it didn't count!

Maxine talked about some of the day-to-day arrangements at home and on the road.

I roomed with Wilma in Fort Wayne. Then when we'd go on the road, the chaperone would pick. You know, each girl had certain ones that they would run around with. Well, on the road maybe you could room with that girl once. But you roomed with other ones too. The chaperone decided. Sometimes we had single beds, more often double beds.

Most generally, once you got through with the ballgame, by the time you come back and showered, went out and ate, come back, wrote a letter or called home, you're ready for bed.

I remember Rita Briggs, our catcher in 1953 and 1954, liked to have me pitch 'cause she said, "You can get 'em out, and we can always catch the last movie of the double feature at the drive-in!"

I asked Maxine whether it was hard to calm down after a game.

No, I didn't have trouble after a game. It was the day and the night before when I knew I was gonna pitch. I'd go to bed, and I could see them girls I had to face, and every pitch. The day I pitched I didn't want to do nothin', no physical stuff, like the laundry or wash the car. I just wanted to read or lay around. Because I didn't weigh very much and I needed all the strength I had!

They tried to get some weight on me. They had me drink Jello. I must have been just a little runt. But wiry or something, or I wouldn't have lasted. I must have been strong.

I asked Maxine about her favorite moment on the field, the best thing that happened to her in her long career. She told me about two "best moments."

Earlene "Beans" Risinger and I went seventeen innings, nuthin' to nuthin'. My leg was so tired I could hardly raise it to throw the ball. The only bad thing about that game was the last inning. It was gonna be midnight and they was gonna call the game. They had Beans walk somebody intentionally, thinkin' they could get a double play or a force out, and damned if she didn't walk the next one too and walked in the winning run.

'Course I was happy as hell, but I knew how she felt. I remember after the game I run out of the dugout and caught her goin' up the steps out of Memorial Stadium. I put my arms around her and said, "Beans, this is a helluva way to win a ballgame, but I'm so tired I can hardly walk." And she said she was too!

Then another favorite game was in Fort Wayne. I pitched a no-hitter in the first game of a double-header. Well, they wouldn't let you go shower, change clothes, and go home, because they might need you in the second game. Eventually the manager took our pitcher out of that second game. It was the ninth inning with two outs, but the bases were loaded. "Max," he said, "is your arm strong enough? Are you sore? Do you think you can go out and get this last batter?" I said, "God, I don't know, let me go out and warm up." I didn't know whether I could throw tight, you know.

Well, I felt pretty good, so he put me in. The batter was Betty Francis. I remember to this day that bitch hit me every time. I hated to pitch to her! And I had to face her. But God was shining on me; I struck her out. And my teammates and the fans just mobbed me!

Maxine also hated pitching to former teammates, her friends who had been traded to other teams.

The manager traded Wilma Briggs to South Bend in '54. Now, you think that didn't hurt, when I had to pitch to her? She came in the League the same time I did, and they made us roommates in Fort Wayne. I liked her, and Betty Foss too, because we all came from farms, and we could talk farm.

Wilma and I, we were buddies. And Dottie Schroeder too. She got traded, and I had to pitch to her. It was a funny feelin'.

But then you thought, why, goddamn, if she's up there, she's gonna hit you. You gotta get her out. I tried not to look 'em in the face, 'cause if I did, I don't know what I'd 'a done, so I just kept my eye on the target. And I think they did hit me, if I'm not mistaken.

I'm just glad I stayed on the same team as the Weaver sisters so I didn't have to pitch against 'em. I remember in 1950 at spring training Max Carey wanted me to pitch to Betty, who'd come up for a try-out. He wanted to see what she had.

She was left-handed, you know, and she took that first swing, and I thought, Jesus God, if she ever hits that, Lord have mercy! I bet I threw her ten or twenty pitches. She'd swing and miss every one. Finally, she hit one and drove that ball right back in my guts. That's all Carey needed. He signed her up. She was just awesome at the plate.

And Betty's sister Jo Weaver, when she came to play for us in 1951, she was like a reindeer. She could hit and run. She was tall and skinny, and when she took a stride, man, she'd take one stride to two or three of my steps. If she'd had a chance to play more than three years, who knows what she could have done.

◆◆◆

Who knows what many of the women could have done, given the chance to play out their baseball careers in an ongoing League? Maxine recalls the end.

> When the League folded, in 1954, I was only twenty-five. Look how many more years I could have pitched. But I will never know.
>
> I didn't know what I was gonna do. Just like Jo Weaver said, here she was real young and she thought that was the way she was gonna make her livin' for quite a while. And here the League folded, and she had to go to the shop and work. It was just like she lost everything.
>
> I did have a job that I could come back to. But who wanted to work in a shop?

Maxine joined Bill Allington's All-Americans, a barnstorming team of former League players, who travelled for four summers after the League ended, playing exhibition games against men's teams. In the winters, and later after Allington's All-Americans folded too, she worked for Jonesville Products—a factory four miles from where she lives now—for almost twenty years, making tubing for gas and brake lines. She lived at home on the family farm, where she took care of her mother, who died in the early 1960s, and her father, who died in 1971. She had met Bob Randall at work.

> We went together off and on, and we just decided we guessed we'd get married. One night goin' to the show we saw this place, the owners settin' here on the porch. "You know," Bob says, "if I had that place, and they had a feather, we'd both be tickled." Later we bought that farm.
>
> Now, we weren't married yet, but I told him I'd buy it with him, we'd pay it off in five years, and then we'd get married. I didn't want to work and keep house at the same time. We bought the house in '68, I moved here in '71 after my dad died, and we got married in '73. I was forty-four years old.

Maxine had finally fulfilled almost all the requirements for a conventional life: she lived on a farm in a small midwestern town only ten miles from where she was born, she was retired from a proper job and married to a respectable man, she was surrounded by brothers and sisters, nieces and nephews.

But her unconventional life as an ace hardball pitcher years before kept resurfacing, resurrected by the rediscovery of the League and by interviewers like me. I asked Maxine about the highpoints of her life, and she responded with a characteristic double message.

The first game I pitched and won. That was a highpoint. And being inducted there at Cooperstown, that was. And of course, marryin' Bob, I got to say that!

Maxine Kline shows off the twenty-three $1 bills Fort Wayne fans gave her in thanks for her 23 wins in 1950, most in the League.

She had shown me a picture of herself proudly holding a string of twenty-three one dollar bills, given her by fans for her twenty-three wins of the 1950 season. At the same time Maxine told me how uncomfortable she still feels about her baseball past.

When I got home after the touring All-Americans, they wanted me to play fast-pitch softball. I thought about it, but I decided I didn't want to go back to underhand, after having played overhand. So that was it, I refused them, and they left me alone.

And everything was fine, until this Cooperstown thing cropped up. And then it was fine again for a couple of years until this movie came out! All of a sudden, here we are in the limelight.

I hope in a year this will all die down, all the parades and interviews and like that. I hate it really. I hate you bein' here today too. Bob says, "Well, why did you grant her an interview if you don't like it?" And I said, "Well, I don't know. Don't ask me why."

In my mind I don't think people approve of what I did. I should've growed up and had children, like the rest of my brothers and sisters.

"I think people approve," I said. "Who do you think doesn't approve?" "Me," replied Maxine, "I guess I don't approve. Look at my family: All married and had children. And look at me! I must be the wild one."

Chicago Colleen catcher Ann O'Dowd holds the compact while pitcher Beverly Hatzell puts the final touches on her make-up. Publicity shots like this promoted the "feminine" image of the League.

Players were expected to wear skirts whenever they appeared in public. Here they have dressed casually for a tour of Fort Wayne's Magnavox factory.

LOOKING LIKE GIRLS, PLAYING LIKE MEN

"No way were we gonna play baseball in a dress."
                                        —Dottie Collins

The tomboys who arrived to play women's professional baseball were shocked at the uniform they were issued: a one-piece skirted tunic with contrasting-colored shorts underneath. They were ordered to say goodbye to the outfits they had grown up with: the jeans of sandlot ball, the satin shorts of softball, the knickers of men's baseball. If they wanted to play girls' baseball in Wrigley's League, they were going to play in a dress.

The skirted uniform was an important part of the image management had chosen in order to market the League: this women's baseball league would be family entertainment where fans could see girls who looked like girls play baseball like men. The image was intended to counter what Wrigley saw as the negative reputation of other women's teams. Girls who had played for the touring women's "Bloomer Girl" teams of the 1890s to the 1930s were sometimes criticized for their "mannish" appearance. The immensely popular women's softball teams of the 1940s were thought to be "hard-looking" and "tough." Neither of these versions of women's ball were feminine enough nor genteel enough to satisfy the All-American Girls Baseball League organizers. A magazine article in 1943 described what was seen as the problem:

> It has been no secret to sports fans in the Midwest that girls' softball in Chicago has been outdrawing the major-league baseball clubs. But the neighborhood games lacked polish. The major-league girls' problem was that of converting a somewhat uncouth Amazonian spectacle into something nearer the Wellesley, Vassar, Smith and Stephens standard of competition.[46]

Clearly it is not the "standard of competition" that bothered this writer and League management, but an appearance they perceived as "uncouth" and "Amazonian," codewords for lower-class and lesbian.

The official League manual is completely explicit about the organizers' conception of the League as "feminine," by which they mean "not masculine." That the League would also appear non-lesbian is never a stated goal, but is implicit in the emphasis on "feminine-type" girls.[47]

> Girls baseball as developed by the All-American League is a clean, spirited, colorful Sports Show . . . whose extraordinary popularity is principally traceable to the dramatic impact of seeing baseball, traditionally a men's game, played by feminine-type girls with masculine skill.

To that end, the League specified standards for the players' "skill, their femininity, and their general deportment," in that order.

It is to the organizers' credit that skill came first. "Every effort is made to select girls of ability, real or potential, and to develop that ability to its fullest power" (emphasis in the original). The system of recruiting, local try-outs, spring training, and serious coaching were all designed to find and develop girls who would play ball at a level worthy of being called professional. This the League achieved; the All-Americans played technically excellent baseball.

But successful professional sports are a medium of entertainment ("Girls Baseball is staged as a Show as well as a competitive sport."). Attracting the fans is its primary purpose. The organizers of the All-American League conceived of the fans of women's baseball as solid, conservative midwestern families, the "best classes of the community," who, they believed, wanted to see nice girls play good ball. "Nice girls" are girls who appear feminine. Thus,

> No less emphasis is placed on femininity, for the reason that it is more dramatic to see a feminine-type girl throw, run and bat than to see a man or boy or a masculine-type girl do the same things. *The more feminine the appearance of the performer, the more dramatic her performance* (emphasis in original).

The League explicitly refused to allow the girls to look like the tomboys they were. They wanted to emphasize gender dimorphism, the differences between men and women, not the similarities, not the androgyny expressed by tomboys.

> Masculine appearance or mannerisms produce an impression either of a masculine girl or an effeminate boy, both effects prejudicial to the dramatic contrast of feminine aspect and masculine skill.

The men of the 1940s—the organizers and owners of the League throughout its history were almost entirely male—believed there was nothing unusual or noteworthy about tomboys being able to play baseball. Tomboys, being "masculine-type girls" could of course do masculine-type things. But where was the show in that? What would attract midwestern crowds was seeing baseball played by people you wouldn't think could hit or field or throw a ball if their lives depended on it, that is, feminine-type girls.

The whole promotion was an exercise in image-making that played upon an artificially dichotomous conception of sex-roles: real men play baseball, real women do not play baseball. It is therefore entertaining when the exception to the rule can be demonstrated, i.e., real women playing real baseball. It is ironic that the same men who gave women the opportunity to excel in sports did so while simultaneously reinforcing the idea that sports are a male endeavor; women playing a professional sport constitutes a "drama."

Real women do, of course, play baseball—over five hundred of them played in the All-American League itself—but they were not stereotypically feminine women. The girls who could play baseball at the level required by the League were non-traditional. They wouldn't have given their young lives over to baseball had they been traditionally socialized. They were available to play precisely because they were tomboys.

◆◆◆

The period in our history when the AAGBL flourished was an era when beauty—how a girl or woman looked—was considered a legitimate element to include in any description of her other talents. The idea that such comments could be sexist was several decades in the future. The 1950 Rockford newspapers commended tennis star Nancy Chaffee and Olympic diving champion Vicki Draves for having been named to the "eight woman varsity all-glamour team" of sports. Gertrude Augusta "Gorgeous Gussie" Moran, another tennis star, didn't make the team. A woman wrestler is described as "an attractive brunette" and "one of the shapeliest of the distaff grapplers." My favorite find in this genre followed the front-page headline in the *Rockford Register-Republic* on May 11, 1950: KILLS HER EMPLOYER, SELF. The lead paragraph read, "Pretty, brown-haired Dorothy Decker shot and killed her publisher-employer, and then committed suicide, authorities said today."

Commentary on how the All-Americans looked in addition to how they played was more common early in the League's history. In 1944 *Liberty* magazine punned "What's a Ball Game Without Curves?" and in 1943 or 1944 the Sunday*World Herald* magazine titled its story "As Beauty Goes to Bat." The tendency never entirely died. In 1952 an article in *Holiday* magazine dubbed the All-Americans "The World's Prettiest Ballplayers."[48]

Free to engage in subjective commentary, different observers naturally evaluated the women's appearance differently. Rockford's account of a Rockford-South Bend game—the first no-hit, no-run game in the history of the League—refers to the Peaches' pitcher Olive Little as a "little chunky righthander." South Bend's report about the same girl pitching the same game calls her an "attractive young lady."[49]

South Bend sports editor Jim Costin's account of the first game ever played in the All-American League on May 30, 1943, a double-header between the Blue Sox and the Peaches (the Blue Sox took both, the first game 4-3 in 13 innings, the second 12-9) perfectly combines the elements promoters were hoping to blend into a successful show.

None of the girls on either team is of the usual sandlot variety. The strong, accurate arms possessed by most of them, and the healthy "cuts" they take at a pitched ball were revelations to most of the onlookers—including this one. Their thoroughly feminine uniforms and appearances also added color to the scene. They play for keeps, too, as evidenced by the manner in which they slide, crash into each other, and generally carry on as though they were out for blood.[50]

Even in this early account the writer's focus is on the game rather than the show. His remark about the uniforms is an aside; he wants to get on to the mayhem of the play itself. Costin called the first game "an afternoon thriller that was one for the books."

Daily sports coverage of the games in local papers soon abandoned the references to appearance and focused on serious descriptions of the games, the strategy, the mechanics, the prospects for the next game. Pretty petite Irene Applegren became lefty Irene Applegren. Nevertheless, the tension between appearance and the game, between the feminine image and the competitive reality, was a constant of the players' lives.

Regardless of when they entered the League, all the players agree they were chosen primarily for their talent on the field. In fact they like to joke about it. I asked the Peaches' Marie Mansfield (who entered the League in 1950) if it was really true that management would have picked a pretty player over a good player. Marie replied, "I don't think so. Everybody on my team was ugly." Daisy Wilma Briggs (who began her career in 1948) knows she never looked like the stereotype the League was trying to project: "I'm certainly not very feminine." Rockford's Applegren (who began pitching in 1944) didn't know of anyone who had to leave the League because she wasn't pretty enough. "They didn't care what you looked like if you could really hit that ball and win for 'em. That made money."

Only a few players described to me discrimination based on appearance that they themselves had witnessed. Isabel Alvarez could remember another Cuban girl who was, in Isabel's words, "too weird-looking" to be chosen even though she was skilled enough to play. Nickie Fox remembers that in 1943 the League was really fussy about short hair: "If you had a 'mannish' hair-do, they'd just send you home, without even a try-out." Feature stories about the League sometimes refer to players released or not chosen because they didn't conform to League standards of femininity, but I have found no confirmation of this as a widespread practice.

Usually, players were simply chosen for their ability. Being realists as well as image-makers, League management knew that players at the skill level they needed were not stereotypically feminine. As Arthur Meyerhoff, Wrigley's advertising executive who in 1945 became the League's Commissioner, always maintained, League organizers would rather try to make a ballplayer beautiful than turn a beauty into a ballplayer.[51] They thus recruited non-traditional girls for their baseball skills, and then tried to make them over with a battery of rules about appearance and deportment and—the ultimate effort at feminization—with Charm School.

In 1943 Wrigley contracted with Helena Rubenstein's prominent Chicago beauty salon to coach the All-American girls in principles of good grooming and ladylike deportment. The girls learned how to sit carefully and sedately without collapsing into a chair, how to walk with poise rather than strutting or shambling, how to apply make-up instead of being satisfied simply with brushing your teeth and putting on your baseball cap. According to Irene Applegren, who attended Charm School in 1944, it was clearly a clash of cultures.

> They had some models there, very pretty girls. They made us look, you know, like "yuk." [She laughs with some discomfort recalling the scene.] That was funny because we were nowhere that feminine, none of us. I hate to have you put this down, but it was kind of a joke to us, really. I think most of us thought it was uncalled for. It was too farfetched, too different from ball-playing. But it was another adventure in our lives.

Irene's mother suggests, "They didn't want you to be tomboys. Actin' and lookin' rough."

Irene responds, "They didn't want us walkin' around with a cigarette in our mouths, or sittin' there with a bottle of beer. Well, none of us did that in the first place."

There was a chasm between the Charm School fantasy of what women's lives should be like and the reality of these girls' experience. Dottie Schroeder went to Charm School in 1943 when it was a daily part of that first spring training.

> We learned how to walk and how to talk. They were deadly earnest about this. Well, being brought up as I was, I didn't outwardly scoff at it, but inwardly I did, because I thought, "They're going to teach me how to be graceful. I learned how to be graceful by playing ball out in the pasture, side-steppin' all the cowpies!"

I asked Dottie how long Charm School went on. She replied with just a hint of sarcasm, "We were charming after that one week."

While Charm School was clearly too much—and was required in its most intensive form for only the first two years of the League—many of the girls appreciated some of what they learned there. They acquired practical social skills, like making small talk with strangers and using the right fork, things working-class families didn't teach their children. These skills were useful later when the girls had to be celebrities at the local Rotary and Lions Club luncheons.

Tiby Eisen, who attended in 1944, told one writer,

> It made an impression on me. I think a lot of the girls needed it. They had no polish. I always figured if you were going to be in the public eye, you might as well have a little class.[52]

Mary Rountree joined the League in 1946, too late to attend Charm School herself: "I'm sorry I missed that. I think I could have benefited from it. In fact I think major-league players could use a little more charm themselves, and maybe a chaperone as well."

By 1950 Charm School was a thing of the past, but the League regulations that specified how players were to look were still articulated with great specificity and enforced. Some of the rules:

Rules of Conduct for Players
ALL-AMERICAN GIRLS BASEBALL LEAGUE

THE MANAGEMENT SETS A HIGH STANDARD FOR THE GIRLS SELECTED FOR THE DIFFERENT CLUBS AND EXPECTS THEM TO LIVE UP TO THE CODE OF CONDUCT WHICH RECOGNIZES THAT STANDARD.

1. Always appear in feminine attire when not actively engaged in practice or playing ball. AT NO TIME MAY A PLAYER APPEAR IN THE STANDS IN HER UNIFORM, OR WEAR SLACKS OR SHORTS IN PUBLIC.

2. Boyish bobs are not permissible and in general your hair should be well groomed at all times with longer hair preferable to short hair cuts. Lipstick should always be on.

3. Smoking or drinking are not permitted in public places. Liquor drinking will not be permitted under any circumstances. Other intoxicating drinks in limited portions with after-game meal only will be allowed. Obscene language will not be tolerated at any time.

The rules were not always observed. Here Sally Meier and Yolanda Tiellet are not only in public in their jeans, but are fraternizing. In 1946 Meier was an outfielder for the Rockford Peaches, Tiellet a catcher for the Grand Rapids Chicks.

The complete list of fifteen rules also required players to get their chaperone's permission to go out on a date, to change where they lived and to choose a restaurant. The manager's permission was necessary for driving outside the city limits. Uniform skirts were not to be shorter than six inches above the knee-cap. Relatives, friends and visitors were not allowed on the bench. Baseballs could not be given away as souvenirs. Everyone had to be in their rooms within two hours of the end of a game. And the members of different clubs could not fraternize at any time during the season. The list went on.

In general, the players observed these regulations. The rules about behavior caused more difficulty than did those about appearance. The rule prohibiting fraternization with players on other teams was the most onerous, flying as it did in the face of the allocation policy, trades and friendship. The nightly curfew was sometimes difficult to meet for young, active girls who were keyed-up after a hard-fought game. Excessive drinking was sometimes a problem, but affected performance so quickly that it had to be controlled. Nearly everyone smoked, though not in front of fans. And I never heard of anyone getting up the nerve to bother a manager about whether or not they could drive out of town.

The admonitions about appearance, however, were in fact reasonable enough that players could conform to them with relative ease. Many players reminded me that wearing skirts in public was simply normal behavior for girls in the 1940s and 1950s. Marie Mansfield said, "It really was not a change at all for me."

The girls might have dressed like ladies most of the time without anyone demanding it, but chaperone Millie Lundahl is not so sure.

> I do think the players liked boy-type clothes. They liked boys' Oxfords, for instance, definitely as unfeminine as anything could be! And they liked slacks and shorts. They often wore shorts when we were travelling, 'cause it was summertime, and hot on those buses, but when they'd get off the bus to get a Coke or go to the restroom, they had to put a skirt on. [The players forty years later complained to me about this particular overly-literal interpretation of the dress rule.] The girls were naturally casual dressers, but they wanted to wear nice clothes. They didn't wear spiked heels, but comfortable heels. They wanted to look nice.
>
> It was the selling point of the League. Women that were really women, not tomboys. Some of our girls were mannish-acting, but there was all the difference in the world between them and the Chicago softball league girls; they were hard-looking.
>
> We never had to be ashamed of the girls.

The rules that established the chaperone and the manager in *loco parentis* for the girls were constricting, but were largely regarded as necessary. Nickie Fox, who thought Charm School was "the most ridiculous thing," still believes the supervision was a good idea. The only way Wrigley's scouts could get these girls away from their families—Nickie's own father was a prime example—was to run a squeaky-clean organization. The League's behavior rules ensured that the relatively inexperienced young women in its charge were protected.

But the pressure to appear feminine coupled with the necessity to play winning hardball produced many contradictions. When spring training was held in Cuba, the players were told what clothes to bring. Among the crucial items were a couple of "nice" dresses, a pair of heeled shoes and "your own glove and spikes (the spikes we wear are men's style...)."

While the girls were being told how important it was to decorate their lips, managers were concerned about something entirely different. Norma Dearfield, a Chicago Colleen, recounts the realities of daily practice.

> I remember them coaching us on ground balls and saying, "You let the ball break your nose or knock out your teeth, but you don't turn your head."[53]

The image haunts me of a player with teeth missing but lipstick carefully applied.

I have a picture of Peaches second baseman Charlene Barnett posed to look like a Hollywood starlet. Alice Pollitt told me,

> Charlene might not have looked like a tomboy, but she was a tomboy too. I think we all had the tomboy in us, every one of us. I always remember her wearin' men's underwear, knit jockey shorts. I thought that was a good idea 'cause they were better than the cotton panties we wore.

Vivian Kellogg's scrapbook has a picture of a player coloring her lips captioned, "applying make-up is important to Ruth Lessing, Grand Rapids Chicks catcher." I asked Kelly whether this was true, was applying make-up important to Lessing? "No," she replied. "It was all just publicity." What was important to Ruth "Tex" Lessing was getting the right call. Her baseball card quotes a Chicago paper of the time that reported that Tex had once been fined $100 for hitting an umpire. Fans sent $2,000 to the League on her behalf.

I asked the players whether anything about the rules requiring them to look feminine actually inhibited their ability to play good baseball. They brought up only one real problem: the short skirts meant that baserunners chronically scraped their thighs sliding, acquiring the dreaded "strawberries." This was a serious matter, discouraging some runners from sliding at all, subjecting others to repeated injuries. Alice Pollitt still has scars on her thighs testifying to the painful outcome of this particularly ill-conceived triumph of image over function.

The skirts may have been "feminine" but they were also, of

course, provocative. They projected what Susan Cahn has called "an ideal of wholesome, feminine sexuality."[54] Peoria Redwings Manager Leo Schrall loved coaching Faye Dancer, a natural crowd pleaser. "When she slid and those skirts went flying up over her head, you should have heard the fans. They just roared. They loved it." Leo understood that the game had to be played well, but it also had to be entertaining. With somebody like Faye, "You're gonna get more people out there. That's what this is all about! That Dancer, she was a wonder."

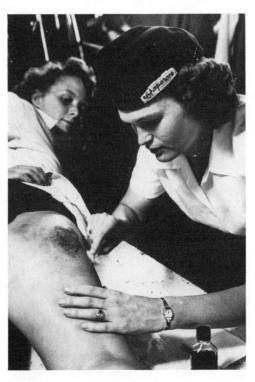

Dottie Green, Rockford's chaperone, attends to a "strawberry" on Lois Florreich's thigh. This routine and painful injury was caused when players slid into base unprotected because of their skirted uniforms.

Irene Applegren understood the ticket-selling combination the League was striving for. "The male fans liked to come out and see a cute little girl with pretty legs and a nice figure who could still throw a ball."

An observer from Major League Baseball's authoritative *Blue Book* studied the League in 1945. His subsequent report was quoted extensively in the League manual. He reflected on the sex-appeal aspect of the League's presentation.

If by "sex" is meant the normal appeal of the feminine mode and attitude, then most certainly sex was an important source of interest and a legitimate element of the league's success.

However, he continues,

The moral tone of the enterprise was beyond reproach. There was not the slightest evidence of sex exploitation in any phase of club management or individual conduct.

The atmosphere [at the ballpark] was such that the crowd did not indulge in indignities. No higher grade patronage ever complimented a sports show, and I have never seen any program of athletic contests which secured and held such a large percentage of middle-aged and elderly women.

I asked the players whether they thought the feminine image they were asked to project had to do with appearing more middle-class (the midwestern version of Vassar) or less lesbian. A few thought that both motivations were at work. Mary Rountree analyzed what she thinks League image-makers were attempting.

They were trying to avoid any criticism of the appearance of masculinity. If we had all appeared to be extremely masculine, dressed in shorts or slacks, there would have been derogatory publicity about it. Detractors would have said we were too masculine, or would have thrown the proverbial homosexual criticism at us. The League didn't want that, and they didn't have that, and I'm glad.

Other players think homophobia was far from the minds of League organizers. Irene Applegren said, "I don't think people thought about homosexuality." Her mother went a step further: "I don't think there was anything like that then." While this is certainly not true, homophobia was less strident because homosexuality itself was so hidden. League management did not have to be explicit about projecting a heterosexual image. They had only to articulate their intention to make the All-American League a high-class Sports Show, to "appeal to the best classes of the community," by fielding teams of "nice girls."

The players agree. To Wilma Briggs the All-American League was a "class act." Fran Janssen saw the League projecting a "more refined" image. "Nice," to everyone, meant genteel rather than straight.

The players, in fact, didn't perceive much of a dilemma between looking feminine and playing hardball. I asked Dottie Collins how she felt about the whole image business.

Well of course women doing something like playing baseball in that particular era was not accepted. They were considered tomboys. But as far as how we felt about it, I don't think we cared. We just wanted to play baseball. They could have put us in men's jeans, and we'd have gone out and played. We just didn't care about the image.

When we California girls saw those uniforms we thought, "no way are we gonna play baseball in that." It was a dress!

I asked if the problem was modesty, the skirt being too revealing.

Oh no, that didn't enter into it because the short shorts we played in in California were revealing. And actually early on the skirts were so long they weren't particularly revealing. They were clear down to the knee. We're the ones who shortened those damn things so we could pitch underhand without getting tangled in all that material. We felt like a bunch of old ladies out there in those damn things.

"So what was the problem?" I asked.

It was a dress! We just were not gonna play in the stupid things. But it was put to us that either you play in 'em or we'll give you a train ticket home. Well, we weren't about to go home.

Mary Rountree had her own solution to the apparent dilemma between being feminine and playing hardball: "I understood the value of having a very fine, feminine image for all the players. And when I was playin', I wasn't thinking about it at all. I was playin' to win."

Kate Vonderau sums up what most of the players thought was going on, now that they have time to think about it.

Women in sports was not quite as acceptable at that time as it is now. So in order for people to accept women playing baseball, to accept women being in professional sports and still being women, it was important not to emulate men in how we looked and acted. So maybe the feminine image was important. I didn't feel it was all that important really, but from the point of view of the fan it might have been.

I suppose it was so the girls wouldn't be too rough or too loud or too something. It was more show for the fans than anything else. I don't know if we accomplished that, but we'll say that we did anyhow. We went to all that trouble!

♦♦♦

Both players and management went to great efforts to attract fans. And their exertions were rewarded. From its beginning, the game of women's baseball was a success, both at the gate and in the hearts of its supporters. As long as it was promoted vigorously, fans turned up.

Promoters were confident that all they had to do was get the fans to the park one time. The girls and the game would then sell themselves. The League manual spells it out for local sponsors:

> In order to attract Customers the first time the Sponsors cannot play up too strongly the Skill and Spectator-Appeal of Girls' Baseball. The girl players will meet every expectation of the new spectator. The sight of girls playing Baseball remains a constant source of amazement and wonder to most Fans—particularly to men who have played Baseball: proof of its soundness as a competitive sport. Every Fan in turn becomes salesman or saleswoman; everybody wants to bring a friend.
>
> Obviously, the more Fans you attract into the park by ballyhoo, the more friends you will send forth into the Community plugging for Baseball played by Girls.

Just how successful the venture was is clear from a retrospective published in a Rockford paper in 1950 wherein sports editor Dick Day reviewed how far the Peaches and their fans had come since Opening Day in 1943. Day recalls,

> The time was early evening of June 5, 1943.
>
> A skeptical and curious throng, glad of something that would take their minds off the war, had come out to the 15th Avenue high school field, "just for the laughs," to see women try to play baseball.
>
> In the back of everybody's mind was the thought that perhaps the draft boards would strip the men's clubs of players and that even the major league parks would stand idle if women couldn't learn the game, just as women were then learning to operate lathes and drill presses.
>
> It's now Labor Day of 1950. And tonight an enthusiastic throng, no longer skeptical, will be out at the Peach Orchard to help the Peaches close out another pennant race.
>
> The emergency for which their league was created turned out to be no emergency at all—but the gals are going stronger than ever and are busy enlarging the niche they have carved for themselves in the sports life of Rockford.[55]

I remember being so excited at the prospect of seeing a game that my heart was in my throat. I always wanted to go again, to have season tickets, to see *all* the games, to give myself over completely to the exploits of my heroes.

My family had other things to do than go to the ballpark every home game, and I was too young and lived too far away to get there on my own. But some fans could and did indulge themselves. Colleen Holmbeck was six years older than I was and lived within walking distance of the Peach Orchard. She and her sister could go every night.

> We had little jackets that our parents bought us and we got the players' autographs on these jackets. Then my mother would embroider the autographs, and we'd wear them proudly to school. This was a treasured thing to both of us.

I'm envious, forty-some years later, talking with Colleen on the phone; I too want a jacket autographed by Snookie Doyle and Dottie Kamenshek and Dottie Key!

Not only did she have a neat jacket, Colleen played on an unofficial Peaches "farm team" for three years. In 1950 the Rockford Ko-Eds girls' baseball team numbered forty girl players, ages fourteen to twenty-one, playing in official peach-colored uniforms cast off by the mother team. Although the Ko-Eds never cut anyone and "welcomed any girl who wishes to turn out to play the great American game," Colleen also remembers how serious they were about baseball.

> It was really important to the team to win. We pitched overhand with the small ball, we practiced sliding in those skirts. We practiced and practiced, and the coach yelled at us, the whole shebang. It was the dream of some of them to play with the Peaches. And for me it was always a fine memory.

Other All-American cities fielded organized junior teams of aspiring girl baseball players. Unorganized girls' baseball also flourished because of the professional example set by the League. Fort Wayne's 1950 Official Program and Scorebook described the impact in that city, at the same time reminding girls of what's expected of them.

It's astonishing to see how many of the young ladies of our fair city have taken to the diamond since the Daisies and their fellow League members moved into the spotlight. Learning that girls do have a place in the national sports spotlight, they have decided to try their hands at fielding and throwing a la Dottie Schroeder and swinging the willow a la Viv Kellogg.

They have the finest examples before them, in the AAGBL stars, that young girls and women can be athletes of the highest magnitude, yet retain the femininity, grace and graciousness expected of members of their sex. They have noted that a lass does not have to be a "musclewoman" or hard boiled to indulge in and make her living in athletics.

All the cities had loyal girl and women fans, "fanettes" to a writer in the same 1950 Fort Wayne program.

Don't get the idea that all Daisy fans are men. Take a look around you tonight. You will see about half the spectators are women. And if you come back to the next game, it will be the same way.

It's just possible that the women fans recall their own pig-tail days and secretly wish they could field and throw a ball with such grace and precision, or slam a three-two pitch out of the park.

Through all the years the All-Americans' fans have never lost their loyalties. When Vivian Kellogg went to the premier of "A League of Their Own," the feature film that fictionalizes and celebrates the 1943 All-American Girls' season, she ran into an old fan.

A girl came up to me and asked "Are you Vivian Kellogg?" "Yes," I says. "Do you remember me?" she asks. "Berg?" And I says, "Yes, you're Bonnie Berg." "Remember how you used to let me spit in your glove for good luck?" she says.

I sure did remember. She was our business manager Ernie Berg's daughter. Way back she was a little redhead, fiery red hair, couldn't have been more than eight or nine years old. Just as I would walk into the ballpark each day she'd grab my glove and ask, "Can I spit in it for good luck?" And every day I let her.

◆◆◆

The players greatly appreciated their fans. The Peaches had "Coke girls," admirers who would buy their favorite player a Coke just as the game ended, wait in the runway underneath the stands, and proudly hand it over as their favorite entered the locker room. Alice Pollitt remembers her girl:

> Every night she'd be there. They spent their money on us, you know. It was probably only a nickel, but it was theirs. When it was her birthday, I'd buy her something.

Stars might have more than one Coke girl. Rookies might not have any for a while. Sis Waddell remembers the girl who took pity on her.

> Some of them, like Kammie and Snookie, they'd have two or three kids buying them Cokes. In the locker room they'd share their Cokes with us rookies 'cause we weren't gettin' any. Finally this one little girl, she saw I wasn't gettin' a Coke, so she started buyin' me one. Sylvia Marinelli was her name. Then every night she was out there with my Coke. We got to be good friends, but I've lost track of her now.

Sis didn't remember any Coke boys, just girls ten, eleven, twelve years old. "We were their heroines you know."

Having fans was of practical importance to a player. It was a chance for a naturally shy girl to develop some social skills. And it was an opportunity to make herself valuable to management. Mary Rountree explains,

> You got over a lot of your bashfulness, your inability to talk to people. You met so many people, and you were constantly thrown into situations with total strangers, people who'd been watching the ballgames but who you didn't know. It gave you a chance to develop your personality. You learned to speak tactfully and graciously and solicitously.
>
> After all, those people were payin' money to watch you play ball, and that's why, in my case, you were gonna be able to go to school. So you're indebted to them, and you better let them know how grateful you are for that.
>
> And right away you develop a following that gives people up in the front office the idea that "She is so well liked that I know this is a person I don't want to trade."

The most loyal and active fans provided housing for the girls, or took several girls ("Never just one," according to Millie Lundahl) out to dinner after the game. They ran the booster clubs, and bought season tickets so they could see every game. Some—once gasoline rationing was over—even travelled to away games. And they were generous with their adulation. Norma Metrolis, never a star, remembers, "No matter whether you rode the bench and warmed the pitchers up or played every day, you had your own fans."

Sometimes, though, the players had to keep the fans in line. Sis Waddell remembers one such fan.

> When I was up in Battle Creek we had a big, heavy-set guy sitting down the third-base line. Every night this son-of-a-gun would show up. He must have hated the world, because he just come out to heckle us. He didn't like any of us. He had paid his money, so he thought he had his right to yell and shout at us.
>
> This one night we could hear him a little better than usual, so we decided we were gonna shut this guy up. We started foulin' 'em off, pullin' 'em foul toward the third-base line. We made a bet. If you hit him, you got so much. If you got close, you got so much. Boy, we had fun that night.
>
> The guy thought the first couple were an accident. But then the people sitting around him moved away and let us have at him. Pretty soon he was sittin' there by himself. He'd move back a little bit, and yell, and we'd drive one at him again. Eventually I remember he hid behind a telephone pole. Finally he got the message and shut up.

Another time Dottie Key protected Waddell.

> This one woman didn't like me too well. One night I made an error in right field, and she was on my case. When Dottie and I came in from the field, this woman was really givin' it to me. Dottie took her glove over, handed it to the woman, and said, "Here, if you can do it better, why don't you go out and play."
>
> I know when Dottie tells the story, she doesn't tell who the player was 'cause I made an error. But it was me all right.

Betty Weaver Foss valued the ladylike image projected by the League precisely because it protected the female players from verbally abusive fans. Having played men's baseball in Kentucky, perhaps she knew what the alternative could be like.

> The rules kept the girls looking like women and acting like ladies, and we were respected as ladies. Some of the new girls thought we would be a bunch of boys, or tomboys, but we weren't them type of people. We were strictly All-American girls.

We fans were of all ages, and both sexes, and had varying degrees of commitment to our team. From the bat girls to the Sunday fans, each of us has brought some lasting memory away from those days. We all took from the experience what we needed for ourselves: a moment of relaxation, a few laughs, the thrill of a close game, the initial shock and then the satisfying commonplace sight of women playing baseball.

For me the tension between the image and the reality was itself important. It was the perfect mirror for my own confusion over sexual identity. Here I was, a tomboy approaching puberty watching older tomboys dressed like girls playing a men's game. And their being accepted. And cheered on.

The All-Americans—without knowing it of course—accompanied me for five crucial years on my own frightening journey. By their example of doing what they loved, even when it was not what nice ladies do, they helped this one tomboy turn into the kind of woman she needed to be.

The All-Americans did for me, and for other girls and women, just what role models should: they showed us that females can do anything. Betty Foss says, "The whole world thought we was nuts." That's the kind of role models we all need, people nuts enough to do the things that can make them our heroes.

Fort Wayne's Betty Weaver Foss, the 1950
League batting champion, connects with the
ball in a night game.

GAME FIVE

Thursday, September 14, 1950

If a student of baseball were to rely on the offensive statistics to determine who won the regular season All-American Girls Baseball League pennant in 1950, she would without hesitation pick the Fort Wayne Daisies. That the Daisies came in second behind the Peaches—although a very close second—would need some explaining.

The Daisies were known for their power at the plate. One would expect this power to be reflected in the number of runs a team can score, and indeed, over the course of the season, the Daisies did score 78 more runs than the Peaches. But the Peaches wound up the season with 67 wins and 44 losses to the Daisies 62 wins and 43 losses. How did the Daisies score so many more runs and still win fewer ball games than their arch rival?

The answer lies in the essentially different character of the two teams. The Daisies were a powerful offensive team. When they won a ball game, they tended to win it big, scoring many more runs than their opponent. The Peaches, in contrast, were a fine defensive team. When they won a ball game it was often by only one or two runs achieved through a combination of excellent pitching, fine fielding and a few well-timed, well-placed hits.

The outcome of the season series between the two teams tells the story. Rockford and Fort Wayne played sixteen games against each other during the 1950 regular season. Fort Wayne won a convincing ten of these games. When the Daisies won, they left no doubt about it; they won by an average of 4.4 runs per game. The Fort Wayne team scored an average of 6.4 total runs per game in those ten games. When the Peaches won, on the other hand, they barely won: Rockford won by an average of only 1.83 runs per game and scored an average of only 3.33 runs in their six victories against Fort Wayne.

The difference is dramatically illustrated in the final scores of the two shutouts the teams played against each other during the regular season. Rockford won the first shutout, on July 8, by a score of 1-0. Two days later Fort Wayne won the other shutout by a score of 12-0. Had the whole season consisted of only these two games, the Daisies would have scored twelve times the number of runs the Peaches did, but still have finished the season in a tie. What counts, as every Peach and every Daisy knew, is not the number of runs scored, but the win.

There was some cause for concern for the Daisies in the timing of their ten wins. Eight of the ten came in the first two months of the season. In August, Rockford won four of the six meetings between the two teams and began the stretch run that left them pennant winners in September. As the season moved toward its conclusion, powerful Fort Wayne must have been feeling nibbled to death by Rockford gnats.

The two teams' overall batting averages were very similar: Fort Wayne's was the best in the League, but Rockford was in second place, not far behind. Fort Wayne players hit a collective .249, Rockford .240.

But the Daisies were more powerful at the plate. Of the seven League players who finished the season batting over .300, four were Daisies: pitcher Ruth Matlock, .361 (in 21 games), Betty Foss, .346, Evelyn Wawryshyn, .311, and another pitcher, Millie Deegan, .309 (in 39 games). Only one Peach, Dorothy Kamenshek, .334, batted over .300.

The Daisies knocked out 133 doubles to the Peaches' 88, although the Peaches—not famous for their power—hit 51 triples to the Daisies' 16. Fort Wayne did clobber three more home runs, 21 to 18, and batted in more runs overall, 402 to Rockford's 358.

The Daisies got on base more, with only seven fewer hits than the Peaches (880 to 873), and many more walks, 422 to 327. Both teams had a number of batters hit by pitches, 35 for Fort Wayne, 34 for Rockford. As you would expect with batters swinging from their heels, Fort Wayne struck out more often than Rockford, 370 strikeouts to Rockford's 320.

Once runners get on base, a team must move them along somehow. Rockford did so with sacrifice hits, 90 to Fort Wayne's 78. But Fort Wayne moved their runners along with many more stolen bases, 306 to Rockford's 225. Fort Wayne did leave 822 runners on base, while Rockford stranded 765. From the number of runs scored, however, we know the Daisies brought a lot home as well.

Rockford was known for its excellent pitching and consistent fielding. Rockford's pitchers had a collective ERA of 2.44, but Fort Wayne's team ERA was only slightly higher, 2.62.

Rockford did register more put-outs than Fort Wayne, 2,904 to 2,770, and more assists, 1,314 to 1,288. The Peaches made a few more double plays, 77 to the Daisies' 71. Neither team completed a triple play. Both teams made 229 errors during the course of the season. And they ended the season with almost identical fielding percentages, .947 for Fort Wayne, .949 for Rockford.

All in all, the 1950 championship series paired two equally skilled but very different teams, one an offensive power, the other a clever defensive team. By the fifth game, these well-matched teams had both found a way to win two games.

◆◆◆

The fifth game is pivotal in any seven-game series that is tied after four games. A win in the fifth game will give one team a decided edge; whoever wins Game Five needs to win only one more to take the series. The loser of Game Five must win two in a row to triumph, a difficult task when two teams are evenly matched.

The significance of Game Five is affected by home-field advantage. (In a seven-game post-season series, the winner of the regular season is awarded the advantage of playing four of the possible seven games at home, games one, two, six and seven.) If the winner of Game Five has home-field advantage for the series, that team need only win one of two remaining games at home, a likely possibility. If the loser of Game Five has home-field advantage, perhaps they can win the next two games at home, a difficult but quite possible task. The loser without this advantage is faced with the uphill task of winning two back-to-back games on the road.

Game Five is thus an intensely fought battle, both parties acutely aware that the outcome can decisively affect the series. The account that follows reflects this intensity. The *News-Sentinel* writer is passionate in his frustration and disappointment with the result of this dramatic game.

Daisies Beaten in 10th; Trail Rockford by 3-2

Fort Wayne News-Sentinel, September 15, 1950

The Daisies' plans to snare their first All-American Girls Baseball League championship were virtually obliterated Thursday night at Zollner Stadium when they blew a 4-3, 10-inning decision to Rockford's Peaches.

The two teams are idle today, but will resume action at Rockford Saturday night with the Peaches leading the best-four-out-of-seven-games series, three games to two, and needing only one victory to wrap up their third successive AAGBL title.

If the Daisies win Saturday, the seventh and final game will be played at Rockford Sunday night, drawing the curtain on the 1950 campaign.

Thursday's loss was a bitter disappointment, because the Daisies could have won with heady play and a break or two.

Freak Play Aids Peaches

Rockford broke up the duel in the first extra inning, but needed a freak circumstance to do it.

Dottie Collins, who had pitched to only 16 batters in the preceding five innings, after giving up five hits and a couple of runs in the first four frames, started the troublesome 10th by retiring Marilyn Jones on a fly to left. Then she hit Dottie Key with a pitched ball. Dottie

Kamenshek moved her to second with a sacrifice. "Snookie" Doyle walked.

Jackie Kelley slashed the ball right back at Collins' feet. She deflected it between second and third. Dottie Schroeder, who had raced to cover second at the crack of the bat, reversed her field, but, in her anxiety to make a quick play and prevent any scoring, kicked the ball and Key raced home with the lead run.

With Helen (Nickie) Fox, who had replaced starting pitcher Gacioch, at bat, Kelley and Doyle then teamed up on a delayed double steal that so confused Collins she did not make a play in any direction until Doyle was at home plate with the second run.

Daisies Rally Again

The Daisies, who had to come from behind to tie the game in the regulation nine innings, almost did it again. Evelyn Wawryshyn led off with a hit off Doyle's glove, her third single of the game. Foss lashed a prodigious blow to right field, which outfielder Irene Applegren tried to snag but couldn't. Sally Meier, Wednesday night's heroine, batting with runners on second and third, socked a liner which Doyle grabbed. The shortstop threw quickly to second trying to double Foss, but the throw was bad, advancing Wawryshyn to home and Foss to third. Schroeder, swinging hard, fouled a second strike back and then bunted straight to Fox, who doubled Foss off third and ended the game.

The Daisies passed up a scoring opportunity in the sixth. With one run in and the bases loaded, Thelma Eisen missed the ball completely on an attempted bunt and Vivian Kellogg was out at the plate. Kellogg shared batting honors with Wawryshyn, also getting three hits.

Summary

Runs - Key 2, Kamenshek, Eisen, Schroeder, Doyle, Wawryshyn. Errors- Doyle. Runs batted in - Doyle, Kelley, Gacioch, Wawryshyn, Collins. Three-base hits - Key. Two-base hits - Foss 2. Sacrifice hits - Doyle, Kamenshek, Kelley 2, Gacioch. Stolen bases - Doyle, Kelley, Eisen 2, Wawryshyn. Double plays - Eisen to Kellogg, Fox to Kelley. Base on balls - Off Collins 4, Gacioch 5. Strike outs - Collins 1, Gacioch 4, Fox 1. Hit by pitch - by Collins (Kelley, Key), by Fox (Collins). Left on base - Rockford 7, Fort Wayne 9. Winning pitcher - Fox. Losing pitcher - Collins. Time - 2:00. Attendance - 1,800.

▲ Dorothy "Dottie" Kamenshek, the best first baseman in the history of the All-American League, stretches for a throw from shortstop. A Florida men's team tried to acquire Kammie's contract in 1950, but she chose to stay with the Peaches.

▶ Dottie Kamenshek talking with the author at the 1992 reunion.

DOROTHY "KAMMIE" KAMENSHEK
Rockford, First Baseman

Statistics: Born: 1925. Home Town: Cincinnati, Ohio. Height: 5 feet 6 inches. Playing weight: 136 pounds. Bats: Left. Throws: Left. Entered League:1943 at age 18. Teams: Rockford, 1943-51 and 1953. Lifetime totals: Batting average: .292. Fielding percentage: at first base, .982.

Dottie Kamenshek was without question the best first baseman to play in the All-American Girls Baseball League. She and Doris Sams, who played the outfield and pitched for the Muskegon and later Kalamazoo Lassies, are regarded as the two best all-around players in the history of the League.

Kamenshek was chosen for the All-Star team at first base seven times in her ten-year career, in 1943 and from 1946 through 1951. She won the batting crown in 1946 and 1947 with averages of .316 and .306. Her 1950 average was .334, fourth overall and the best batting average for a Peach that year.

Kammie's dependability at the plate was legendary; she could connect with the ball. In 3,736 lifetime at-bats, she struck out only 81 times. In the 1950 season she fanned only 9 times in 341 trips to the plate.

Her fielding was also unparalleled. Kamenshek committed only 192 errors in 1,005 games of professional baseball. During that time she made 10,423 put-outs, the most of any All-American player. Her lifetime fielding percentage was .982. Wally Pipp, who in the 1920s played first base for the New York Yankees, told the Associated Press in May 1950 that Dorothy Kamenshek was "the fanciest fielding first baseman I've ever seen, man or woman."[56]

♦♦♦

I was no different than any other Peaches fan in 1950; Dottie Kamenshek was not only a hero, she was someone to regard with awe. I thought of her as a different type of being than her teammates, more grown-up, more serious, a person of substance not to be taken lightly.

In September 1992, when I approached the motel desk in Fort Wayne to register for my room at the All-American Girls Professional Baseball League Players' Association's mini-reunion, I overheard Vivian Kellogg checking in. I introduced myself, and with her usual enthusiasm, Vivian dragged me by the hand over to meet four or five players grouped in the lobby. She singled out a player at random and said, "You remember Kammie, of course."

And there she was, looking older, of course, but just as I remembered her, still serious, still more grown-up than any of us, a person of stature. I shook her hand—I hoped with sufficient vigor—and said, "Yes, of course I remember," trying to sound all of my fifty-two years. I felt ten years old again, awestruck, thrilled to be in the presence of my girlhood idol. I felt a bit light-headed and it wasn't until several hours later that I could recover sufficiently to ask Dorothy Kamenshek to meet me in my hotel room for an interview.

♦♦♦

Dottie Kamenshek began playing vacant-lot ball with the neighborhood kids: "We just chose up sides and played." She was ten years old, and all the other players were boys; there simply weren't any girls in her Cincinnati neighborhood. I asked whether the boys cared that she was a girl.

> They never said anything. I don't think there was the emphasis on boy-girl competition like there is now. We were just doing what kids in our neighborhood did.

Dottie's father died when she was nine, and her mother, while not overly enthusiastic, didn't oppose her daughter's ball-playing. "It kept me out of trouble," explains Dottie. When at about age thirteen young Kamenshek got into the industrial leagues, playing for a local meat-packer, her mother became actively supportive, attending all her games.

Dottie's mother was poor, and had to work full-time. Her only child was often on her own, what we'd now call a latch-key kid.

She was a matron, basically a janitor, at Proctor and Gamble for years and years. She was born in Rumania and had only a third-grade education, but she was a very brilliant woman. I was the first woman to go to college in my whole family. And the only way I could do that was with the money I saved from playing baseball. It paid for my first semester's tuition.

When in 1943 Wrigley sent out the word to baseball men around the country that he wanted girl ball-playing talent, Kamenshek's manager organized try-outs in Cincinnati. About fifty girls showed up. Six were sent to Chicago for further try-outs and two made the final cut to join the first sixty players in the League. I asked Dottie how she felt trying out. Dottie recalls,

I felt like it was an opportunity. I just had enthusiasm to try to make it. I thought, this is my chance. I'm sure I was nervous, but it didn't dominate me, in the sense of making me freeze up or anything.

I'd never played first base, I'd always been an outfielder. But at the try-outs in Cincinnati I heard them asking everybody to say two positions they could play. Well, I thought, what does a left-hander do if she doesn't pitch except play the outfield and first base? So, I told 'em first base.

In Chicago we spent a week running, throwing, fielding, batting and so on. They graded us on each of those skills. Then, once they'd chosen the girls they wanted, they used the points they'd given each girl to divide us up into comparable teams. And that's what they did again each year at spring training, reassigned players when necessary so as to equalize the teams.

I was fortunate enough that Rockford always wanted me, and I got to stay there.

Kamenshek attended that first Charm School in 1943. I asked her about the feminine image the League tried to create.

Well, well. Let me think about that. [She pauses to collect her thoughts.] I think most of us came from very poor families. I don't think there was a real middle class back then; there were either poor or rich. The rich were going off to finishing schools, and the poor just didn't learn social skills.

My mother didn't wear make-up, so I didn't either. I had never eaten out in a restaurant until I went to Chicago, so I knew nothing about which fork to use. I had been on one train ride prior to 1943, so I was unfamiliar with tipping. I wasn't uncouth, I just wasn't educated about these things.

Charm School was fun. I didn't like the way they put make-up all over my face, and I never wore it. To this day I don't cover up my wrinkles, I just wear lipstick. But I didn't feel Charm School was too extreme. I think we all took parts of it that we thought were good for us, and eliminated the other. We laughed about it like mad, but I think every one of us picked up things from it.

Dottie played the first thirteen games of her career at center field, and then became Rockford's first baseman. I asked her if someone taught her to play first base.

No, it was natural. I had watched baseball. My mother used to take me to the Cincinnati Reds games every Ladies' Day. I wasn't there just to rah-rah the team. I paid attention to their technique. I guess I was an observant person.

I've always been serious, too serious, everybody says. About everything. I'm a deep thinker. I'm a minor in philosophy, so you become a deep thinker.

I think I was a team leader. I used to try to help the rookies out when they'd come to the team. They had pressures, you know. Especially the ones who came in the later years. Since by then we were playing baseball rather than modified softball, they had a level of performance to achieve that we early players had grown up with.

I'd try to help 'em relax. Tell 'em it doesn't mean everything if you made an error. I tried to help them psychologically more than with their skills.

I asked Kammie if even a fine player like herself improved her skills.

Yes, I did. Through practice, a lot of practice. Bill Allington was our manager, and he was a great teacher. And I was willing to work and practice.

He taught me how to bunt for hits. We worked for hours on the drag bunt, a bunt that I as a left-hander would ease down the first-base line, sort of dragging it along with me as I started to run toward first.

I wondered if Dottie thought there were advantages to being a left-hander in baseball.

A right-hander would say so! Actually, there might be, because as you're swinging, your momentum is already going towards first. It might give you one more step. And, of course, you're literally closer to first base when you're standing in the batter's box.

I brought up the fact that left-handers also have an advantage at first base; they are traditionally chosen to play that position because their gloved hand is toward the inside of the diamond where more balls will be hit. "Right," said Kamenshek ruefully. "And you get eliminated from all the others, except pitching and the outfield."

Kamenshek explained the subtle adjustments a first baseman makes, depending on which infielder is throwing the ball.

> You knew what their ball did as they threw it. Alice Pollitt threw a straight riser from third base. Snookie threw a very very heavy ball to catch, one that hurt when it got to my hand; it broke to my left. Charlene Barnett threw very accurately, a straight ball from her second-base position.
>
> If I had pick-ups to make, it would be from Snookie or Al, not Barnie. Not because they were less accurate, but because they were further away. They may have gone into the hole, deep between second and third base, to make the catch. Then they had to get rid of it fast, before they had a chance to square up. There are a lot of technical things you have to accomplish before you can throw a ball straight.
>
> As they released it, you knew if it was gonna be in the dirt, or high, or to your left or right. I wasn't real tall, but I could jump, I could move.

In 1950 Kamenshek's excellence at first base drew her to the attention of the men's major leagues. Former Yankee Wally Pipp had issued his public opinion that Kamenshek was "almost up to big league standards."

> You should see that girl. She's a slugging 135-pounder who would wow 'em in the east. Manager Bill Allington of the Peaches has a piece of baseball property that might bring some dough, if the majors were game enough to try using girl performers.

Pipp predicted that the next great innovation for the major leagues was the introduction of "lady ball players . . . and within the next five years."[57]

Shortly after Pipp's pronouncement, the president of the Florida

International (minor) League and an official of the League's Fort Lauderdale club wrote Kamenshek to ask who they should contact to discuss offering her a contract to play for them. Fred Leo, President of the AAGBL, and later the League's Board of Directors turned down the offer. Leo was particularly concerned that Kamenshek would not be able to hit for extra bases in the men's game. He went on to explain, "Rockford couldn't afford to lose her. I also told them [the Florida negotiators] that we felt that women should play among themselves and that they could not help but appear inferior in athletic competition with men."[58]

Dottie's reasons for not wanting to play with the Florida minor-league team were quite different than Mr. Leo's, though she acknowledged a difference in physical strength between men and women.

> I said no, because I thought at that time it would be more of a publicity stunt than a sincere desire for the calibre of ball I could play. In that era, I don't think it would have been a legitimate offer. Also, I don't think women have the body build. I weighed 135 pounds. There's no way I could hold up for a whole season competing against men. As much as women are after equalization, we aren't built to compete with men. In terms of skill, I think I had the abilities, but I did not have the body.
>
> So I said, "No, I'm very happy where I am." Now whether my judgment was right or wrong, I don't know.

Kamenshek appreciated working for Bill Allington, but like so many others, she found him formidable.

> I thought he was a great baseball manager. But he was difficult to get along with off the field. You didn't like him for some reason. He was too intense, too controlling of all his players. He wanted you to eat and drink and sleep baseball, twenty-four hours a day. No fun. Baseball was his life.
>
> He was an excellent teacher, but he drove people too hard. I would talk back to him sometimes, for myself and for the other players too, to try to protect and defend them. He'd listen, but whether he heard me or not, I don't know. Sometimes he would change.

I asked Kamenshek if she had a favorite memory of a moment on the field, some wonderful play or perhaps a timely hit.

It's all blended together for me. I think the greatest things were our championships, we won more championships than any other team. That's why everybody picks on the Peaches. Everybody likes to talk about when they beat the Peaches, but they don't mention it's the only year they did beat us!

I showed Kamenshek the clipping of an important 1950 game where she had batted 4-for-4, and asked if she remembered that.

Nah. I remember winning the game. But I'm not a statistics person. I knew I had won a couple of batting championships, but I didn't know my yearly or lifetime stats until the baseball cards were made up.

There's one thing Allington taught me that I remembered all of my playing years: Get one walk a game, and hit two balls hard, even if this time they're outs, and you'll hit .300. So, if I went zero for four, I didn't care, if I had hit two balls hard and got a walk. So when I see I hit four for four, I want to know how well I hit them; maybe only two of those were hit well.

I'd be disappointed if I couldn't help the team win with hits, or a bunt, or a walk, or a steal, but the individual stats didn't matter to me. I just enjoyed the game, the offense, the defense, I enjoyed the entire game.

I led off a number of years and hit second a number of years. Your first and second hitters are supposed to get on base however they can get there. I was a good runner, I could steal bases, so I was always first or second.

When I was trying to steal, I'd pay attention to the pitcher's movements. I'd observe them if I was on base, but I would already have observed them from the dugout. You weren't through playing just because you were sitting on the bench.

Maybe one of the reasons I was a better player was that I was always paying attention. You have to have some natural ability, and you have to develop the skill, and you have to develop the mentality.

I wondered whether to serious-minded Kamenshek, baseball felt like fun or like business. She replied definitively,

Fun! I don't think anybody in our League would say it felt like a business. We were doing something we wanted to do, that was first, and getting paid for it, that was second.

I appreciated the fans. I didn't pay any attention to cheers or boos, though. Either way, it meant they noticed you. You'd have a certain following of fans. They might go out to eat where you ate or even drive to away games. You had a relationship with them.

I didn't pay much attention to the organization. At seventeen or eighteen or nineteen years old, if you get your paycheck and you can play ball, you don't care about anything else. You don't know organizations.

I asked Dottie the difference between being on a winning and on a losing ballclub. How did it feel to her and the other players?

You knew if you were a contender or not. And you developed a confidence level if you were. You felt like the other team had to beat you. Rather than thinking, "I've got to beat them," you go in with the attitude, "They have to beat us." That's the best way I can describe the difference.

If you ended up in the playoffs the year before, you knew you'd be a contender. And if you won the championship, you knew darn well everybody's gonna be after you. So you went out there the next season and played hard all the time to maintain your status.

Everyone I interviewed on the Peaches team—and some Daisies as well—expressed their admiration for Dottie Kamenshek.

Alice Pollitt, Rockford's third baseman:

Now Kammie, I don't think there was any other player in my mind than Kamenshek. I liked the way she played ball. She made me look good. Sometimes I'd throw a curve to her, and she'd pop up and say, "So, you're gonna be a pitcher now?"

I think she was the best first baseman in the League. She'd stretch, she'd jump, she was a good hitter. And she knew baseball, she knew what to do. I don't think there was a first baseman better'n her. She was a natural. She made a lot of us look good.

Rose Gacioch, Rockford's pitcher and rightfielder:

Those major-league boys nowadays, they don't know how to catch a ball at first base. Kammie should teach 'em. Kamenshek could teach 'em how to play first.

Marilyn Jones, Rockford's back-up catcher:

I had this thing about Kammie. She was one that I always really liked. I just admired her, she was so graceful, and she could hit! And she was nice to you. And she was . . . well, I was an impressionable young woman . . . and Kammie was the greatest!

My scrapbook includes a clipping from the August 20, 1950 Rockford Morning Star that describes a special event that accompanied the previous night's ballgame. The article reads, in part,

"Dottie" Kameshek Receives Gifts, Tributes from Public

A girl baseball star who has been called one of the greatest defensive first basemen—man or woman—of all time, who has been honored by sports writers all over the nation, and whose diamond services have been sought by professional baseball, was honored by the folk in her adopted home town Saturday night.

More than 3,000 baseball fans braved frigid temperatures to pay tribute to the Rockford Peaches' Dottie Kamenshek. It was "Kamenshek Night" at Beyer Stadium.

In one of the most successful celebrations ever held in Rockford to honor an athlete, Miss Kamenshek was presented with $780.69 in contributions from the fans. She also received a $50 war bond from her teammates, another $50 war bond from her mother, and hundreds of other gifts, ranging from an electric cooker to a corsage, from friends and fans.

Among the gifts was one from the Grand Rapids baseball players, a group of girls who haven't been paid for more than three weeks because of financial difficulties in Grand Rapids.

Even the opposition was appreciative. Dottie Schroeder, Fort Wayne's shortstop, thought Kamenshek was "one of the greatest players of all time."

Kamenshek explained how she and Snookie held the team together and kept everyone's minds on the game.

> You have to have an attitude, and you have to have a leader, or leaders. I'd say Snookie and I were the Peaches' leaders.
>
> We hated to lose. If we did, we tried to figure out what we could have done differently to help the game. We'd sit in the clubhouse before we showered, and talk it over. The rest of the team kind of hung around to see what we were talkin' about. Pretty soon they'd realize, "Well, we better think about the game." Then you get your rookies listening too, and pretty soon it steamrolls. This is what develops champions.
>
> If, when we thought about it, we decided we couldn't have done anything differently, then okay, forget it. If it was the right play, and you didn't get 'em, that's fine. We'll go out and get the next one.

But if it was the wrong play, remember it! Maybe we would have thrown to the wrong base, tried to get the runner at second when we should have gone to third, that kind of thing. We'd think, Why did we do that? How many outs were there? Was that the right play?

Everyone's gonna make physical errors. They bothered you, but you knew it would happen. It's the mental errors you have to minimize to be a winner. I didn't mind losing if we played well. But I think Rockford had a winning attitude.

◆◆◆

Dottie Kamenshek retired from the League in 1952 with a bad back. In 1953 the organization prevailed upon her to return for home games to help the team both in the field and at the gate. She retired permanently after that season. She completed her college degree in physical therapy in 1958, from Marquette University in Milwaukee, Wisconsin.

In 1961, she and Marge Wenzell, a utility player for eight years and nine teams in the League—but never the Peaches—moved to California. Kamenshek began working as a physical therapist, and eventually became chief of Crippled Children's Services for Los Angeles County, with two hundred physical therapists working under her.

I worked with children with cerebral palsy, spina bifida, muscular dystrophy, amputees, all the long-term problems. The children did not know they were handicapped; they were children first. So you could work with them as children, and then work with the family to get the parents to accept their handicapped child. Which was difficult. Probably eighty-five per cent of the families ended up divorced because of their handicapped child. But I loved it.

In 1980 Kamenshek took an early retirement from supervising others, and went back to part-time work in patient care. She is now fully retired. Dottie continues to share a household with Marge, who herself had a long career as a purchaser in the electronics industry. Their home in Cathedral City, California, is right next door to Snookie Doyle and her friend Pauline "Heddy" Crawley.

Kammie thinks the rediscovery of the League has been wonderful for everyone.

It's great for the whole group, really. I think it's brought a lot of smiles to everybody's face; it's made us feel young again.

♦♦♦

At the end of the interview I asked Kammie whether she thought Rockford was the best team, thinking over the twelve years of the League's existence. She answered without hesitation.

Yes, we were the best. Back then I don't know if I would have said that. No one really thought about it. But since Cooperstown, and all the interviews, all the looking back, you see who won the championships. So yes, I'll say it now.

And who did she think was the second best?

I wouldn't want to comment on that. I'll just stick my neck out and say we were the best!

Dorothy "Dottie" Schroeder, Fort Wayne's fine shortstop, leaps and pivots in the air to throw out a runner. Schroeder was the only woman to play all twelve seasons of All-American baseball.

THE PLAY
OF THE GAME

*"We played good baseball. That's not brag-
ging. That's a fact."* —**Kay Blumetta**

The women of the All-American Girls Baseball League were good
athletes when they entered the League, some of them outstanding
natural sportswomen. Jo Weaver, the dominant player the last three
years of the League, says, with characteristic understatement, "It's
something that you're kind of gifted with."

Not everyone—in fact hardly anyone—enjoyed natural gifts comparable to Jo's, but everybody could learn the game. It was during
their tenure as professional players that these women mastered both
the fundamentals and the nuances of high-calibre baseball. They
came to understand how to play baseball and, more importantly,
how to think baseball. As Faye Dancer says, "Baseball is a learning
sport."

Many players made the distinction between their natural athleti-
cism and the demands of professional-level performance. Irene Applegren felt that, "most of it came natural to us, but we probably had
never thought about it all that much. We had just played ball and had

a good time." Fort Wayne utility player Helen Ketola explained, "You have natural ability, but you have to practice like anything. Of course, at that age you didn't know it was practice; it was joy really."

Not every All-American felt she had natural ability, at least not to the degree of those around her. Dottie Schroeder, Fort Wayne's shortstop who was a natural, evaluated center-field teammate Thelma Eisen: "I always admired Tiby greatly. She didn't have the natural ability a lot of the players did, but she worked hard and made up for it by hustling." Tiby agreed. "I wasn't a natural athlete. I had to learn."

Whether natural athletes or not, to be successful in professional baseball all the players had to master the game at a higher level than they had ever played it before. They had two places to turn for the knowledge they needed: they could learn from each other and, if they were lucky enough to have a devoted and knowledgeable manager, they could be taught by him. Rockford catcher Ruth Richard drew from both these resources to master a new way to hit.

> I was a left-handed batter, and had a lot of trouble hitting left-handed pitchers. There's just something about their delivery, especially if it's a little bit from the side, that is very difficult.
>
> But if their ball is outside, you can hit it to the opposite field. I used to watch Kamenshek, who also batted left; she was good at it. And Bill Allington, our manager, was himself left-handed. He'd say, "Wait for that outside pitch." So I'd get up there saying to myself, "Now I'm not gonna try and pull the ball; I'm gonna try and wait for an outside pitch and punch that ball over third." If you waited for that one pitch, you could hit that thing to left field all day long.
>
> If I got a hit like that, that was the greatest. I'd really practiced it, really had to work on it, and made it into a success.

◆◆◆

Most of the girls who entered the All-American League had played softball at levels of expertise that brought them to the attention of their managers. A few were so good at another sport that coaches figured they could play baseball too. And a handful were already playing baseball on men's teams.

Whatever their experience, what they found in the All-American League was something different than what they were used to. Some of the skills the women had to learn were simply the finer points of high-calibre baseball, like hitting to the opposite field, returning signs, and executing the hit and run or the double-steal. Most important of all, they had to learn to pay attention all the time. Fort Wayne centerfielder Tiby Eisen absorbed that lesson.

> The key to being a good player at any position is to be ready. You can't have your mind wandering. You're set, you're ready, you're balanced on your feet, just like a fighter. The minute the pitcher winds up, you're ready to go in any direction. If you lose that concentration, you lose half a step, and that will mean you miss the ball.
> When I learned to play baseball I found out I could think!

Players also had to develop particular skills depending upon the rules they found when they entered the League because the rules of play changed throughout the course of its twelve-year history.[59] When Dottie Schroeder, Dottie Kamenshek and Nickie Fox began playing in 1943, the game was modified softball. The diamond was a little bigger (65-foot basepaths), there were nine players on a defensive team rather than ten, the pitcher's rubber was moved back a bit, gloves were required for all players, and leadoffs and stolen bases were permitted. The pitchers, however, still threw the familiar twelve-inch softball underhand.

Gradually the ball shrank and the basepaths lengthened. Sidearm pitching was allowed in 1946 and required in 1947. In 1948 overhand pitching was introduced, a change that seriously affected players' careers, as underhand pitchers were thereafter required to throw either sidearm or overhand. Batters had fifty feet to pick up the pitch, and the ball now measured 10-⅜ inches.

The following year another five feet were added from pitcher to batter, and the ball shrank again, this time to an even ten inches. The 1948/1949 dimensions characterized the rules of women's professional baseball for the next four years, 1949 to 1952, the longest period players enjoyed when the parameters of the game did not change.[60]

The point of all these changes was to add speed to the game and runs to the score, thus making for more exciting entertainment. League President Ken Sells explained, "Softball was considered as very much a pitcher's game and it was felt that more hitting, baserunning, and spectacular fielding would have much more fan appeal."[61] The men who ran the All-American Girls League wanted their girls to play the kind of ball these men were familiar with; all the rules changes on the field moved in the direction of making the women's game more like the men's.

Pitchers bore the brunt of the on-the-field changes. Some excellent underhand pitchers, successful for the first four or five years of the League, could not adapt to the sidearm or the overhand pitch. Rockford and Kenosha pitcher Mary Pratt, for instance, could not learn the sidearm pitch. Pratt was a successful underhand pitcher from 1943 to 1946, but left the League after a brief appearance in 1947, in time to become Fort Wayne rookie Helen Ketola's junior high school heroine.

Rockford's Nickie Fox made the changeover from under- to overhand successfully, but understandably preferred her underhand career, when she lead the League with earned-run averages of 1.81 and 0.93 in 1943 and 1944, respectively. In 1943, Nickie won 31 games and lost only 8.

> My most effective pitch was really my underhand pitch. It was a rise ball, it used to go almost to the plate and then lift up. I'd do it all with my wrist. A writer from Racine once said I could have thrown my mitt in and nobody could have hit that either!
>
> I did change over when they brought that overhand pitch in. I had a pretty good curve, and a drop ball, and of course my fastball. But you have to be careful to keep a fastball either inside or outside. If you throw it across the center of the plate, all they have to do is swing and that ball goes a country mile.
>
> Overhand is an altogether different way of throwing. And I'm sufferin' for it now. My back, you know.

Dottie Collins entered the League in 1944, pitched underhand for two years, sidearm for two years, and overhand for two years.

> The change turned out to be easy for me. I had thrown a curveball underhand and a knuckleball too; so I just reversed them both. I held the ball the same way, and just threw it overhand. It was just easy for me.
>
> Lots of the girls couldn't change. It depended on the individual. Connie Wisniewski was a great athlete. She could run, and she was a hell of a hitter, so she went to the outfield. She was just a great ballplayer.
>
> If I had not been able to make the conversion, I'd have ended up

back home because I was a lousy hitter, and I never could run. Pitching was it for me, period.

Maxine Kline entered the League when overhand pitching was already the style. But even she had to adapt somewhat.

> That last year, 1954, they made the ball even smaller [9 to 9-¼ inches] and went to 85-foot basepaths [from 75-foot]. That 10-inch that we used for five years was a good-sized ball. The 9-inch ball didn't fit right in your hand, it seemed to be heavier, and it hurt your arm to throw it. I didn't like it. But that 10-inch was wonderful.
>
> Those extra ten feet on the basepaths, you could tell the difference in them too!

Softball played at a high calibre is indeed a pitcher's game. Scores tend to be low, and pitchers' earned-run averages are correspondingly low. With the introduction of overhand pitching to the League, earned-run averages moved upwards, as did batting averages and the numbers of runs scored. Nickie Fox's lowest ERA was in 1944 (0.93), and her highest in 1952 (2.80). Dottie Collins' career reflects the same external influences at work: her lowest ERA of 0.93 was achieved in 1945, her highest of 3.46 in 1950.

What is difficult for pitchers is a gift to hitters, of course. Dottie Kamenshek's lowest batting average was .257 in 1944; her highest, .345 in 1951. Dottie Schroeder, for most of her career an average hitter, was helped by the changes at the plate, though she had to keep beefing up her throw.

> My throw from shortstop to first kept getting longer. But the overhand pitch and longer pitching distance made me a better hitter. It improved my average. Of course the older I got, the more I was thinking. The last year I hit something like .304, I think.

Dottie Schroeder hit exactly .304 in 1954. In 1943 she had hit .188.

All the rules changes meant that All-Americans who played in different eras were playing different games of baseball. It makes little sense to compare a batting average squeezed out against a softball fired underhand with one banged out against a hardball delivered overhand. Nor is it very meaningful to compare pitcher's records achieved under the different pitching rules. All-American statistics as often reflect differences in the rules under which they were compiled as they do differences in the performance levels of the players who compiled them.

Base-stealing records were affected by the expanded infield measurements. While longer basepaths should have meant stealing was more difficult, this was offset by the increased pitching distance and distance from home plate to second base. Since runners steal not only on catchers (challenging the speed and accuracy of their throws), but on pitchers (using the time it takes for their wind-up and their pitch to reach the catcher), base-stealers may have had to run farther, but pitchers and catchers had to throw farther to catch them.

Sophie Kurys' phenomenal 1946 record of 201 bases stolen in 203 attempts—a record not yet broken in the history of professional baseball, men's or women's—was accomplished on 72-foot basepaths. Betty Foss, thought by some to be even faster than Kurys, was running on 75- and then 85-foot basepaths in 1953 and 1954. In 1953 Foss stole 80 bases, first in the League. Kurys was running against underhand or sidearm pitching from a pitching distance of 43 feet. Foss was stealing bases from overhand pitchers throwing 60 feet to the plate.

In a perfect world, it would be ideal to stabilize the rules of the game before comparing athletic performance. In the real world, rule changes always deliciously complicate the comparison of sports achievements, and players and historians of the League argue enthusiastically about who played better when.[62]

All the players agree, however, that although classic softball is a fun game, baseball, whatever form is being played, is infinitely more interesting and more difficult.

Snookie Doyle did not play during the 1951 All-American season, but played softball in Arizona instead.

> When I went back in '52 it was very difficult because I was not in shape. It was difficult going from softball to baseball. Going from baseball to softball was easy, because I don't think your skills have to be as good. The ball bounces truer on softball fields because they are skin [dirt] infields with no pitcher's mound.
>
> On a grass baseball field with a mound you can get bad bounces, and you really have to watch the ball into your glove.
>
> Also, a baseball goes much faster than a softball.

Softball is easier on your body as well. Tiby Eisen compared the two:

> I thought softball was much easier to play. You don't have to run as far, you don't have to slide. You can see the bigger ball better. After you've played baseball, softball was a cinch.

The All-Americans played a brand of offensive baseball classically referred to as the "scientific" style, to be distinguished from the "slugging" style that relies on hitting the long ball. "Scientific" baseball is characterized by bunting, stealing, the hit and run, and sacrificing. Less reliance is placed on power hitting, a great deal of reliance on fine pitching and defense.[63]

The All-American League manual appreciatively quotes an "intensive study of Girls' Baseball," made by the authoritative *Baseball Blue Book* in 1945. The *Blue Book* observer visited several Fort Wayne Daisies games and submitted this detailed analysis of what the girls' game was like. Even though couched in the rather intricate language of the 1940s, the pacing and character of the game are clearly conveyed.

> 1. In method, in the number and deployment of players, whether at bat or in the field, the girls played real Baseball. They could run, steal, slide and do what was a revelation to most men—throw, throw hard and with precision. Moreover, in that basic thing—game strategy—the girls' league exhibited Baseball according to high standards—those comparable with major league performance.
>
> 2. A constant, never-suspended physical attitude of alertness was required by every player and was supported by continual player "chatter," by (snappy) conference "huddles," by signaling and other conventional devices. The girls secured a far superior psychological effect from these devices than is obtained by the average (men's) minor league organization. "Stalling" was minimized; umpire baiting was limited; games (9 innings) seldom consumed more than one hour and 20 minutes.
>
> 3. Most important of all was a fast moving procession of what one might call spotlighted episodes subordinate to the game contest. These challenged the attention of the spectator throughout the game. For example, if a runner was on base the spectator was kept on edge by the runner's constant threat to steal. At the same time you were keyed up by the uncertainty of whether the batter would swing, hit

and-run or sacrifice. If two were on base, there was constant maneuvering for a double steal.

When long hits inside the park were accomplished, most of them involved close plays at second, third or the plate. These plays, which gave spectators time to build up suspense and interest through periods ranging from seven to fifteen seconds, punctuated every game and held the crowd in breathless suspense, as contrasted with synthetic home runs over the fence and their frequent destruction of the suspense period.

The chances for success in base-stealing were just about the right proportion to make the effort count in game strategy. Scoring was comparatively low and therefore produced in a large percentage of the games the psychological effect of a close contest.

There were more intentional passes, strike-outs and bases-on-balls, and a larger proportion of runners left on bases to runs scored than in standard baseball practice. But this condition produced a surprise element for this observer. It brought about a continual pressure and movement toward the plate—an around-the-diamond threat, linked up all the way from first to third, to reach that focal point of game interest, the home plate and what it means in Baseball.

◆◆◆

The training that would produce the kind of play appreciated by this Blue Book observer was the responsibility of All-American League managers. They were the source of their players' sophisticated knowledge of baseball. The calibre of the manager had an enormous effect on the calibre of the team. Fort Wayne's catcher Mary Rountree told me,

> To have a good team you need the talent and motivation of the players and you need a good coach. When my teams did not win, I feel we just didn't have good coaches. Somebody who's scientific enough to get out there and figure out: How can I beat this team? There are ways you can beat another team even if your team doesn't have the most extensive talent.
>
> When you have a combination of a most outstanding coach and talent that's just waiting to be used, that's it! You don't have to go any farther.
>
> The League just didn't have a lot of outstanding coaches.

Mary is right. The role of the manager is critical, especially in nondemocratic organizations like baseball. The girls looked to their manager to teach them and to lead them. When he couldn't, the team floundered.

The League's managers were almost always men. Tiby Eisen managed two teams in the League for short periods, the Peoria Redwings in 1946 and the Daisies in 1948. Both times she was only a temporary manager, until a regular male manager could be found. I asked her if she would have liked managing on a more long-term basis.

> Well, yeah. I think I could have. I always liked outsmarting somebody. You have to know your players, especially your own catcher and pitchers. And you have to know the players on the other team. You have to remember who hits where and what they can do, what could happen and what could not happen. And then you compete against them. You have to outsmart them. That's my thinking. That's what managing is, with some luck of course.

Mary "Bonnie" Baker managed longer than any other woman. Baker had begun her playing career as a catcher in 1943, and in the course of nine years in the League, played every infield position. In 1950 the Lassies had folded in Muskegon, Michigan, and moved to Kalamazoo. League officials hired Baker to manage the new team for the remainder of that season, but the following winter club directors passed a resolution officially barring female managers on anything but an emergency basis. The next year Ernestine "Teeny" Petras managed for a few weeks in Kenosha.

Other players were sometimes *de facto* managers, doing the work inept nominal managers left undone. Doris Tetzlaff played this role for the Fort Wayne Daisies in 1952, during Jimmie Foxx's tenure. Dottie Green effectively led the Rockford Peaches before Bill Allington took control of the team in 1944 and also during his absence in 1947.

The calibre of managing varied greatly. The League's publicity-conscious organizers hired a number of retired major-leaguers with famous names; some of them could indeed lead a team, like Max Carey, the Daisies' manager in 1950 and 1951, and Johnny Rawlings, Rockford's manager in 1953 and 1954. Some could not, like drinker Jimmie Foxx, who stumbled through the 1952 season with the Daisies.

Tiby Eisen played for Max Carey in 1944 during his first season as manager of the Milwaukee Chicks and again when he managed the

Daisies. In 1944 Carey guided the Chicks to the pennant and the League championship. Tiby remembers Carey with affection.

> He was a wonderful father figure. He really took care of his girls. And he was just a wonderful teacher. He taught me everything he knew about being an outfielder, and running, and stealing bases. And he knew plenty. He played major-league baseball for twenty years, mostly for the Pittsburgh Pirates, and led the National League for ten years in base-stealing.
> I was lucky because he was great. And he really helped me.

Other managers had never played major league ball or did so for only a short time, but were knowledgeable baseball men. Some of them could manage and motivate girls; some could not.

Major League Hall of Famer Max Carey was central to the League's success. He served as president from 1945 to 1949 and skillfully managed the Milwaukee Chicks in 1944 and the Fort Wayne Daisies in 1950 and 1951.

Leo Schrall was an industrial league coach and a member of the board of directors of the All-American Peoria Redwings when a shake-up in 1947 made him their manager. Leo is eighty-five years old now and has made a career of baseball. Next to his wife Mildred, it has been the love of his life. Next to Leo, baseball has been the love of Mildred's life too.

I interviewed them in their attractive middle-class home in Peoria. Helped by a very few notes, Leo could remember in great detail his career with the All-Americans. When his memory would falter, Mildred could fill in. He began by telling me how he came to manage the Redwings, a story that demonstrates that the players were not completely devoid of the power to influence their own fortunes.

When the team came back from a road trip toward the end of that 1947 season, their chaperone called the chairman of the board and asked him to have a meeting of the board of directors, right then. So we all got together for a lunch meeting. Three of the girls, I remember Faye Dancer was one, came to represent the team. [Faye remembers that the whole team was present, but that she and two other players threatened to quit if the manager was allowed to continue.]

They started right in, "We want to tell you that we feel like we are a better team than what we're playing. We should be winning games that we're losing. And we're gonna fall out of the playoffs if we don't get into fourth place." The girls were four games out of fourth when they came in, with only sixteen games to play. "We have nothing against Johnny Gottselig, but we would like to see a change made."

Well, we listened to the girls and then they left and we all talked. The first thing I said to them was, "Now, look, if you let Johnny go, who you gonna replace him with?" And also I said, "We can't just take the players' word for everything." Well, we argued around for awhile, and the chairman finally put it to a vote. I abstained because we hadn't given Johnny a chance to be heard. Well, the vote was nine to two to fire Gottselig, and that's what we did.

Then one of the directors said, "Leo, why don't you just finish the season?" I was managing a real good men's industrial team at the time and had 'em on top of the league. "You gotta be kidding. I don't know anything about girls' baseball." "Well," he said, "you know enough about baseball to finish the season."

I said, "Now, look. The chances of them getting into the playoffs are not very good." And they said, "We don't care so much about that. What we want is to keep these girls satisfied so that they'll come back next year."

Well, we had a game to play that night! I had about twenty minutes to talk to them. I said, "Look, I've never coached girls before, I've never coached girls' baseball. I'm new at it, just as much as some of you are. But I do think I know baseball. So, we're going to play base-ball my way, which is the men's way, and if you bear with me," I said, "you're going to be a lot better ballplayers." They were all in agreement; they even clapped a little bit.

So then we had to play the game, and we beat Kenosha. We beat 'em three to two on a squeeze play in the eighth inning. I remember it very well. The girls executed. They put on the squeeze, a run scored, and we won.

Well, they were crazy! They were runnin' around like it was the World Series. I could hear 'em in their dressing room right next to mine. That was fine. I was glad they had that enthusiasm.

We had three games at home against Kenosha, and we won all three. But after the third game, we had to go on the road. We trav-elled the 375 miles by bus to Grand Rapids for a game the following night. We'd just gotten started when one of the girls asked the driver to stop. He pulls over at this tavern, and one of the players—a big one who loved beer—gets out and comes back with two cases for the girls. Well, I didn't say anything then.

We arrived about six in the morning, and had a meeting first thing that day. I went over a few rules of discipline, like curfew and only three beers after a game and so on. And that was the only time I had to do that. After that, they abided by the rules. I can't say enough for them; they were a great bunch.

And there was no question that they wanted to win. When they won that first game against Kenosha, they thought they were gonna get back into fourth place. I knew that was almost impossible. Well, we won two out of three in Grand Rapids, but we lost one. Then we had to go to South Bend, where again we won two, but lost another one. So we're still two games behind the fourth-place team.

We come home again and had to face Fort Wayne and Dottie Col-lins, one of the best in the League. I knew we were in for a hell of a battle, and it turned out that way. She beat our pitcher Mueller one to nothing. And that did it; it knocked us out of the playoffs.

The girls felt good and they felt bad, we came so close. I told them how proud I was. "Now next year I'm comin' back," I said, "I've al-ready signed a two-year contract, so if some of you don't like me or the way I coach, just tell me and I'll try to trade you." Nobody came forward, and they were all there for spring training the next season.

The contract Leo signed gave him $7,500 a year plus a share of the advertising revenues. In 1948 his Redwings drew 125,000 fans in a community of under 100,000 population, the record for attendance up to that time for any sport in Peoria. One night during that season over 7,000 fans attended a game against the Muskegon Lassies. Leo, normally a serious man, hides a small smile, "I was the most popular man in Peoria in those days."

Leo was a rich source of detailed information about the day-to-day situations he encountered coaching women's baseball.

Leo Schrall, who made baseball his professional life, guided the Peoria Redwings for two seasons, 1948 and 1949. "Girls' baseball left its mark on me," he says.

The catcher decided what pitch to call, but I had them look to the bench in a critical situation. Then I'd give them a curveball or a fast-ball sign. Nobody threw a changeup, which is really just a slower fast-ball. It's a great pitch in men's baseball, where the fastball is so much faster. But in women's baseball, a changeup would have been too slow, the batters could've hit that. The slider was just comin' in at the time, but I wouldn't even think of lettin' 'em throw a slider. It tears up the elbow.

The squeeze sign was one of the best things in the business. I asked them what Johnny's squeeze sign was, and they said when he went skin to skin. [Leo runs through a few quick motions, ending with a touch to his cheek, then his hand.] I said that was okay, we'd use it, but we'd change it at the end of the fifth inning so the other manager or players wouldn't figure it out.

Then I asked them, "What return sign did you have?" And I got nothin' but sixteen blank stares. Well, they didn't have one. "Look," I said, "here's the situation. There's a runner on third, and I give the squeeze sign. Now when both of you, the runner and the batter, pick it up, you need to tell each other you both have it. That's the return sign. With no return sign, if the girl at home plate misses the sign, the girl at third won't know she doesn't have it. She'll break for home on the pitch, the batter won't bunt the ball, and the runner will be out."

Now, to the girl on third I said, "I want you to be standing on the bag. If you get the sign, I want you to kick the bag with your foot once, just like you're kickin' it to get your bearings. It's a simple sign. Now, for you at home plate, to make sure that the girl at third knows you've got it, I want you to wipe the side of your skirt with you hand."

Faye Dancer said, "Well, we never had anything like that!" And I said, "Well, we're gonna have that from now on." And it always seemed to work.

You know, I was talking to Faye on the phone just the other day, and she said, "You were the only coach I ever had that had a return sign. I was always amazed at how beautifully it worked all the time."

I told Leo I'd never heard of a return sign either, and what a good idea it seemed to be. "It's simple," he said. "That's baseball."

I asked Leo his opinion of some of the other managers in the

Bill "the Silver Fox" Allington, who managed the Peaches from 1944 to 1952 and the Daisies in 1953 and 1954, is remembered as the best all-around manager in the League.

League, especially Rockford's Bill Allington and Fort Wayne's Max Carey.

Max Carey was a great baseball man. He was very sound. And he was a good commissioner for the League. But he disliked me from the word go, and I know why: I was not a big-league friend of his. I only played in the minor leagues, and I don't know if he ever even knew that. He never spoke to me.

Bill Allington was a good manager, a smart manager. His players played sound, fundamental baseball, and that's the tip-off of good coaching. And he also had discipline on his ballclub. Everything was serious business with him, just like it was with me.

We liked to see things done the right way, and we didn't like mistakes, mental mistakes. I said to my players, "Any time you make a physical error, you'll never hear me say anything. I'll never criticize you; because you're human, you're gonna make 'em. The ballplayers in the big leagues make 'em so why shouldn't you make 'em? So when you make a physical error, all I want you to do is keep your head up, forget about it, and go on and play your own game. Get the next one. And the next one."

"Now mental errors are something else, and I'll have to correct you. I won't do it on the bench during the game—well, maybe once in a while I might—but mostly we'll have a meeting before every game and go over these things."

At such a meeting I would say, "Now, look. A play came up last night where the runner on first went to third when the ball was hit to you in right field. Now, you didn't think ahead, did you?" The girl would say, "No, I didn't." And I said, "I knew that, because you picked the ball up and immediately threw to third base. And the girl who hit the ball went around first and headed for second. Now they got runners on second and third, the tying run's at second, and we have no chance for a forceout or a double play."

"See, you gotta think. Every player on the field has to think ahead: If the ball's hit to me, what am I going to do?" I had to get them to think.

I wanted to know what differences Leo had found between coaching men and coaching women. I asked him if he yelled at men more.

Yeah. I yelled at the girls too, but there was a difference. I can't really lay my fingers on it.

Men were harder to get into good physical condition. They'd quit halfway through and I'd make them do whatever exercise it was all over again. The girls would either do it the first time or fall flat on their faces trying. Which you had to give 'em credit for.

I expected more out of the men, I think. I knew the women had certain limitations, like problems every month the chaperone was supposed to keep me informed of. When that time came around, I would give them a day or two off.

But coaching the men was much harder. The women were eager and they listened. They paid attention. In fact they were the finest, most responsive people I ever coached when it came to discipline. Much better than the men.

The women's game itself was different than the men's game. When I coached there was only one real power hitter in the League, Audrey Wagner of Kenosha. She hit nine home runs one year. Mostly the girls would hit singles, or hit the ball between the outfielders and run like hell. Those that could run had a triple! I remember Dancer had two in-the-park home runs.

Running was one of the strongest parts of the game. The teams with speed were the ones that won. For instance Racine, that had Kurys. She didn't swing that hard; she choked up a bit and was a line-drive hitter. But every time she was on base I closed my eyes. I knew she would steal, and I just didn't want to see her run!

And pitching, of course. When you looked at the championships, the teams that won had the best pitchers.

Leo also remembered more about his team than how they played baseball.

After I left girls' baseball, I just have never forgotten much of it. It left its mark on me. It was part of my life, a big part of my life. My wife Mildred was able to go with us on the bus. The girls loved her.

And I'm gonna tell you something, they could sing. We'd get on the bus, I'd sit up front with the driver, the girls would get into their jeans, and sit around on the seats and on the floor and start to sing. They had one song that was always the most beautiful, "My Happiness." They could harmonize. I even put my tenor in a few times. And I tell you, it did something to you inside. And every time I hear that song today, it just gets me.

◆◆◆

The better players in the All-American League learned this business of thinking ahead that the good managers taught them, managers like Schrall and Allington and Carey. But thinking ahead wasn't all there was to it. Learning to think together was the essence of team play. Ruth Richard, the woman many think was the League's best catcher, remembers how the Peaches thought together as a team.

Our infielders were so good. We played good together. You always knew what the next person was thinking, as far as what plays were coming up.

The whole team always went over each batter before the game, how to pitch to 'em. We'd go over the opposing line-up, and Bill would say, "Well now, this one, we'll throw her a lot of curves. And this one, throw low and away." So then you'd remember what each batter's weaknesses were.

The whole team had to be there because how a batter is pitched determines where you're gonna play them on defense. If you're in the infield, and the pitcher's gonna give somebody a lot of curves, you'll play 'em a little different than if they're gonna be hitting at fast-balls all the time.

We were always thinkin' ahead, something I know all the teams didn't do.

And we'd try to out-think the opposition with special plays we agreed on, though they didn't always work out right. I remember one time Boston Mansfield was pitching. I purposely went out to her and said, "Now, Boston, there's a runner on first and a runner on third. They may be gonna double-steal. After you pitch the ball, I'm gonna throw it right back, hard, as if I was trying to catch the runner at second. But you're gonna intercept that ball, and throw it to third, picking off that runner."

So we have a plan, and here we go. She pitched it, I fired that ball back, and what does she do? She ducked! The ball went dribbling into center field. And I felt like an idiot. It looked like I didn't know what the heck I was doin'.

Boston was very smart when it came to playing ball, but that time she just couldn't have been thinkin', not at that moment.

Bill found a lot of ways for us to score runs, even if we might not be the greatest hitters. He'd have different plays. I remember one we practiced a lot of times. When you have runners on second and third, the runner on second always takes a big leadoff because they figure everyone's thinkin' about the runner ahead on third. So I would watch, and if the second-base runner got way over, say beyond the shortstop position, I called for a pitch-out, and threw the ball to Al Pollitt at third. It looked like we were tryin' to pick off the third-base runner. But Al would turn and fire to the second baseman, and we'd trap that runner between second and third.

We practiced that play for so long, and I think we only ever tried it once. But it worked! You had to be thinkin' every minute, and everybody had to be thinkin' the same way!

Rockford's players delighted in recounting their successful execution of special plays Allington had taught them. As they talked I realized that the women remembered these moments with special affection because they had expended so much effort practicing for an eventuality that almost never occurred. When the moment did arrive, if they recognized it and the play worked, all the hours of practice came together in a perfect moment of team accomplishment.

◆◆◆

Baseball is, of course, a team sport. Working together toward a goal gives the team player both a sense of security and a thrill. Rockford's centerfielder Dottie Ferguson Key knew what it took to have a winning team.

It takes nine players. You have to trust the rest of your team. We had a running team. And we worked together.

I think we did it because of Bill. He was such a wonderful manager. On the bus, after we'd lost a game, we'd be real quiet. We might have won three of them, but we lost that last one, so we'd feel bad about it.

No sooner would we get goin' on the bus afterwards than Bill gets everybody into the conversation, talking about the game. If I made an error, what happened? Why? He was nice about it, but you didn't want it to happen too many times.

We all looked up to Kammie as a leader, and Snookie as a leader, but really we all worked together. If a clique of some kind formed, if some players wouldn't join the rest of us, it was taken care of, like with a trade or something.

Dottie Kamenshek identified some of the things she thought had made the Peaches the best team in the All-American League. A lot of these things had to do with being a cohesive team.

Our skills as players, of course, made us a good team. Also, playing together. Sacrificing for each other. Cheering each other up if someone was blue or lonely. And including everyone. That's important. I think some teams could have won more if they'd been more cohesive off the field. Some teams had their cliques within the team, and it hurt them on the field.

Baseball today is not like baseball was in the 1940s or 1950s. There's a lack of team play now. Everyone's only thinking about their own individual records. "I gotta get my average up so I can get big bucks." They don't think about the team.

Almost everyone at some point in the interview acknowledged the satisfaction they had gotten from being part of a team effort. Fort Wayne's Vivian Kellogg reminded me that no one could be a star without eight players behind her. Helen Ketola, who played only sporadically in her rookie season with the Daisies, nevertheless told me,

> I felt I was contributing to the team in a small way. Not a big way, but I didn't feel I was a left-out member. I felt I was part of the team.

I asked Rockford catcher Marilyn Jones the difference between playing an individual and a team sport. "I don't know, " she said, "except that on a team you had everybody else helpin' you!"

◆◆◆

The women who played professional baseball believe there are distinct differences between the way men and women play the game. Dottie Schroeder summarizes the differences.

> The men can hit the ball farther, and they're stronger, of course. And most of them can run faster than the girls. But we have the ability and the grace and the knowledge of the game. Even though we're not as strong and can't run as fast, we still have the same skills, on a graduated scale. We could still do it. In fact I think the girls are smarter than the men.

The organizers of the All-American League wanted to field women's baseball teams that performed at a professional level of excellence. How they expressed this expectation was that they wanted their girls to play like men. This was a laudable aspiration if what it meant was that the players were to take baseball seriously, learn from their coaches, develop their skills, execute the fundamentals, work together as a team, think ahead, and be ready for anything.

In saying that they wanted their girls to play like men, League organizers and managers were simply reflecting their experience, limited to seeing only men play baseball. Now that the League they created is part of baseball history—now that we know how the All-American girls played—we can amend that phrasing. When we want females to play at their highest pitch of dedication and skill, we can say we want them to play like women. Or, even more to the point, we can simply say we want them to play baseball.

◆◆◆

One of the years Leo Schrall was coaching the Redwings he was also coaching the men's baseball team at Bradley University in Peoria.

> Big-league scouts used to come to our games at Bradley. One day a couple of them came over after the game and said, "What in the hell are you doin' coachin' the girls?" He was rippin' me, of course. And I said, "Jim, Bill, the game's tonight at 7:30. I'm gonna give you two tickets. I want you both to come out. If those girls don't sell you on girls' baseball, I'll take you both out to dinner tomorrow night."
>
> So they finally agreed. They came out there that night, and they came out early the next night too. They came in to see me after the game and said, "My God, Leo. I'd never have believed that if someone were to tell me on a Bible. I never saw girls play baseball like that. That's not softball, that's baseball!"

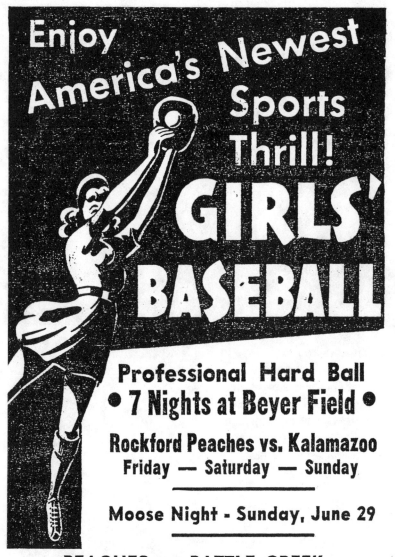

Enjoy America's Newest Sports Thrill!

GIRLS' BASEBALL

Professional Hard Ball

• 7 Nights at Beyer Field •

Rockford Peaches vs. Kalamazoo
Friday — Saturday — Sunday

Moose Night - Sunday, June 29

PEACHES vs. BATTLE CREEK
June 30, July 1, 2, 3

Admiral TV CONSOLE Attendance Prize Mon., June 30

C. I. O. NIGHT - JULY 2

V.F.W. Flag Presentation - Thurs., July 3

Attendance Prizes Every Night

▲ In 1948 Peoria fans came to the ballpark in record numbers. On the night of September 4, 7,000 (some remember 10,000) fans turned out to watch the Redwings play the Fort Wayne Daisies.

▶ A 1952 Rockford Peaches program. Pictured in the upper left corner is Alice Pollitt.

American Girls
BASEBALL
L
E
A
G
U
E

BOOST
THE
Rockford
Peaches

OFFICIAL 1952
PROGRAM
Price 10 Cents

All Home Games Played At BEYER FIELD
(15th Avenue High School Stadium)

GAME SIX

Saturday, September 16, 1950

Like the pennant race that preceded it, the 1950 Championship Series of the All-American Girls Baseball League developed into a closely-contested nail-biter. After five games fought under wet, windswept conditions, Rockford led the Daisies three games to two. With Game Six the contest moved back to Rockford, giving the Peaches a chance to end the series at home. The Daisies needed to win Game Six or retire for another long winter, once again succumbing to a stronger Rockford team.

Overall, the teams were nearly identical in total runs scored over the first five games; Rockford had scored twenty runs to the Daisies' eighteen. Rockford, however, was hitting better than Fort Wayne, with forty-two hits to the Daisies' thirty-six. Rockford's team batting average was .282, Fort Wayne's .236.

Individually, the Daisies' second sacker Evelyn Wawryshyn was leading all batters with a stunning .550 average (11 hits in 20 at-bats).

Betty Foss, who had nosed out Dottie Kamenshek for the batting title during the regular season, at first had trouble hitting Rockford pitching in the series, getting only two hits in her first eight at-bats. She regained her stride, though, and going into the sixth game was hitting .294. Wilma Briggs, in right field, was hitting .316. Sally Meier led the Daisies in runs batted in with three.

Among the Peaches, Dottie Key was hitting .400, Dottie Kamenshek and Rose Gacioch .353 and Snookie Doyle .350. Doyle had batted in five runs, and Jackie Kelley, Rose Gacioch and Dottie Key three each.

That women's baseball relied on speed and team play rather than individual power is clear from the statistics for the first five games. No one had hit a home run, and the only triple was Dottie Key's in Game Five. Eight players had hit doubles, however, with Wawryshyn connecting for three and Foss for four.

On the other hand, eleven players had stolen bases, Tiby Eisen and Evie Wawryshyn three each, Jackie Kelley and Dottie Schroeder two each. Eight players had moved teammates along with sacrifice hits, two each for Jones, Kamenshek, and Kelley.

Rockford had left thirty-three runners on base, Fort Wayne thirty-four.

Among pitchers, Nickie Fox had finessed Rockford to two of its three victories, Louise Erickson accounting for the third. Fox had lost Game Four and Peaches' ace Lois Florreich Game Three. Fort Wayne's Dottie Collins and Maxine Kline had each won one game and lost one, while the Daisies' Millie Deegan had suffered one loss.

Bill Allington knew Fort Wayne's run-scoring potential. He sent Louise Erickson, winner of Game Two, to the mound to try to hold the powerful Daisies in check just long enough to win one more. Max Carey's Daisies desperately needed Game Six to tie the series and force a seventh game; he chose Maxine Kline, his victor in Game Four and the League's winningest pitcher in 1950, to still the Rockford bats.

Saturday night, September 16, 1950 was clear and cool. The growing intensity of the contest and the first good weather combined to draw the series' highest attendance, 3,385, to the Peach Orchard for what local fans hoped would be their team's title game.

Daisies Blank Peaches, 8 - 0, Square Series Title Is at Stake Here Tonight

by Harry D. Milne
Rockford Morning Star, September 17, 1950

Betty Foss' line drive over Eleanor Callow's head in the third inning for a home run with the bases loaded was the blow that crushed the Rockford Peaches' hopes of ending the championship playoffs Saturday night, and Fort Wayne went on to defeat Rockford 8-0, and even the series at 3 all.

The seventh and final game of the series will be played at 8 o'clock tonight at Beyer stadium. Manager Bill Allington has named Nickie Fox to pitch for the Peaches, and Manager Max Carey of Fort Wayne is expected to call on Millie Deegan. Fox did a fine job of relief pitching for the Peaches in the pennant winners' 4-3 victory over the Daisies Thursday night in Fort Wayne.

Louise Erickson was on the mound for the Peaches Saturday night, and her lack of control got her into trouble several times. She started the game by walking Thelma Eisen, who promptly stole second. Eisen was sacrificed to third by Wilma Briggs and scored on Evelyn Wawryshyn's bunt.

Walks First Batter

In the third Erickson caused trouble for herself by walking Maxine Kline, the first batter to face her in that inning. Eisen sacrificed her to second and Briggs bunted one that nobody could field in time. Erickson then walked Wawryshyn to load the bases. Foss got a hold of one of Erickson's fast ball pitches and drove it on a line over Callow's head to hit the jackpot.

The Daisies picked up another run in the fifth on Wawryshyn's single, stolen base and Rose Gacioch's poor throw to first from right field trying to cut Foss down on her hit.

Two Fort Wayne insurance runs were added in the ninth. Ketola scratched a hit and Kline walked. Eisen sacrificed them up. Briggs' single scored Ketola. Briggs and Kline pulled a double steal, the same play with which the Peaches beat the Daisies in Fort Wayne, with Kline scoring the final run.

While Kline gave up eight hits, she kept the Peaches' blows scattered with the exception of the sixth inning, when the home team made two hits but failed to score. A double play unassisted by Foss ruined the Peaches' chances of scoring in the sixth. Callow beat out a bunt and Marilyn Jones singled, both advancing on Erickson's infield out. Dottie Key then hit a line drive that Foss grabbed before doubling Callow at third.

The Peaches loaded the bases in the second inning with two out on a fielder's choice and two errors by Helen Ketola, rookie shortstop who replaced the injured Dottie Schroeder. Dottie Kamenshek popped to the pitcher to end the threat.

Play of the Night

The best fielding play of the night was made by Rose Gacioch, who ran to the right field foul line to make a one-handed catch of Kellogg's drive to right field. Gacioch was the only Rockford batter to get more than one hit off Kline.

She got a ground rule double, which would easily have been a triple but for the wire fence in right center, and a single.

Summary

Runs - Eisen, Briggs, Wawryshyn 2, Foss, Ketola, Kline 2. Errors - Foss 2, Ketola 2, Gacioch. Runs batted in - Briggs, Wawryshyn, Foss 4. Home run - Foss. Triple - Eisen. Double - Gacioch. Sacrifice hits - Briggs, Wawryshyn, Eisen 2. Stolen bases - Eisen 2, Foss, Wawryshyn 2. Double plays - Foss (unassisted). Base on balls - off Kline 1, Erickson 5. Strike-outs - Kline 2, Erickson 1. Left on base - Fort Wayne 5, Rockford 11. Time - 1:34. Attendance - 3,385.

▲ Rose "Rosie" Gacioch
played for the All Star
Ranger Girls "Bloomer Girl"
women's baseball team in
1934 and in the All-American
League from 1944 through
1954. Rosie, who could play
any position including
pitcher, and hit as well, thus
linked these two important
eras of women's baseball.

▶ Rose Gacioch outside her
home in Michigan where she
talked with the author in
1992.

ROSE "ROSIE" GACIOCH
Rockford, Rightfielder and Pitcher

Statistics: Born: 1915. Home town: Wheeling, West Virginia. Height: 5 feet 6 ½ inches. Playing weight: 160 pounds. Bats: Right. Throws: Right. Entered League: 1944 at age 28. Teams: South Bend, 1944; Rockford, 1945-54. Lifetime totals: Batting average: .238. Fielding percentage: in right field, .960; as pitcher, .950. Pitching statistics: Games won, 92; games lost, 60. Winning percentage: .605. Earned-run average: 2.44.

At age thirty-five, Rose Gacioch played all seven games of the 1950 championship series, six as Rockford's rightfielder and one as the starting pitcher for Game Five. Affectionately called "Grandma" by her teammates, Rose was the next-to-the-oldest player in the League, two weeks younger than Racine's Irene Hickson. Rockford Manager Bill Allington assigned Rose the critical fourth position in the batting order for all seven games, the "cleanup" spot where a batter's consistency and power are expected to bring baserunners home. For the series she batted .381, knocked in three runs and scored one herself. In the game she pitched she struck out four, walked five and gave up five hits and two runs in 6-1/3 innings.

The 1950 series was a thrilling experience, but it was just one among many for Gacioch. Her career with the All-Americans was her second professional baseball experience. In 1934 she had played one season for Maud Nelson's All Star Ranger Girls, a Chicago-based barnstorming team of professional women players. Seventeen years later, Rose had her best season with the All-Americans, pitching a career-high twenty wins to seven losses for the season, with an earned-run average of 1.68.

Rose Gacioch's career spanned two decades and forms a link between the professional "Bloomer Girl" teams of the early years of the century and the professional league play of the mid-century All-Americans. Throughout it all, whether called "Petunia," for her love of flowers, or "Grandma," for her age, Rose was doing what she most cared about: "I loved baseball that much I didn't care what they called me."

◆◆◆

Marie Mansfield, an eighteen-year-old Rockford rookie in 1950, remembers she and her buddies "used to think Rosie was 108 years old then. She must be 150 by now." In fact, Rose is seventy-seven, lives in a modest trailer home in a suburb north of Detroit, and occupies herself visiting with friends, nieces and nephews, bowling ("I'm a good bowler yet") and fishing ("I feel so comfortable when I'm fishing. You go out there and think about everything that's happened. It's so peaceful.")[64] We talked at her kitchen table, surrounded by scrapbooks and pictures, baseball and bowling trophies. In a distinctive, husky voice, she told me stories from a quarter-century of ball.

Rosie's baseball career did not start auspiciously. She was born in 1915 into a poor Polish Catholic family in Wheeling, West Virginia, a small town dominated by coal mining and factory labor. She was the youngest of a large number of children, only four of whom she remembers well. Her father, a factory worker, died five months before Rose was born. Her mother took in people's washing and rented out rooms in their house.

> I went through the Depression. One time when I went out to the ballpark I found a little purse and brought it home. We didn't have no sugar, and I didn't have no shoes. My mother opened it up and found thirteen dollars in there. "Oh, we can't use this," she said. We asked neighbors all around and waited almost a month and a half for someone to say they'd lost it. Nobody came forward, so I got a pair of shoes, and we got a bag of sugar.
>
> It was hard. If you ate a bowl of soup you got one piece of meat in it. That's how it was when we were young.
>
> My mother said playin' ball wasn't for girls. She and her sister were born in Poland, so they didn't believe in the girls playin' baseball here. Plus she used to say I was a baby.
>
> I was the baby of the family and had to take care of her. She was

sick a lot so I missed a lot of school. The nuns said, "You might as well quit because you'll never graduate, your mother bein' sick like that." I was just promoted to seventh grade, but I can still read in Polish now.

I wasn't a good kid. She used to make me kneel on rice when I was bad, because she was too sick to hit me.

Rose and her mother struggled with each other, many of these conflicts occasioned by Rose being a tomboy when her mother was determined to have a more conventional daughter.

I liked to play ball with the boys, because they treated me nice. And I tell you, nobody could get smart with me when I was on the field. Nobody. We had some good games. And some good fights too. I remember once I gave my sister a black eye in some argument over the batting order.

The first game I pitched, I pitched in a skirt! Now we're talking overhand-pitch baseball, you understand. Paul Melko, the Little Cardinals manager, asked me to pitch. I said, "No, I can't, I got my skirt on." He says, "I think your mother won't mind." So I started the game.

Pretty soon somebody yelled, "Rose, here comes your mother!" So I snuck off the field, went across a creek into an old cemetery, and hid there until my mother went home. Then I finished the game. I had nineteen strikeouts that day.

In fourth grade I snuck out of school to see Babe Ruth and Lou Gehrig, in town for a barnstorming exhibition game. Sister Michael said I shouldn't go, but I had to. I got to the ballpark all wet 'cause I had to crawl through a tunnel. I was cryin' 'cause I had no money to get in. This guy saw me, gave me his big handkerchief, told me to wash my face at the water fountain, and let me in. He was real nice. I wish I knew where he lived now.

Of course I got a whipping for skipping school. But I didn't care if my mother made me kneel on rice for five hours. It was worth it because Lou Gehrig shook my hand.

Sister Michael was a good friend to me. She'd play ball and turn a rope for me. She liked sports, used to listen to the ballgames and the next day ask me the score. She was good. She used to say "If you like it, keep it up." So she's the one that really kept me goin' at baseball.

She didn't like my butch haircut though. My friend's father was a barber, but of course he only knew how to cut boys' hair. So when I asked him for a short haircut, it turned out just like a boy. Sister Michael took me from one class to another to "show off her new boy." I had to wear a little dust cap for about three weeks 'til it growed in a little. And I got a whippin' from my mother for gettin' a boy's haircut.

Rose's mother died of cancer when Rose was sixteen. Rose moved in with her older sister, told the Wheeling Corrugating Company she was eighteen so they would hire her, and officially joined the Little Cardinals, a town boys' baseball team. The year was 1931 and Rose was on her own.

Rose showed me a picture of the Little Cardinals team. Fourteen players form an inverted "V", each boy's hands on the shoulders of the boy in front of him. They are dressed in long socks, knickers, white shirts, and caps emblazoned with "LC". The manager is kneeling in the center with antique ball gloves scattered around him and a trophy recording the year, 1931. On the back of the picture Rose has inscribed the names of thirteen boys, Joe Zarnock and Alozy Czapinski and Leon Owoc and one girl.

Manager Paul Melko and his 1931 Little Cardinals boys' baseball team of Wheeling, West Virginia. Rose Gacioch joined the team as a standout pitcher when she was sixteen. She's seventh from the left.

"Now find me on there," Rose challenges me. "I think that's you," I venture. "Nah, nah. I was better lookin' than that when I was younger! Come on, give me a break!" I get it right on the second try. Rose is second from the tallest, standing at the point of the "V", relaxed, gaze clear, a self-assured youngster looking into the camera. "I was a good-lookin' girl," she says.

Rose remembers practicing her pitching.

> I learned how to pitch out in the hills. Between two trees. My girlfriend would go behind the trees, and I'd throw the ball with a twist like this [she demonstrates] and it would go through and curve around the tree. We got an old mattress and cut a hole in it. My friend would hold it up and I'd practice pitching through the hole. Then I added arrows to right and left and practiced pitching inside and away.

All the practice, the experience with boys' teams, and the struggles to maintain her own tomboy identity in the face of a disapproving and violent mother were about to coalesce into Rose's opportunity. The president of the corrugating company where Rosie worked knew of her play and of the women's touring baseball teams owned by Maud Nelson. He arranged for a try-out for Rosie, and when Maud saw her play, she was signed as an infielder and a pitcher for the All Star Ranger Girls' 1934 season.

Maud Nelson, nearly unknown today, was the principal force in women's professional baseball from 1897 until 1934.[65] For forty years her name was synonymous with "Bloomer Girl" baseball, so named for the outfits they wore—loose-fitting knickers originally designed and worn by Amelia Bloomer, a pioneer of women's rights who believed women needed the freedom to move if they were to exercise other freedoms.

Maud Nelson pitched for the Boston Bloomers and the Star Bloomers, and created, owned and marketed the Western Bloomer Girls, the American Athletic Girls and the All Star Ranger Girls. Typically the teams fielded six women and three men, the men playing catcher, shortstop and third base. Maud's teams and others like them barnstormed the country, challenging men's teams to games of hardball. The owners were paid from the gate receipts and a variety of promotions, and in turn paid their players well. Women were playing professional baseball.

The All Star Ranger Girls were known for the excellence of their ball and their flashy off-the-field uniforms: cowboy hats, silky jackets and flared skirts. Rose loved those uniforms, "They were made for me." Rose played for the 1934 team, arguably the best Ranger Girl team fielded by Maud Nelson, but women's baseball as a whole was in decline by then, being replaced by softball, a less expensive game that relied on one superior player, the pitcher. Rose was only able to play one year of women's professional baseball before the game itself disappeared.

For ten years Rose worked back home in Wheeling, making galvanized steel tubs and playing softball. She could bring home fifty dollars for a weekend of play in Ohio or Pennsylvania. She travelled a bit with former major-leaguer "Sad Sam" Jones' barnstorming teams. She played softball in Madison Square Garden and saw the World's Fair in New York. But baseball had been her love, and baseball seemed nowhere to be found.

> It was 1944 and I was workin' in the factory. One day I'm eatin' lunch and readin' a little New York paper I had a habit of buyin'. There was an article there about the All-American Girls. I showed it to my friends and said, "You know, I'm gonna be on that." "Oh Rose," they said, "you're full of shit. You're twenty-eight years old."

> About a month later this guy from the machine shop came up to me. "Rose, I hear you want to play with the All-American girls. I can fix it for you." "How can you do that?" I asked. He said, "My daughter's the chaperone for South Bend, Indiana! She's comin' here after the season's over to visit me, so I'll get her to look you up."

> So she came, took me out to my old neighborhood ballpark, hit fly balls and such to me, and said, "You'll be hearing from me." That winter I got a letter from Mr. Wrigley to report for spring training.

Maud Nelson died in February 1944. Later that same spring her Ranger Girl player Rose Gacioch was signed to play with the All-American Girls League. Rose thus became the woman who links the barnstorming and League eras of women's professional baseball.

◆◆◆

Rose's first year with the All-Americans was spent with the South Bend Blue Sox. Manager Bert Niehoff, a former major-league player who occupies a place in the history of earlier women's professional baseball,[66] created a new fielding arrangement for rightfielder Gacioch.

> Bert said, "Rose, I'm gonna put the second baseman closer to second, and the first baseman closer to first. Now you've got all that terri-

tory in between. Come in and flip the ball to first." Batters would see a big space in right field, hit toward it, I'd run in, field the ball, and throw them out at first! Twice in my career I had thirty-one assists from right field, a League record.

The next year the South Bend President, "gave away Gacioch because she used poor English," according to a Blue Sox chronicler, who concluded, "The loss of Gacioch was felt for years to come."[67] Rose played the rest of her career with the Peaches.

She liked working for Rockford Manager Allington.

> I thought he was one of the best. He was one of them that loved the game. You take a person that loves it, you know they're gonna help you. Bill had us enthused about it. He had us talkin' and eatin' and sleepin' baseball. He always had us thinkin' ahead of time. You could tell he loved it, that's why I liked him.

> He knew how to work with me too. One time I was complaining 'cause an umpire in Grand Rapids wasn't calling strikes for me. "Bill, I'm puttin' 'em in there. I'm cuttin' corners real nice. And that umpire ain't givin' it to me." Well, I'd gained a little weight, and you know what Bill said? "Well, you got so damn fat, maybe you can't throw the ball up there." That got me so mad, I went out there and they didn't get a hit off me after that!

> He just knew how to get after you. Maybe I was gettin' lazy. I was gettin' older too, you know. So he just pepped me up a little bit. Just got me mad enough to think, I'll show you!

I asked Rose if it was okay with her that Allington used those tactics.

> Oh, yeah. He was more right than I was. He could see it where I couldn't.

More than one Rockford player told me of a game against Fort Wayne where Rockford was leading by so many runs that fans turned off the radio broadcast and went to bed. When they got up the next morning, Rockford had managed to lose the game in the bottom of the ninth.

> It started to rain a little bit, there in Fort Wayne. It was muddy and Fort Wayne had those big Weaver sisters. They were good ballplayers. They started hittin' that ball. Nobody could get it. When a ground ball was hit, the girls couldn't throw it 'cause it was wet. It was terrible. We

were leading by twelve or fifteen runs or something like that. That was my most embarrassing moment.

Bill was fit to be tied. I'm not saying what he said to us afterwards 'cause I liked him too much. He called us something that I'd never heard him say. He had a right to say it. Now if we were only two or three runs ahead, it would be different, but not that many!

1945 was Rose's best year at the plate and as an outfielder. She set the assists record from right field and led the League with nine triples and forty-four runs batted in. She was thirty years old. But by 1948 Allington was noticing Rosie might have slowed a step or two in the field.

He says to me, "Rose, look, you've got a lot of territory to cover in right field, and you're gettin' older. Why don't you become a pitcher again now that we're overhand?" So I practiced and practiced and became a pitcher again. All I had was that little territory to cover when someone would bunt the ball or hit it right at me. Well, I knew how to catch the ball.

Rose pitched from 1948 until the League ended in 1954. Alice Pollitt, Rockford's third baseman, remembers both Rosie's pitching and her attitude.

Rosie had confidence in herself. She would say, "I'm gonna go out there and win. I'll throw the ball over the plate and you girls are gonna field for me." And we did. She was a 20-game winner one year.

Now if you talk to Richie [Ruth Richard, Rockford's catcher], she'll say Rosie didn't have nothin' on the ball. You wondered how she did it. Well, she had control. Richie'd signal inside, and she could put it there. She had control. But her curve wasn't really a curve. We called it a "wrinkle."

Snookie Doyle remembers Rosie's play and her personality.

She had more assists than any other outfielder that played in our League. She could field that ball in nothing flat. She'd field what looked like a single and throw them out at first. She was fantastic. A good hitter too.

And she was a good person. She's a little older than some of us, and she always had a very deep voice. She was a nice person. She taught me some Polish once, how to say "Give me a little kiss" in Polish.

Gacioch was a wonderfully versatile player. In addition to her pitching and outfield roles, she sometimes played as a utility infielder. In 1952 she was voted to the All-Star team as a pitcher, in 1953 as a utility infielder, and in 1954 again as a pitcher.

One time the last game of the season, Bill let me play every position on the field. I caught, I pitched, I played first, second, third, all around. Every inning I'd come out and play someplace else.

I had a lot of fun with baseball. I enjoyed it.

◆◆◆

Rose was playing when the League ended after the 1954 season.

It never hits you when it ends. It's when spring training is supposed to start again that you really notice. But you just had to make the best of it because you knew it ain't gonna be no more.

I give credit to Mr. Wrigley for starting it. I think he done a lot of good for these girls. Because they were a nice bunch of girls, and they worked hard. Sure they got paid for it, but they deserved it. And they made the people, the fans, happy, I'll tell ya. The people just loved those girls.

Just before the League's final season Rose and her bowling partner Fran Stennett won the national women's doubles bowling championship. Rose stayed in Rockford doing factory work for many years. She never married.

I do what I want to do. When I was younger this guy wanted to marry me. I liked him very much. "Rose," he said, "when we get married you gotta quit baseball. You gotta quit bowling. You gotta . . . "

I said, "Go to hell." Excuse my language, but I said that because I wasn't gonna be his slave. I was on my own too long already.

I'm glad I didn't get married, but sometimes you sit here and wonder what kind of kids you'd have had. I'd be a good mother, you know? I'd teach 'em how to play ball.

Rose retired eventually and moved near Detroit where her remaining family lived. She maintained her independence from family too.

My whole family's good to me. We do things for each other. My sister wanted me to move in with her, but I said no. I like my own place. I'm happy here.

Rose has a wealth of family support, but has been financially poor her whole life. Society has rewarded only marginally both her lifetime of factory work and her long career in women's professional baseball. She herself is satisfied with her life, though, and happy in her independence: "You tell 'em, I'm gettin' along good."

Rose's niece and children went to Cooperstown with her to celebrate the inauguration of the Women in Baseball exhibit.

It was a good feeling, seeing that exhibit at the Hall of Fame. Because that don't happen to everybody. I always say, now I got something on Pete Rose. I got there before he did!

My niece's daughter had a lot of fun. A little boy asked her for her autograph. She said, "I don't play ball." He said he didn't care, he wanted her autograph anyway. That tickled her. No kiddin'. That made her so happy.

At Cooperstown we players had trouble recognizin' each other. When we were younger, we looked different. But they all recognized my voice. "Here's Rosie!" they'd say, as soon as they heard me.

I got a heavy voice. I always did. You play out in right field, hollerin' and it'll do that. One time a doctor in Rockford said, "Let me operate on ya, make your voice sound like a woman." I said, "Get outta here! I like this voice."

Manager Bill Allington kept women's professional baseball alive for four years after the League ended in 1954. Allington's All-Americans toured the country and played men's minor league and industrial teams. Pictured are: Manager Bill Allington and players Joe Weaver, Dottie Schroeder, Katie Horstman, Joan Berger, Gertie Dunn, Ruth Richard, Dolores Lee, Jean Smith, Jean Geissinger and Maxine Kline.

THE YEARS

AFTER

BASEBALL

"I didn't want it to end, ever, ever."
—**Marie Mansfield Kelley**

Dottie Schroeder played in the first game of the All-American Girls Baseball League on May 30, 1943. Her South Bend Blue Sox team hosted the Rockford Peaches, and won both games of a double-header, the first 4-3 in 13 innings. Dottie's team then won the night game 12-9 with a four-run rally in the bottom of the eighth.

Schroeder also batted in the deciding run in the last game of the All-American Girls Baseball League on September 5, 1954, "climaxing her best year in the League."[68] Schroeder's Kalamazoo Lassies, who finished fourth in the regular season, upset the pennant-winning Fort Wayne Daisies to take the post-season championship three games to two.

The Peaches finished the final season in fifth place, the only one of the five remaining All-American teams not to make the playoffs. The season never opened in 1955, and women's professional league baseball was at an end.

I asked Dottie Schroeder whether she had any idea that the final game of 1954 was the final game not only of that season, but of the League itself.

I think I did. The League was in decline because it was several years after the war was over, and people had more money to spend and could travel, and television was just coming into its own. So it was over.

You know, lots of people say they think they were born too soon. I don't, because if I'd been born thirty years later, I'd have missed playing in that League. We were born at the right time.

That right time was now at an end. Bill Allington kept women's baseball alive for another three years by creating a barnstorming team, Allington's All-Americans, that travelled around the country playing exhibition games against men's teams at county fairs and the like. Dottie Schroeder, Betty Foss, Jo Weaver, Maxine Kline, and Ruth Richard, from the 1950 Daisies-Peaches rosters, played some or all of these final years. After the summer of 1957, women's professional baseball died. It has not yet been reborn.

Many factors contributed to the demise of the All-American Girls Baseball League. A combination of sound central management plus strong local backing in small communities had made the League work.[69] By the mid-fifties, critical elements of the formula had been withdrawn.

Central management of the League had been dissolved after the 1950 season. The new owners based in each city no longer had a commitment to team parity throughout the League, and the allocation system was abandoned. Certain teams became perennial powerhouses, others chronic also-rans, and this lack of good competition was reflected in lowered attendance figures.

Before its demise, the central organization had maintained generous funds for publicity. Individual boards of directors cut this money, trying to balance budgets in a shrinking financial situation. Lack of publicity took a further toll on attendance.

The fans themselves had more entertainment alternatives once World War II and the Korean War were over. They could buy gasoline and travel, or they could buy their first television and stay home. Either choice meant skipping the ballpark right down the road. Television itself was so new that team owners had no idea how to exploit the medium to promote interest and therefore attendance. Instead of being a powerful ally, television operated solely as an enemy of live sports entertainment.

Central management had handled player recruitment, spring training and player development for all the teams. Now, in an era when players had to come directly from their amateur softball experience into professional League baseball, neither spring training nor extended player development was available. City-owned teams allotted only two weeks before each season opened for players to make the difficult transition. Few players could adapt this quickly, so much of their training had to go on during season games. That, in turn, lowered the quality of play in the early weeks of a season.

The lack of a player development system was a problem for the League throughout most of its history. Dottie Kamenshek explains,

> In the last years of the League many of the original players had quit. You had good ballplayers later, but not enough were coming up to pick up the slack from those of us who had retired. To keep a league going you need a system of minor leagues to develop player talent. This, with the exception of the 1949 and 1950 touring teams, the All-Americans never had.

The League also died because society has a relatively limited attention span for women's sports. Under "normal" circumstances, men's activities, among them sports, preempt the attention and the money of both men and women. Men watch and support other men—rather than women—doing almost anything. Women have less money and are less accustomed to supporting other women. Instead, women's attention is focused on supporting men in their activities. So, when the special situation created by the war years of the 1940s and 1950s was over, the League foundered. Many individuals—players, fans, booster clubs, chaperones, managers, owners—made prodigious efforts to keep the League alive, but these were not enough to reverse society's overall bias toward male public performance.

Nonetheless, the midwestern men, women and children who came to the ballpark for twelve years to watch the All-Americans did a better job of supporting women's team sports than has ever been achieved in this country before or since. At the height of the League's popularity in 1948, 910,000 fans watched ten teams play women's baseball. By 1954, however, less than a third this many fans came out to the ballpark in the five remaining League cities.

The women playing in the last years of the League were bitterly disappointed when the end came. Maxine Kline, still pitching for Fort Wayne, was shocked. "I didn't know what I was gonna do." Jo Weaver, an unofficial Daisy in 1950 because she was only fourteen years old, had begun playing in 1951. By 1954 she was already compiling impressive statistics, but she was really just hitting her stride. Jo's regret is palpable forty years later. "When the League folded, it was devastating. My dream was there. I would love to have seen what I could have accomplished."

I can't help thinking, so would we all, Jo. So would we all.

♦♦♦

Both Maxine Kline and Jo Weaver extended their ballplaying days by joining Allington's All-Americans. But then even they, like all the players before them, took up life off the ballfield. Kline returned home to her small Michigan town and worked for twenty years bending tubing for brake-linings and such, first by hand and arm strength, later with air-powered equipment. She married late in life. Jo Weaver stayed in Fort Wayne and worked for thirty years for Essex Wire. Jo never married.

The women who played baseball for the All-American League were unconventional, before, during and after their ball-playing days. As youngsters they were tomboys, interested in active outdoor lives thought inappropriate for their sex. As young adults they played women's professional league baseball, the only women to do so in the nation's history. As older adults they continued a pattern of choices unusual for the average woman of their day.

Women who reached adulthood during and just after World War II had the highest marriage rate in the history of the United States, just over 96 percent.[70] Some observers have assumed that the All-American girls left baseball to follow this pattern, to become conventional wives and mothers. A 1989 article in the Smithsonian magazine, for instance, contributes to this myth by imagining the fate of the players thus: "Whereupon the players, most still in their athletic prime, put down their bats and balls and gloves, and went on to raise families and often to coach their children."[71]

Actually a minority of the women who played professional baseball married. Of the 557 All-Americans included in *The Baseball Encyclopedia*'s player roster, only 150 (27 percent) are listed with married names.

Likewise a minority of the 1950 Peaches and Daisies players chose marriage and families. Half of the twenty-six players I talked to ever married at any time in their lives. And only eight, less than one-third of the group, both married and had children.

Of the thirteen players who married, seven led family lives typical of the post-war years: they stayed married for a long time and birthed and raised children within this nuclear family setting. Dottie Key looked back to the change from baseball to family. I had asked her if she played any sports after baseball.

> No. When baseball was over my husband Don and I knew it was finished, and I got pregnant right away. No sports. I was home then. I didn't have to go to work, and we had our children; it was family then.

Dottie Ferguson Key, Alice Pollitt Deschaine, Louise Erickson Sauer, Helen Waddell Wyatt, Dottie Wiltse Collins and Helen Ketola LaCamera all married and had two children. Evie Wawryshyn Litwin Moroz's first husband died after two years of marriage, and she's been married to her second husband now over thirty years. She has six children. All these women are still living with their husbands except Alice Pollitt Deschaine, who was widowed in 1991.

Their children were a joy to them, and some of their kids played sports, though few knew much about their mothers' professional careers.[72] Alice Pollitt Deschaine described how it was with her son and daughter.

> I don't think my ball-playing was ever mentioned for a long time; my scrapbooks were in the attic. The kids knew I played ball, and when they were little I used to get my glove out and play ball with 'em. I thought I pushed my son too hard, 'cause I think when he was one year old I had a glove on his hand! He don't seem interested now.
>
> I didn't push my daughter at all. When she started workin' she said, "Well, they got a softball team, and I'm gonna play ball." I thought, "Oh, good!" I'd go out there and help and cheer. She could hit, but neither one of my kids could run.

Six other players married, but the circumstances or outcomes were less conventional. Marie Mansfield Kelley's husband drowned two months after they were married in 1959. Marie was pregnant; she never remarried and raised her daughter as a single mother with help from her family. Dorothy "Snookie" Harrell Doyle married twice, once for two years and a second time for fourteen years. Betty Weaver Foss was briefly married, and Helen Nichol "Nickie" Fox was married for one year in 1946.

> I got married to a Canadian in 1946. I got him a good job and he went one day to this job. He said, "Well, you're makin' good money, and I don't intend to work if you're makin' the money you are." He just thought I was gonna take care of him. So that finished that.

Marilyn Jones Doxey and Maxine Kline Randall both married late in life, after they had established work lives and passed child-bearing years. Marilyn was forty-two, Maxine forty-four.

Half the Peaches and Daisies never married. Six of these thirteen women are currently living with female friends. Dottie Schroeder is living with her twin brother, and Irene Applegren with her mother. Five of the never-married women are living by themselves. Of the four women who were briefly married, two are living with female friends, Marie Mansfield Kelley is living with her brother, and the fourth is living alone.

The All-Americans as a group gave themselves more choices of what we would now call "lifestyle" than was common for their day. Some lived with husbands, some raised children, some lived alone, some lived with other women. As it turned out these women were as creative about their intimate later lives as they had been creative in scoring that winning run on the diamonds of the 1940s and 1950s. Mary Rountree, for instance, has created, in effect, a present-day team for herself. The purpose is no longer to win, but to help each other out.

> We have a whole bunch of ladies here in Miami, all of whom are widows except myself, and we hang together. If one is sick, we all try to go and help that one. If there's a problem with their children, we try to help with that. If somebody's car has broken down, we'll go and pick 'em up or take 'em where they have to be. It's a community of ladies for convenience and helpfulness.

Reflective of the working-class background from which a majority of the women came, only five of the players went beyond their high school education. Mary Rountree is a medical doctor, and Kate Vonderau (backup catcher to Mary in Fort Wayne in 1950) went on to get a doctorate in physical education. Three other women are college graduates: Wilma Briggs, Dottie Kamenshek and Snookie Doyle. Snookie attributes her college degree to Kamenshek's example.

Kammie was an inspiration because she started back to college when she was playing ball in the late 1940s. I admired her for that. I started college when I was twenty-nine, graduated in 1958, and started teaching physical education in junior high.

But most players never went beyond a high school education, except perhaps for training courses sponsored by their employers. Seventeen of the twenty-six are high school graduates and four never completed high school. For many, braininess in the classroom just wasn't their thing.

Dottie Key: "I hated school. With a passion. But any sport, I loved it."

Vivian Kellogg: "I didn't excel in school. I wasn't an 'A' student. And so I excelled at sports. I played every sport there was . . . I've been in sports all my life."

Dottie Schroeder: "I had a real good education playing baseball."

The amount of education these women acquired in large part determined the kinds of jobs they would hold throughout their lives. And they did hold jobs: the All-American women supported themselves and contributed to the support of their families throughout their working lives. This fact further distinguishes these women from most other women of the time. In 1954, when the League ended, thirty-six percent of American women worked outside the home. By contrast, twenty-four of the twenty-six ball players—a definitive ninety-two percent—worked for significant portions of their adult lives. Many worked in offices, doing a variety of clerical and administrative tasks. Many worked in factories. Three were teachers, one a dental assistant, another a physical therapist, another a physician.

Regardless of the arena in which the women worked, what characterized many of their careers was their longevity. Fifteen of the twenty-six women worked twenty or more years for the same company or in the same field. Wilma Briggs first worked for twelve years for a knife company, went to college, and then taught elementary school for twenty-three years. Norma Metrolis was an inspector for the U.S. Department of Agriculture for thirty years. Fran Janssen has sold insurance for twenty-five years. Ruth Richard has worked for more than twenty-six years in the same gauge factory in which her father worked as a molder before her. The All-Americans transferred the loyalty they gave to baseball, to the League and to their individual teams to the jobs they held once baseball was over.

The women vary in their evaluation of how satisfying their work lives have been. A few, like Kate Vonderau (teaching physical education at the college level) and Mary Rountree (the doctor), have been involved enough in work that their ball-playing days seem dim in comparison to the achievements of their later years. Kate said, "So many things have happened that were over and above what I did in those days." But most, I believe, would echo what Dottie Schroeder says. "I only played ball for twelve years. And I've been at this job for thirty-five years. I wished I could have played ball that long."

Women's professional baseball was an opportunity for working-class and farm women to be paid while achieving excellence at an activity they loved and for which their skills best suited them. Once the League was at an end, they returned to the more limited options that society offers to workers with a high school education or less. The current lack of women's professional team sports in effect cripples all those women who could otherwise find meaningful work in professional athletics. Working-class men blessed with special physical skills can hope to put these capacities to use in sport; working-class women cannot.

◆◆◆

When the League ended, a great silence settled over this era of women and baseball. Those of us who were there—as fans or as players, chaperones, managers or owners—privately remembered the League with great fondness, but found little public occasion to talk about it. Dottie Schroeder, for example, didn't share her experience with her co-workers.

> Very few people where I work knew I had played ball. I never told them. It's not that I didn't want to, but they'd never seen a game, never seen me play ball, so these people wouldn't have the slightest idea how good these girls were.

The women probably felt like Norma Metrolis did: "It was a whole different lifestyle, and the only people that really understood it were other people that played."

What people uniformly failed to understand was that these women had played baseball, not softball. Many of the women told me they'd experienced a version of this interchange:

> Player: Well, yes, I used to play baseball with some pretty good players.
> Friend: You mean softball.
> Player: No, baseball.
> Friend: Girls don't play baseball.

Rather than argue, these fine ballplayers simply shut up.

They were also discouraged from talking about their experience because they feared that what they'd done was too unconventional—too "un-feminine"—to be accepted. Mary Rountree, whose ball-playing salary sent her to the first year of medical school, never mentioned it once she became a doctor.

> When you get into private practice, you don't say a word about having played ball. It's not something that girls normally do. You're a little bit out of your feminine area, to have played ball.

The players also didn't realize what a unique place in history they had enjoyed. They were young and simply wanted to play ball. When it was over, they were sad, but had to get on with their lives.

A few, like Rose Gacioch in Rockford, found jobs in the cities where they played. Dottie and Don Key also stayed in Rockford because Dottie had made her reputation there: "I had it made down here." Snookie Doyle got her first teaching job because she had played baseball. But she went to her interview assuming her baseball history would work against her.

> I had to put the baseball on my resume, you know. Well, the principal started quizzing me about playin' ball, and I thought, "Oh, I probably won't get the job." I was afraid he'd think, "One of *those*, are you?" They think you're a bunch of Amazons because you're a girl that's good in athletics. This was all goin' through my head.
>
> But actually, it was the baseball that got me the job. At the time this junior high had about twenty percent black children plus mixed whites, Asians and kids of Mexican descent. He felt that playing in

sports I'd have a better understanding and a better working relationship with different races.

Snookie's experience was the exception. Women's careers are not commonly advanced because of an association with sports. Fifty years after the All-American League was formed our society still generally equates being a woman with a femininity that excludes competitive team sports.[73] Nothing spontaneously arises in a woman's life to make the telling of her sports triumphs relevant or desirable. Nobody thinks to ask a young woman her high school batting average or average number of points per basketball game. Sports experiences fade for women because nothing in adult life reinforces them. As a result, the significance of the experience fades for the women themselves.

This happened to the All-Americans. Many of the women told me they had no way of knowing how important their experience had been. Helen "Sis" Waddell Wyatt, the Peaches' utility infielder for two years, says,

> At the time we didn't realize it was the thing it is now. I was just playin' baseball because I liked to play baseball. I didn't know I was doing anything special or sensational. My kids knew I played baseball, but that was it.

I asked if her children knew her playing was a big deal.

> No. And I didn't know it was such a big deal either.

While the players almost uniformly stopped talking about the details of their professional baseball days, they did incorporate into their adult lives important things they'd learned from the experience. Mary Rountree felt her baseball helped her be a better doctor.

> My ballplaying was absolutely magnificent for me. You had to meet a lot of people so you learned to get over your stage fright, your bashfulness. Because you had to do personal appearances, you overcame your inability to talk to people in a very quick amount of time. I think that it allowed me to be totally at home with patients.
> It gave you a chance to develop your personality.

Ruth Richard agreed with Mary: the experience gave her a self-confidence she didn't have before.

I think it gave you more confidence, really. Before that you maybe didn't have that much confidence in anything, and then you realize, I guess being able to do what I do in front of all those people, I should be confident.

When the stands would be full some of the players would be afraid of the crowd, and I'd say, "Why be afraid if you know what you're doin'? If you're doin' a good job, you shouldn't be afraid."

Dottie Kamenshek learned to trust her own perseverence. "Baseball taught me that if you worked hard enough, you could do what you wanted to do."

The All-Americans took with them from baseball a host of memories, a new-found self-confidence, a social ease with different kinds of people, and a fully-developed competitive spirit. Most of the women threw their energies into other sports, usually softball, bowling and golf.

The Amateur Softball Association kept retired All-Americans out of Association play for two years because, they reasoned, "your calibre of play is so much greater." According to Tiby Eisen this was true. She and other Californian ex-All-Americans, among them Lois Florreich, organized a team that played exhibition games against ASA teams "and beat the hell out of 'em!" After the two year waiting period, Tiby and Snookie Doyle joined the famous Orange Lionettes and "went on to win more championships in softball!"

Other All-Americans could not return to softball once they'd played baseball. Dottie Schroeder was one of them.

The manager of a girls' fast-pitch softball team wanted me to play, but I turned him down. No doubt they're good players, but it just wouldn't have been the same, not after playing baseball. So I just quit playin', just like that. And I haven't thrown a ball since.

Other All-Americans excelled at a variety of sports. Vivian Kellogg has more bowling trophies among her memorabilia than she has baseball awards. Racine Belle Joanne Winter played on the Ladies' Professional Golf Association tour. Sixty-six-year-old Fran Janssen had just taken a twenty-two-mile bicycle tour the weekend before our interview.

The All-Americans have been active throughout their lives: they play golf or go bowling once a week, or walk or take a bike ride, whatever their health will allow. Few are completely sedentary. The players are now in their late fifties to late seventies, and they look in good shape for their ages. Some may be a bit overweight and limp on their bad baseball knees, but on the whole they're vigorous and vital. Some look like they could play again tomorrow. Marie Mansfield Kelley assured me, though, that she and her sister players don't feel like they used to.

I don't think former athletes take better care of themselves than just regular people. At least not in comparison to today where everybody is so figure-conscious and health-conscious, keepin' in shape and eatin' the right foods. We didn't have any of that. We were young, and we were in shape. It's only when you get older that you start gettin' middle-aged spread.

Women who were once accustomed to their bodies serving them so well do not accept the ravages of age gracefully. Jo Weaver, not only a great hitter but a League-leading base-stealer in the 1950s, endured a shocking experience just trying to play a little softball twenty years after her playing days.

It's very very hard to know what you used to be able to do but can't do any more. Your mind says you can do it, but I tell ya, your body can't. When I was forty-two my company wanted me to play slow-pitch. When I tried to run to first, I actually fell down because my body wouldn't take me down there the way I wanted it to.

Nickie Fox puts it succinctly, "You hate to get old."

Regardless of age, however, an old ballplayer can turn on the television or go down to a local ballpark and watch a good game. Many of the homes I entered on a September afternoon had a major-league game on the television.

The All-Americans are sports fans, but they have a special problem watching; they know too much about the game to watch as happy amateurs. Dottie Key can't help thinking strategy.

I don't even enjoy going to watch a ballgame. Everybody else is yellin' "Come on!" And I'm sittin' there thinkin', "Okay, there's a runner on first and a runner on third. How many out? Okay, what's the play gonna be?" I'm thinkin' of what would happen if I was playing.

Nor can Lou Erickson keep her pitcher's mind out of the spectating.

I watch a lot of Cubs games on TV. But I get nervous watchin' a game now. I know what that pitcher should be doin', you know, and it drives me bugs the way he's doin' it. Once you been through it, it's hard to shake. I just like to see 'em all do so well, and if it doesn't turn out that way, why I have a hard time.

I like the one Cubs commentator 'cause he was a pitcher. He says he'd do it this way, and I'm thinkin' the same way. I'd throw him the same pitch.

These women can't help but watch—after all, baseball was their life—but they also can't help but notice the discrepancy between the kind of publicity and pay the men receive, and the quality of their baseball thinking. Dottie Schroeder was aghast.

Two or three years ago *Sports Illustrated* had a picture of every player in the major leagues and how much money they made. They never should have done that. When I saw what some of those guys were making, and some of them as dumb as dirt when you watch them play . . . it's amazing.

Outfielder Rose Gacioch didn't think much of some major-league play either.

They don't know how to run back after a ball. They don't go to the end, then turn around and catch it. What's the matter with them? They don't follow the ball good. I see guys that gets thousands and thousands of dollars missin' a ball that I'd be ashamed to admit I missed it. And I'm a woman. And they get paid that much! I just laugh at it.

Dottie Collins doesn't think too much of their stamina either.

I pitched and won both games of a doubleheader once pitching underhand. I think I could have pitched a doubleheader overhand too. I don't think it would be that hard. Nowadays the men can't do it, but hell, they can't do nothin'.

Mary Rountree thinks the boys could use another aspect of the All-Americans' training.

I wish I could talk to some of the college and professional coaches, because they need to have chaperones in college and some kind of authority in the professional leagues. I want to explain to them that you can't take a poor young adult out of the ghetto or off the farm, and put him on the mound for the New York Mets or Yankees, and expect him to know how to behave. They need help, just like we did.

◆◆◆

For twenty-five years after the League ended, the All-Americans went on with their separate lives, working, paying attention to their marriages and other important relationships, having children, playing golf or bowling, and watching baseball with a critical eye. Some players took up housekeeping with other ex-players and sustained those relationships over years. And some of the players kept in touch by mail with a few others. But most of the friendships formed during the League experience waned with the passing of the years.

At the same time the All-Americans went on with their private lives, however, something was happening in the larger society that would create for them the chance to enjoy the second miracle of their baseball lives.

World War II had produced a social climate that encouraged women's baseball. The All-Americans had been alive at the right time to seize the opportunity given them. Then, in the 1970s, the feminist movement created another climate that would benefit these women. Feminists wanted to know about the hidden history of women, and one of them, Sharon Roepke of Kalamazoo, Michigan, wanted to know about the women in her area who were rumored to have played baseball. The conditions for the All-Americans' second miracle were being born.

Roepke searched old newspapers and phone books for the names of ex-players, and eventually made her way to June Peppas, a Michigan woman who had played seven years in the League. Peppas had retired and opened a print shop, and Sharon Roepke by this time had located about sixty ex-players. The result was the first newsletter, written and published by Peppas in October 1980, the first time any players from the All-American Girls Baseball League had been in formal contact with each other since 1954.

The newsletter has been published several times a year since. Players send in news of their lives: about new jobs or retirements; about anniversaries and births; about how their partners and husbands and children and grandchildren are getting on; who they've seen lately from the League and how they are; where they've been on their travels; how their health is holding up and what surgery is in the future, or being recovered from; what tasks they're undertaking around the house; and what the weather has been like. They send old and recent photos, and newspaper clippings about themselves and their exploits. They encourage each other to keep up good spirits in the face of aging and ill-health. And they look for former players, managers, chaperones, bat girls, and others associated with their history who have not yet been found.

The editor copies the pictures and articles, edits the letters, and reproduces it all for everyone on the mailing list three times a year. The last issue I read, April 1993, was thirty-nine pages long. To give a flavor of the entries, the August 1991 issue included the following letter from Rossey Weeks, a Rockford player in 1947:

> I read about the players who have medical problems and I have joined their club. Since last October I had a pinched nerve in my back, both eyes operated on, and a plastic joint in my ring finger. Couldn't write or see, but now everything's great. So before another part breaks, I thought I would drop you a line.
>
> I saw the movie "Field of Dreams" the other night. Brought back memories of Max Carey and others. I drove over to the ballpark and just sat there. The young kids were having a great time practicing. I wanted to go out there, but I knew they would think I was crazy so I stayed in my car.
>
> Had a note pad with me, thought you would like to read the poem I wrote called "Play Ball."

> I was driving by the ballpark the other night.
> There was to be a game and someone had turned on the lights.
> I used to play there years ago.
> I wondered if now I was too slow.
> I thought "Could I run the bases once more?"
> Getting my legs out of the car was quite a chore.
> I pushed myself up with my cane.
> When I was young, I never had this kind of pain.
> I walked out on the field;
> The pitcher hurled the ball across the plate.
> I swung my cane, hoping I wasn't too late.
> I heard the roar of the crowd, "Run, run, run!"
> As I made it from base to base I thought, "Lord, what fun!"
> Then I slid into home.
> I turned to wave at the crowd. They were gone!

An attendant yelled, "Lady, are you for real?
Quit tearing up my field.
Old lady, you're playing ball in the windmills of your mind!"
"True! True!" I said, "And I hit home runs every time."
As I walked past him, I thought, "Such a young face."
I started to punch him with my cane and put him in his place.
I told him, "I know more about being young than you do about being old."
I guess I got him told.
I could have warned him that youth doesn't last.
But he will learn;
Everyone gets a turn to look back into the past.

The newsletters and some informal get-togethers of players in the early 1980s generated interest in more formal reunions. In July1982, two hundred All-Americans met in Chicago for the first national reunion. The event was organized by many women, but was chaired by Ruth Davis, a South Bend Blue Sox bat girl who was signed to play with the League in 1955, the season that never happened.

Alice Pollitt Deschaine was there.

> When we first got together in Chicago I think we stayed up all night. We all got together in Richie's room, Joanie [Berger, a Peach from 1951 to 1954] and Boston and me and I don't know how many. We got in there, and everybody's talkin': "Do you remember this? Do you remember that?"
>
> These reunions bring back a lot of memories. You had put it all in the back of your mind, you know, and there it was.

Ruth Richard hadn't seen Alice since her retirement from the Peaches after the 1952 season.

> Al Pollitt was probably my best friend. We roomed together in Rockford. I still kept in touch with her, but hadn't seen her for thirty years. Now, since our League got together, she comes east now and then to see me.

Dottie Schroeder was also at that first reunion.

> It's like your high school reunion. You're a little bit hesitant at first. You have nametags, but once you got there, you recognized most of them. All of us are older, grey-haired. Most of us are retired. But once you get to talkin' to these "girls," we're still the same: the same personalities, the same voice, the same laugh. And if we were younger, we could still play ball too.

Peaches pitchers Louise Erickson and Lois Florreich both retired after the 1950 season. Lou described the ritual with which they ended their playing days.

> We were so sure we were quitting, she gave me her glove and I gave her mine: "That's it; we're not coming back." I didn't see her again until 1988, thirty-eight years later. I had to look twice to recognize her. Luckily we had badges on. Then we put our arms around each other, just like we'd seen each other yesterday.

The renewed contact, both through the newsletters and reunions, has changed how the women relate to each other. Vivian Kellogg feels differently about the girls she used to play with now that she's come to know their adult selves.

> Sometimes your feelings toward them change. Now maybe there was a certain player that I didn't particularly care for when I played ball. It might have been a situation that happened while we were playing that made me think I didn't like her. Now I'd probably give her the shirt off my back.
>
> Also, I only played on the Daisies. I didn't have much communication with other teams. So I'm really getting more acquainted with the girls now, after all these years, than I did when I played ball.

Even with the allocation system and the trades, the girls of the League knew their own teammates best. Now, with fourteen years of newsletters and yearly regional reunions since 1982, they have broadened their friendships far beyond those original team allegiances. They may still identify themselves as a Peach or a Daisy, as an early or later-era player, but they now know women who played for all the teams over all twelve years. Their identification is most significantly with the League itself. Dottie Key says: "What this has done in my life, I've got a lot more sisters. We're friends, not used-to-be-ballplayers."

Dottie Schroeder is aware of something especially important about her newly-found friends.

> A lot of these girls that you never played on the same team with, you get to know now, and find out what nice people they are. They all have that spirit.

"That spirit" is right. I attended the mini-reunion in Fort Wayne in September 1992 and was at first stunned and perplexed at the mood and energy of the more than seventy women gathered there. It was the first time I had seen All-Americans together in a group since 1954. What is it, I kept asking myself, that makes these women together so different from other women's groups?

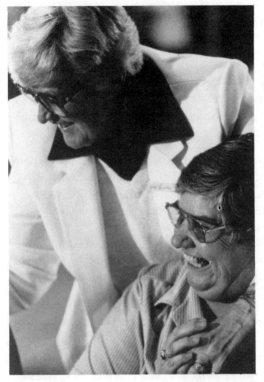

Vivian Kellogg and Ruby Heafner at a reunion.

Many of the women who played professional baseball may be shy as individuals, but they are outgoing and rambunctious as a group. When they meet, the formerly quiet, sedate hotel lobby rings with "Hi's" and "How are ya's" and "Where's so and so?" They are delighted to see each other. They hug and slap one another on the back, punch each other in the arm, and hang on, arms encircling the nearest shoulder. They look comfortable, informal in their dress, practical in their hairstyles, comfortable in their bodies and affectionate with each other. They grin a lot.

A group of All-Americans at a table in the hotel dining room dominates the rest of the room. They talk, they gesture, they get up and move around, they laugh, they charm the waitress. They're loud and take up a lot of space. They're unselfconscious in their happiness, and the room reverberates with their joy.

It occurs to me by contrast how quiet and constrained women are taught to be, how aware of the impression we're making. We talk in low voices, keep our legs crossed and our arms close to our bodies, laugh politely. When we're with other women we are easily distracted, our attention alert for surrounding male needs or threats. We appear solemn, anxious and troubled and are easily overlooked.

The All-Americans are not easily overlooked. Everyone who experiences them senses something very different, something wonderfully different. Dot Montgomery, who played from 1945 to 1947, is quoted in one of the newsletters as saying, "You can always tell a ballplayer; there's something about the way they carry themselves."

Ruth Richard: "When we have these reunions, people think 'Oh, here's a bunch of old ladies.' But by God we got more pep and gumption than a bunch of teenagers! Hey, those ballplayers are the greatest. A special breed, I'll tell ya."

Evie Wawryshyn Litwin Moroz, Fort Wayne's second baseman, attended the 1986 Fort Wayne reunion with her husband.

> Henry said he couldn't believe the energy that was in that room. It was like a glow, he said. Whether it's the love of doing something together, I don't know, eh? He says, "You can't imagine, when those players all get together, that feeling just radiates."

When the girls of the 1940s and 1950s got together to play baseball they were doing something they loved, something physical, something that engaged their bodies and spirits. And they were doing it together. When these women reunite, the same energy inspires them. They are physically expressive, their love for each other is palpable. Their spirits are rekindled and they remember how it was. They are young again.

Fort Wayne's catcher Mary Rountree positions
herself to catch a pop fly.

GAME SEVEN

Sunday, September 17, 1950

Fort Wayne had unleashed its big guns in Game Six, scoring eight runs on nine hits, one a grand slam by Betty Foss. Meanwhile, Daisies pitcher Maxine Kline had shut out the Peaches who, while pecking out eight hits, had been unable to score, leaving eleven runners stranded. Foss also contributed to the Daisies' defense, completing an unassisted double play to snuff out a Peaches scoring threat.

Had the series ended here, we would have concluded that Fort Wayne power finally overcame Rockford precision. But the series had one more game to go. Fort Wayne's 8-0 win had tied the championship match and forced the seventh and deciding game, the contest that would determine whether Rockford could maintain its dominance, or whether an upstart power would overthrow the League's traditional rulers.

Three and a half months of struggle had come down to one final confrontation.

Peaches Wallop Daisies, 11-0, to Clinch Play-off Crown

Kamenshek Is Hitting Star
Potent Bat Helps Fox to Post 3rd Series Win

by Dick Day
Rockford Register Republic, September 18, 1950

Early last spring, Max Carey, the former National league base stealing champion, sat in the visitors' dugout at Beyer stadium and pointed to Bill Allington and his Peaches going through their infield practice.

"There," said Max, "is the best team in the league—they oughta win the pennant."

All of which makes Max a good prophet, even if he is deprived of the honor of leading a winner. Because last night when the Peaches humiliated his slugging Fort Wayne Daisies, 11-0, it gave Rockford the post-season playoff championship to go with its 1950 pennant.

It took the full seven games to do it, but the 3,235 customers who watched the wind-up last night must have been moved to wonder at times why the Peaches hadn't sewed up the trophy in four games.

Foxy Nickie

Nickie Fox, just as foxy as her name, called on a tired arm to befuddle and baffle Fort Wayne's heavy hitters, and the Peaches, led by Dottie Kamenshek, came to her rescue with some stylish stick-work of their own.

Statistically, the game was a mass of contradictions. Both teams got 11 hits, but only the Peaches got any runs. Reasons, of course, were Nickie's crafty pitching in the clutches, four Fort Wayne errors, and the fact that the Peaches collected their blows when they counted.

Kamenshek led the way with four hits and five runs in four times at bat. A home run and a triple were among her more solid blows.

Only 3-Game Winner

By her victory, Fox became the only pitcher to win three games in the championship playoff round. She appeared in four of the seven contests and was charged with one defeat. An injury to Lois Florreich brought Fox to the firing line again last night, and she coaxed a bit more magic out of her weary flipper. The Daisies hit her in nearly every inning, but all the good it did them was to leave ten runners stranded on the sacks.

Millie Deegan, who was routed on her first appearance here, tried again last night, and again her ex-teammates gave her a hot reception. She lasted just two innings after letting four runs cross the plate. A walk to Kamenshek and a sacrifice by Snookie Doyle set the stage in the first inning. Rose Gacioch was hit by a pitched ball and Charlene Barnett walked to load the bases. Jackie Kelley then singled to score Kamenshek and Gacioch.

Serves "Gopher" Ball

An error by Betty Foss put Marilyn Jones on base to open the second inning, and, with two out, Deegan served a home run pitch to Kamenshek. Dottie Collins took over in the third, but Eleanor Callow greeted her with a double, Gacioch sacrificed and Barnett belted a single for one more run.

Collins lasted one more inning, and the Peaches treated her harshly in that one. Fox opened with a single, Dottie Key sacrificed, Kamenshek singled, Fox taking third, Doyle was safe and Fox scored on Foss' error. Callow then drove the ball to Evelyn Wawryshyn and the Fort Wayne sacker first bobbled it and then threw wild for a double error that let in two more runs. Barnett's sacrifice brought Callow home from third, where she had found haven during all the excitement on the previous play.

Kamenshek Tops Club

Frances Janssen replaced Collins to start the fifth and got through that inning without mishap. Kamenshek was the first batter to face her in the sixth, and Kammie whaled a single into left field. Doyle and Callow followed suit with hits of their own to score Kamenshek. The Rockford first sacker walloped a triple with one out in the eighth and scored on Callow's double.

For the seven-game series, Kamenshek led the Rockford team with 11 hits and a .440 average. The best hitting of all, however, was Wawryshyn's .520 average and 13 safe blows for the seven games.

Summary

Runs - Kamenshek 5, Gacioch, Jones, Callow 2, Fox, Doyle. Errors - Foss 2, Wawryshyn 2, Doyle. Runs batted in - Kamenshek 2, Callow 2,

Barnett 2, Kelley 2. Home run - Kamenshek. Triple - Kamenshek. Doubles - Kelley 2, Meier. Sacrifice hits - Wawryshyn, Doyle, Barnett, Key. Stolen bases - Eisen, Kamenshek, Gacioch, Jones. Double plays - Barnett to Doyle to Kamenshek. Strike-outs - by Fox 3, by Janssen 2. Base on balls - off Deegan 2, off Collins 1. Hit by pitch - by Deegan (Gacioch). Left on base - Rockford 5, Fort Wayne 10. Winning pitcher - Fox. Losing pitcher - Deegan. Time - 1:45. Attendance - 3,235.

The Daisies' overthrow of the Peaches was not yet to be. Dottie Kamenshek played one of the best games of her life, she and her teammates blasted eleven timely hits, and the combination of Rockford's defense and pitcher Nickie Fox frustrated Fort Wayne's power, preventing eleven Daisies hits from accounting for even one run. The Rockford Peaches won the 1950 championship series, and in the end won it big.

Two days after Fort Wayne's defeat, Bob Reed of the *Fort Wayne Journal-Gazette* wrote an obituary in his "Sports Roundup" column. Under the headline "Daisies Still Did All Right," Reed analyzed the season and its outcome.

> The Daisies are back in the home balliwick, packing their belongings and getting ready to scatter to their homes far and wide. They'll be going to many parts of the country, from Los Angeles in the West to Boston in the East, from Miami in the South to Saskatchewan in the North.
>
> It wasn't exactly a happy ending, that 11-0 setback in the closing game of the series. Too bad it couldn't have been something like 2-1 or 3-2, but the Daisies had the consolation of knowing they trimmed Rockford just the night before almost as badly. The overwork of the pitching staff through August finally caught up with them a little too soon. Had the hurlers been going in late August and September as they did in July, there would have been nothing to it.
>
> If there are any regrets, they should be over that game here last Thursday when the Daisies were time and again just inches away from a victory which, as events proved, would have made them the champions instead of the Peaches. Nobody was to be blamed especially, even though there was plenty of difference of opinion on strategy at times and considerable second guessing. A series of bad breaks, hard drives that started as potential base hits and wound up as just another putout, and a couple of mental slips that came when they hurt most, told the story.

We have no doubt the gals hope the fans will forget that 11-0 finish and remember that they gave Fort Wayne the best season it has had in the league, financially and artistically, finishing just two games away from the championship over the season's schedule and one game short of taking the play-off title.[74]

The outcome of the 1950 season made it look as if everything in the All-American Girls Baseball League was proceeding as usual: Rockford won and another team came in second. But 1950 was a watershed year, both for the League and for the fortunes of the Rockford and Fort Wayne teams. After that year, everything changed; 1951 was the transition to a new era in the All-American League.

Ownership passed from the central office to individual boards of directors in the various team cities, and the eight teams in the League played a split 1951 season. The Grand Rapids Chicks won the first half and the South Bend Blue Sox the second. South Bend took the championship. Fort Wayne finished second in the first half, and Rockford second in the second half.

From 1952 through the final year, 1954, Fort Wayne was formidable. The Daisies were powered by both Betty Weaver Foss and sister Jo and, with the consistently excellent pitching of Maxine Kline, won 67 of their 109 games in 1952 (a .615 winning percentage), 66 of 105 in 1953 (.629), and 54 of 94 in 1954 (.574) to take the pennant all three years.

Certain Fort Wayne players retired after the 1950 season, notably Dottie Collins, who wanted to be with her new baby, and Vivian Kellogg, battered and bruised after seven seasons in the League. Rookie Helen Ketola stayed home after her one season, and Norma Metrolis finally gave in to her bad knee. Max Carey retired after the 1951 season and Evie Wawryshyn left to marry the following year. Tiby Eisen found a job too good to turn down after 1952.

Over the next few years, Kay Blumetta, Wilma Briggs, Fran Janssen, Mary Rountree, Dottie Schroeder, and Kate Vonderau were all traded to other teams. But new players emerged to take the places of these veterans, and the team developed into a consistent winner. Fort Wayne blasted most of its opponents, and, because of her "explosive power," Betty Foss was dubbed "girl baseball's answer to the atom bomb."[75]

Rockford in the meantime suffered the retirement of key players who were never replaced with girls able to establish a comparable winning tradition. Of those on the 1950 roster, only four players were still in Peaches uniforms in 1954: Rose Gacioch, Dottie Key, Marie Mansfield and Ruth Richard. Nickie Fox was pitching home games only.

Pitchers Lois Florreich and Louise Erickson both retired after the 1950 season, as did second baseman Charlene Barnett, who became a flight attendant. Helen Waddell married and did not return after 1951, and after 1952, Snookie Doyle left to begin college in California. Alice Pollitt Deschaine had a baby, Jackie Kelley joined the Marines, Dottie Kamenshek returned to college full time, and Irene Applegren moved to the Chicago softball league, all after the 1953 season. Chaperone Dottie Green also left after 1953 to become an administrator with the Massachusetts prison system.

Even Bill Allington, after eight seasons directing the Peaches, left Rockford to manage the Fort Wayne team in 1953 and 1954. Marilyn Jones, traded from Rockford after the 1951 season, wound up playing again for Allington, this time in Fort Wayne in 1954.

Rockford's winning ways were at an end, and the team finished third in a League of six teams in 1952, fourth of six in 1953, and dead last, the fifth of only five teams in 1954.

Ironically Fort Wayne was able to win the pennant, dominating each All-American season from 1952 through 1954, but the team never won a championship. When Fort Wayne and Kalamazoo met in the deciding game of the last championship series, Dottie Schroeder found herself playing, not for her beloved Daisies, but for the Lassies. She remembers this win as one of her favorite moments in a career that spanned the history of the League.

> If you want to pick out one big, thrilling thing for me, it was when we won the final game of the championship in 1954. That was great. It was a little bit sweeter because I had played for Fort Wayne for so long until they traded me.
>
> Even though overall Fort Wayne probably had a better team than Kalamazoo, I think we had a bit more desire, which helps a lot too.
>
> Those were the days, I'll tell ya. And that was the very last game.

▲ 1950 was Fort Wayne second baseman Evelyn Wawryshyn's All-Star year, "a very delightful season for me." She batted .520 in the championship series against Rockford.

▶ Evelyn Wawryshyn Litwin Moroz in 1993 at her home in Winnipeg, Manitoba, Canada.

EVELYN "EVIE" WAWRYSHYN
Fort Wayne, Second Baseman

Statistics: Born: 1924. Home town: Tyndall, Manitoba, Canada. Height: 5 feet 4 inches. Playing weight: 135 pounds. Bats: Right. Throws: Right. Entered League: 1946 at age 21. Teams: Kenosha and Muskegon, 1946; Muskegon, 1947; Springfield travelling team, 1948; Fort Wayne, 1949-1951. Lifetime totals: Batting average: .266; Fielding percentage: .942.

1950 was the best year of Evelyn Wawryshyn's professional baseball career, as she says, "A very delightful season for me, eh?" She ended the season with 124 hits and a batting average of .311, both accomplishments placing her third in the League. Only teammate Betty Foss and Rockford's Dottie Kamenshek had higher averages (among players who appeared in at least fifty games), and only Racine's Sophie Kurys and Betty Foss had more hits.

In 1948 Wawryshyn had been named to the third All-Star team at second base. In 1949 she was named to the second team, and in 1950 was chosen the best second baseman in the League.

Evie played spectacularly in the seven-game championship series against the Peaches. She batted an astounding .520, 13 hits in 25 at-bats. She batted in three runs, made three sacrifice hits, stole three bases and scored five runs. She made eleven put-outs and twelve assists from her second-base position. She played errorless ball until the double error in Game Seven that allowed two Rockford runs to score. But the Daisies were already six runs behind, and the additional runs were inconsequential.

Evie was unaware that she had batted over .500 for the series. When I told her, she responded happily, "I never knew that. Hey, you made my day! I feel a lot better about that last game now!"

I asked Wawryshyn why she thought 1950 was such a successful year for her. Evie's response tells much about her attitude toward life and the good things life has brought her.

I don't think any athlete can give an answer to that. Everything just seems to work together, eh? I don't know why it is so. One year you're just great. And the next year you can't seem to do anything. Whether it's emotional, whether you're on a high . . . I don't know.

But I do know one thing. I think our Supreme Being has a lot to do with this. If He decided to do it right for you that particular year, then everything just goes great. I don't know any other way to explain it.

◆◆◆

Evie Wawryshyn Litwin Moroz is a quietly and deeply spiritual person, a woman who credits elements beyond human control for the decisions we make, the forces that create turning points in our lives, the elements that contribute to our triumphs and tragedies. I have not yet met Evie face-to-face. We talked on the phone for a couple of hours, I at home in Anchorage, Alaska, she at home in Winnipeg, Manitoba, Canada. We were thousands of miles apart, but Evie's manner is so distinctive, so caring and loving and somehow graceful, that I had to keep reminding myself we'd never met. Her voice has a Canadian prairie lilt that ends sentences with an "eh?" drawing you into the conversation, creating the impression she is offering you her ideas as a gift, checking occasionally to be sure you're still connected with her.

◆◆◆

Evie Wawryshyn grew up in a town of five hundred people in Tyndall, Manitoba. Her Ukranian father's family immigrated to Canada from Austria when he was four years old, and her mother was born in Canada of Czechoslovakian parents. Both were multilingual, her mother in Czech, German and English, her father in Ukrainian, Polish and English.

Evie's parents were small-town proprietors, helping to settle the prairie. Her father ran a grocery store and was a local politician. Her mother raised their children and took in boarders.

My father was an eloquent speaker in various languages. There were a lot of other immigrants who couldn't speak English. With Dad having the store, people used to come to him for help in understanding what was going on, eh? And so he spoke for other people who had high hopes for themselves. He didn't speak for himself as much as perhaps he should have. I guess he always figured "My turn will come."

My mother kept busy raising us four kids, myself and my older and two younger brothers, and she also took in teachers from the local school. We always had four or five teachers living at our home. She loved to do that. She was a good cook and enjoyed the few dollars it brought in.

As I was growing up there were very few children to play with, so I tagged along behind my older brother Archie a lot. There was never enough to make up a baseball team, so they'd say, "Ah, let Evie play first short," at that time a position between first and second, like a shortstop on the other side of the field. They were okay with my playing there 'cause hardly anything ever came to first short.

I played by myself a lot too. One side of our house was quite large, with no windows, and I threw a ball against that building and caught it for hours on end.

Evie Wawryshyn graduated from high school in 1942, received six weeks' training, and left home to teach for a year in a prairie school. She then travelled to the big city of Winnipeg for a one-year education course, and returned to the prairies to teach. It was in Winnipeg where, at the suggestion of older brother Archie, she began to play organized softball for the Canadian Ukranian Athletic Club Blues.

Archie was quite a motivator for me in sports; he gave me a lot of direction. So I figured, I better do what Archie says. Of course my love of the sport was great too, eh?

During one of the CUAC games a scout from the All-American League was watching. He came down from the stands, stopped me on my way home and asked if I wanted to go down to the States to play this type of ball. Well, I'd never heard of girls playing baseball for money, so I thought it wasn't a true story. I told my mother about it, and then just forgot about it and went on my way. I went out to Flin Flon, Manitoba to teach.

I think destiny has a funny hand in things, you know, because that scout talked to some relative of mine, and at Christmas playing ball down across the line came up again. Archie says, "Why don't you give him a call?" so I did. In April a telegram came, "Would you be prepared to go and play immediately?" The girls I was living with in Flin-flon said, "You better go! Look at all the money you're gonna get!" So I did.

I must have been apprehensive, but you must remember we were young and eager for adventure. I wasn't afraid. And besides, the League treated us first-class. They sent a plane ticket, met me at the airport, helped me to the hotel, gave me a beautiful room. The whole procedure was so well taken care of, all I had to do was follow it.

I came in as a shortstop, but as soon as I got there, they said to play second base. So I said, "All right. I'll go for second base." And I played that all the rest of my career.

A lot of things, I think, are not within your control. You don't do the decisions. They're made for you. And it worked out well for me.

I wondered how Evie felt treated in the League as a Canadian, remembering that Rockford's Helen Waddell was sufficiently sheltered to regard meeting a Canadian for the first time as a major event. Evie recalls being treated well.

They welcomed us so warmly, they couldn't have treated us better. There was no "Well, you're a Canadian; you shouldn't belong," you know? There was just no distinction, no different treatment at all.

Evie was assigned to play for the Kenosha Comets, but after just a couple of weeks moved on to the Muskegon Lassies. She stayed there two years, but never got to play consistently.

The regulars played even though they were hurt. They loved the game and besides you don't want to go out of the game not knowing when you're gonna get back in. The competition for those positions was keen, and the girls were good.

So if you weren't a regular you just had to wait and hope to get lucky. It's a lot harder playin' only once in a while. The pressure is on you to play extraordinarily well when you get a chance, which is very hard to do when you're not used to playing.

After her years with Muskegon Evie was assigned to the Springfield Sallies, one of the teams that travelled during the 1948 season. Evie had played in 73 games in her rookie season, 1946, but only 36 games in 1947. With the Sallies she played 118 games, the most in any single season of her career. Finally Evie had a chance to play regularly, to develop and then to demonstrate her skills.

It's important to play every day to develop your confidence. Because some days you have a bad day, some days you have a good day, eh? If you can't do it one day, and you happen to be lucky and do well the next, it takes care of the bad one. It restores your confidence in yourself.

Evie was named to the third All-Star team for her second-base play with the Sallies in 1948. The following year she was assigned to the Fort Wayne Daisies where she held down the second-base position until her retirement three years later. She had finally made it to a regular starting position in women's professional baseball.

Evie particularly appreciated being able to play second base to Dottie Schroeder's shortstop.

Second baseman Evie Wawryshyn and Shortstop Dottie Schroeder were a doubleplay combination that snuffed out many an enemy rally. Here they give the "V" for victory sign.

I think the key to being a good second baseman is just like the key to playing any other position well: you have to determine your own style, what is comfortable for you. There's just a certain sense you have when you get it right.

At second base you have to be prepared to cover first too, and to participate in double plays. I played with Dottie Schroeder, a wonderful shortstop. She made things easy, eh? She seemed to be able to give you the ball freely, at just the right speed. It seemed to work for us. I think Dottie and I executed our plays pretty well. I hope she feels like that.

I asked Wawryshyn how she dealt with losing when winning was so important, with playing poorly when playing well was supremely valued.

There's no logic sometimes to why things go as they do. Everybody has those days when they feel terrible about some error, and you're wondering how your teammates feel about you too, eh? But it's funny how you can put one game behind you and go out the next day; you never seem to have two bad games in a row.

Players do get in batting slumps, but then the rest of the team carries you. Sure, the individual is hurting, but you can still carry on with a good play in the field, not making any errors. And what counts is the way the team as a whole is doing, not just one individual.

When you're in a batting slump you wonder when the next base hit's ever gonna come, and you do anything to help it along. We'd count white horses. The superstition was that the first person to see a white horse gets a hit. Once you get desperate for a hit, you find yourself lookin' for horses.

When I didn't get a base hit for three or four days I'd go for something with tomatoes in it, like tomato soup. It seemed to work every time. And of course to this day tomato is one of my favorite foods, eh?

Winning, of course, is the ideal. If you can win, and win fairly, there's a nice feeling about it, a delicious feeling. And when you do it as a group, it's special.

Evie remembers one particularly humorous moment in the field.

I was playing second base for the Sallies, and June Emerson was in right field. Someone hit a Texas Leaguer high in the air between June and me. I start moving out, and June starts coming in. As we got closer to the ball June said she had it, so I backed off at the last moment. I guess she must have lost it right then because it hit her on the head, bounced up in the air again, and I caught it on the rebound.

The umpires had a little trouble calling it, but it was a legal out. And ever since, June has been nicknamed Venus, the player without arms.

Evie was never bothered by the League's emphasis on femininity.

I had no trouble with that at all, really and truly. It was just a rule, and I figured I had to adhere to the rules. So you wore skirts in public; you got used to it. It just came naturally to put on your skirts and blouses and saddle shoes; it's a nice, comfortable look.

I asked whether the necessity to look feminine inhibited her play.

You mean, would you not perform as well because you had that feeling that you should be feminine? You must perform daintily? No, I didn't do it that way, and I'm sure the other girls didn't put something on or pretend to be something they weren't; they played just the way God intended them to play.

◆◆◆

Evie Wawryshyn retired from professional baseball after her 1951 season with the Daisies. She married a Chicago boy in 1952. "You figure it's time to start a family, time to get on with another phase of life." Evie's first husband died of a heart attack two years later. In 1960 she married her current husband, Henry Moroz, one of the teachers who had lived with the family back in Tyndall: "I think Mother must have had this in mind!" They have six children and seven grandchildren.

You do miss playing. For years I had dreams, these vivid dreams. I'd be going back to spring training and getting myself all worked up again. Or I'd be hitting. After the League folded, and for some years after, I did have these dreams. So I guess psychologically you missed it a lot, eh?

Evie returned to Canada and settled down to a life of raising her children. But Evie Wawryshyn didn't let the League die quite as dead as it did for some players. In her quiet way, she let her son and five daughters know about her years in the League.

My scrapbooks were there, if they wanted to look at 'em, but they didn't come out very often. We like to sing in this family, though, so I used to sing the League song a lot, the one Pepper Paire wrote during our playing days. And my girls all know it. You know the one? That starts, "Batter up, hear that call, the time has come for one and all, to play ball."

"Yes," I said, "of course," amazed that Evie had taught her children this song, the League rallying cry, its victory song. The women of the League sang it often forty years ago, and they sing it now at every opportunity, at reunions, at the Hall of Fame opening, in the movie. It goes:

For we're the members of the All-American League,
We come from cities near and far.
We've got Canadians, Irishmen and Swedes.
We're all for one,
We're one for all,
We're All-American.
Each girl stands,
Her head so proudly high,
Her motto DO or DIE,
She's not the one to use
Or need an alibi.
Our chaperones are not too soft,
They're not too tough.
Our managers are on the ball.
We've got a president who really knows his stuff.
We're all for one
We're one for all
We're All-Americans.

"My kids knew this song before the movie even came out," says Evie proudly.

The release of the movie "A League of Their Own" has, of course, brought Evie Wawryshyn, just like all the other All-Americans, to the attention of local, regional and national sports organizations. Just one week before Evie and I talked she had been inducted into the Province of Manitoba's Baseball Hall of Fame. I asked how her family liked having a famous mom.

Oh, they're just so enthusiastic, and so happy for me, that they're delighting in it too. You gotta give them all credit, you know. They're all so supportive and enjoying this thing. And that makes it nice, eh?

◆◆◆

Evie and Henry attended the 40th reunion of the League in Chicago, in 1982, and Evie talked about what that reunion meant to her.

Back in our playing days there was such camaraderie on the teams, and such a good support system. Everybody was for the next person. You made your finest friends there, friends for a lifetime.

When you get back to the reunions, there are these same people, and you feel just like you've never been away. You just fall in and carry on the conversation.

There's a warmth about the girls. They're just delighted to be together. And you can't help but get delighted with them!

Doing something like our playing baseball, getting together to make a win . . . well, forty-some years later you still get excited about it! Just talking about it. Once you start reliving these moments, you feel the heartbeat comin' back up again, eh?

Players intently follow a 1986 reunion game. In front, Elizabeth "Lib" Mahon. On the bench: Marge Callaghan Maxwell, Betsy Jochum, Jean Faut Eastman, Beatrice Kemmerer and Wilma Briggs.

A NEW GENERATION OF FANS

"It's like goin' back and playin' again."
—**Nickie Fox**

Many human enterprises have their miracles, but the women of the All-American Girls Baseball League seem to have had more than their share. No one was exempt. Norma Metrolis, a backup catcher for Fort Wayne in 1950, was a utility player for four teams in five years, never a star, someone other players might have trouble remembering. Her career was uneven and injury-plagued, yet graced with a transcendent experience.

I was with South Bend at the time, it was before I got hurt. One of the games I was catchin' I knew everything that was gonna happen before it happened. When the batter walked up, I knew whether they were gonna hit. Every ball that was hit, I knew where it was gonna go and who was gonna catch it. When I came up to bat I knew if I was gonna get a hit.

I could anticipate in my mind everything that was gonna happen. It went on for the whole game. It was almost like a dream. It was a weird feelin', a really strange feelin', and I thought, "Well, this is the ultimate, right here."

Norma was the only player to tell me about an experience of precognition, but all the players would agree that their baseball-playing days were a very special experience.

Now, however, two events have occurred that rival—well, almost rival—that original miracle. In November 1988 the National Baseball Hall of Fame opened an exhibit dedicated to women in baseball that prominently honored the women of the All-American League. Organized baseball finally took the first step in recognizing the women who have played and been otherwise important to the game.

Four years later, in July 1992, the film "A League of Their Own" was released. This comedy about the fictional exploits of two sisters and their teammates during the first year of the League's existence became a summer hit. Millions more people have seen the movie about the League than ever saw the League itself, and the real All-Americans have a new generation of fans who—true miracle of miracles—know they played baseball, not softball.

◆◆◆

While miracles do play a part in the rediscovery of the All-Americans, a lot of hard work went into creating them. For several years in the early 1980s the women who had played baseball together were satisfied to find each other again, read and contribute to the newsletters, and travel to reunions to cheer, laugh, hug and remember. In 1986, however, a small group met at Fran Janssen's home in Fort Wayne to think about a more formal organization, some structure for the League that would allow it to move beyond pure sociability. Sharon Roepke, the original catalyst for the players' finding each other, was there, as were Fran, Dottie Collins, Karen Kunkle, Earlene "Beans" Risinger, and Jean Geissinger Harding.

The outgrowth of this meeting and other organizational get-togethers was the All-American Girls Professional Baseball League Players' Association, formed in 1987 and dedicated to "focusing international attention on the role of the AAGPBL in baseball history."

The Players' Association continued to sponsor reunions and put out newsletters, and now the formal organization of ex-ballplayers and new-found friends had a vehicle for more ambitious efforts as well. The first new achievement was entering into an agreement with the Northern Indiana Historical Society in South Bend, Indiana, to accept and protect memorabilia about the League and its players in an official archive.[76] The archive now houses more than 1,500 catalogued pictures, player scrapbooks, bats, balls, gloves, uniforms and other items. When I can bear to let go of my pictures and scrapbooks, I will have a safe place to send them.

The National Baseball Hall of Fame is located in Cooperstown, New York, the site of what is now called Doubleday Field, where, myth has it, the first game of baseball was played. For decades the Baseball Hall of Fame, founded in 1936, recognized only players from the National and American Leagues; it was largely the White Male Baseball Hall of Fame. Both the African-American men who played baseball in the Negro Leagues from 1884 until 1950, and the women who played baseball from the days of the Bloomer Girl teams to those of the All-American League, were excluded.

Jackie Robinson, who had integrated Major League baseball in 1947 when he was signed to play for the Brooklyn Dodgers,[77] was inducted into the Hall of Fame in 1962. In 1971 the Hall appointed a special committee to consider players from the Negro Leagues, and through 1992 ten of the 179 players inducted into the Hall were elected on the basis of their careers in the Negro Leagues. A special exhibit is devoted to Negro League history.

The All-Americans and their supporters agitated and negotiated for several years to convince the Hall of Fame to recognize women's contribution to baseball. Finally, in November 1988 an exhibit devoted to women and baseball opened to much fanfare. As curator Ted Spencer told a reporter, it was "the rightest thing we ever did."[78]

The All-American portion of the exhibit includes several pictures of players, Dottie Kamenshek leaping for a high throw at first prominent among them. There are three skirted uniforms, one of them Dottie Key's peach-colored road uniform, a glove, a pair of shoes, and six baseballs demonstrating how the ball shrunk as the League approached the dimensions of men's hardball. Most important to the players is a list of the names and years in the League of every woman who played, a list that will be updated as new names come to the attention of the Players' Association.

The opening ceremony for the women and baseball exhibit was attended by seven hundred people including nearly one hundred fifty of the players, the only formal opening of an exhibit the Hall of Fame has ever hosted. Many of the 1950 Peaches and Daisies made a point of being there. Irene Applegren remembered the experience vividly.

> It gave you goosebumps, walking in there. It's unbelievable they had us in there with all those famous ballplayers. It's a real honor, just kind of overwhelming.

Dottie Key is aware of the chance for immortality.

> The Hall of Fame is where they'll remember me after I'm long gone. I keep pinchin' myself—am I still alive?—'cause usually you're dead and gone. They're doin' this for us while we're still alive.

The youngest All-Americans are now in their late fifties. Many are in their sixties and early seventies, and the two oldest turned seventy-eight in 1993. But many All-Americans have already died. Jackie Kelley Savage, for instance, was able to attend the fortieth reunion in Chicago in 1982, but died six months before the Hall of Fame opening. Her local paper reported how family helped her attend anyway, by bringing to the opening some of Jackie's ashes and sprinkling them on Doubleday Field.

Applegren's goosebumps are accompanied by a certain resentment she feels toward the Hall of Fame.

> I just felt like the recognition was a little bit too late. I think they should have done that a long time ago. We should have got credit years ago, all the girls should have. 'Cause a lot of them are already gone.

While the women of the League are grateful to organized baseball for beginning to recognize their efforts, some are taking subconscious revenge on the Hall of Fame by granting to themselves a status not officially conferred: they routinely refer to themselves as having been "inducted into the Hall of Fame." This is not so on several counts, and the Players' Association attempts to educate players about this, often to little avail. The wish to be inducted and the belief that the League should be inducted are too strong to be inhibited by technicalities.

People—for all practical purposes, men—who are inducted into the Hall of Fame must meet the criteria established by the Hall's

Charter and by the Baseball Writers Association of America, the group that selects inductees each year. Among other things, players being considered for induction must have played for ten years in the major leagues. The Hall of Fame does not consider the All-American Girls Baseball League a "major league."[79] Furthermore, since the All-American Girls Baseball League lasted only twelve years, only fifteen women played long enough to meet the longevity qualifications for induction if the standard rules were applied. Special rules would need to be devised, and these the Hall of Fame has to date been unwilling to consider.

A further problem arises because only individuals are considered for induction. And here the rules of the Hall of Fame collide with the "all for one, one for all" philosophy of the League and its Players' Association. Members of the Association, with a few exceptions, are unanimous in accepting only those types of national accolades that recognize all the players of the League, not just the superstars. As Fran Janssen says, "We were all stars."

When Karen Kunkle, upon her retirement as Executive Director of the Players' Association in the fall of 1992, was awarded a lifetime membership in the Association, she articulated her version of this philosophy.

> I have been committed to making the effort toward an organization for all former players regardless of team, years played, type of ball played, or record. I have been a true believer that after fifty years, the one for all, all for one philosophy is fitting and appropriate. It is everyone who made the League historically significant, and it is everyone who will perpetuate its history and legacy. To have been a part of the history in any form is significant and all should be recognized and made to feel a part of that history.[80]

In 1990 the Women's Sports Foundation approached the Players' Association about the possibility of some players being inducted into the Foundation's Hall of Fame as pioneers of women's sports. The Association responded,

> Due to the intent of our members upon organization of the AAGPBLPA, we committed ourselves to being recognized as a group and not as individuals. We feel we cannot designate one member to be more outstanding in her accomplishments than another.
> If your organization ever decides to recognize and recommend in-

ductions for group organizations, we would be tickled pink to even be considered eligible for nomination. We were true pioneers. We feel we do have a special place in the history of women's sports.

The girls of the All-American League were loyal members of their teams when they played. The women of the League Players' Association are loyal team players to this day.

Doris Sams loaned the Hall of Fame the Player of the Year trophy awarded her in 1947 and 1949. But, since it was to be on public display, she insisted on one change. Doris asked that the trophy's plate inscribed with just her name be replaced with a plate bearing the names of all the women chosen players of the year from 1943 to 1954.

◆◆◆

While the women were overjoyed by their inclusion in the Hall of Fame, and are sincerely moved and grateful for this recognition, they feel a bit more ambivalent about the movie and the furor it has caused. Almost everyone has seen it, almost everyone liked it, and everyone is appreciative of the attention it has focused on the League's history. A year after the movie's opening, however, some have grown tired of so much media exposure. Dottie Schroeder says, a bit wearily, "It'll be nice when we sink back into obscurity."

The movie came about, as such things do, through a happy combination of lucky circumstance and focused effort. Helen Callaghan Candaele St. Aubin was an accomplished left-handed batter and outfielder for the Minneapolis Millerettes in 1944 and the Fort Wayne Daisies in 1945, 1946 and 1948. She captured the League batting crown in 1945 with "the kind of swing you associate with Ted Williams or Will Clark," according to son Kelly Candaele. In 1986 Kelly and friend Kim Wilson produced a documentary about his mother's League that aired on public television in 1987. Hollywood producer and director Penny Marshall saw the documentary and approached Candaele and Wilson about the possibility of a feature film about the League.

The result was "A League of Their Own," released in 1992, a comedy about the competitive and loving relationship between two fictional sisters, one a catcher for the Peaches, the other a pitcher for the Racine Belles. Set within a Hollywood-inspired, semi-realistic version of the League's first season, the movie became a major hit, grossing $107.1 million for Columbia Pictures in the first six months of its release.

Some of the players themselves made it into the movie. The film began and ended with scenes from a reenactment of the Hall of Fame opening that included a ballgame among women from the original League who had auditioned for the chance to play once more, this time before millions of fans in theaters.

The movie was positively reviewed ("a good movie, amiable and ingratiating,")[81] and turned out to be a hit with the players. Realistic action shots of hitting, catching, throwing and sliding clearly showed how hard they worked and played. There was plenty of dust and sweat in the movie as well as funny scenes of Charm School and the League's other exploitations of femininity. Doris Sams reviewed the movie in a letter printed in the April 1993 newsletter:

> I thought the movie was very funny. Everybody I talked to enjoyed it. I told them I thought it was about thirty percent truth and seventy percent Hollywood. All in all it made a pretty good story.

The women were initially apprehensive at how a Hollywood comedy might treat them. By now, almost everyone has seen it more than once, but that first time was scary. I too had to swallow my fears to get myself to the theatre, afraid of what popular culture might do to my memories.

Irene Applegren recalls how nervous she was at first.

> I didn't care too much for it the first time; some of the things the coach did made me kind of angry. But I really liked it the second time. I could laugh then. I thought it was a cute movie.

Dottie Key had the same experience, her critical mind evaluating things the first time through, her feelings taking over in later viewings.

> The first time I went to see it I was paying attention to particular scenes. The second time I sat back and really watched. I sat there and I cried and I cried and I cried, because all the memories came back. Especially when they played our song.

Dottie had a lot more self control than I did; I started crying at the opening credits the first time through. I was simply overwhelmed with an awareness of how much I had missed my heroes. It was as if, having been deprived of the thrill for thirty-eight years, a season of girls' baseball was beginning again.

The players naturally paid close attention to how the film portrayed their technical skills, and they disagree about how well the movie did in this respect. Some think the actresses and their doubles did a creditable job; others feel more like Applegren: "If you really looked at them, most of them couldn't throw the ball." Snookie Doyle liked the movie and felt it was valuable in bringing the League to the public's attention, but—ever an Allington protegé—she still worries about getting the rules right. In one scene rock star Madonna, who plays center field, snares a pop fly in her hat. Snookie frets, "I just hope moviegoers realize that we know the rule that catchin' the ball in a hat would be a free base, not an out."

Reportedly the actresses who worked on the film were diligent in their baseball practice and concerned that they represent the players the best they could. The producer told *Entertainment Weekly* that, "The first question they asked me after we had a rough cut was, 'How did I look playing ball?'"[82] But no actress, regardless of effort, can hope to satisfy a professional baseball player. The players took it with a sense of humor, though. As Pepper Paire said in a newsletter piece, "I only wish they had actresses who could play ball. Everybody knows ballplayers can act!"

Just before the movie was released, Columbia Pictures promoters informed every newspaper, radio and television station in every town in the country where a League ballplayer lived that not only was this entertaining picture coming out, but they had an original ballplayer in their back yard.

The players were inundated with calls for interviews, to the extent that Dottie Key became sick with the stress. Rose Gacioch was interviewed incessantly, then treated to the opening of the movie in her nearby town. The next day she got thirty-two phone calls from friends wanting to celebrate her fame. As she says, "There's too much going on."

The ballplayers were celebrities again, and as Helen Ketola LaCamera admitted, "I truly came out of that movie with a little puffed-up chest." Helen Waddell Wyatt discovered that her new-found fame preceded her everywhere.

A little while after the movie came out I walked into my doctor's office for my yearly check-up. I'm sitting on the table, totally naked, with one of those little paper drapes over me.

Now my doctor is this older German fellow, very quiet, very businesslike, never says much. This time he walked in with a grin on his face from ear to ear. In the twenty-five years I've gone to this doctor I've never seen him grin like that. He says, "I am in the presence of greatness! I didn't know you were a ballplayer, Helen. That's fantastic!" He just started gushing and going on and on, and I'm sitting there naked!

Mary Rountree, who had been so careful throughout her career not to burden fellow physicians with information about her athletic past, found herself forced into prominence.

The regular speaker didn't show up one Friday for a seminar I always attended at a local hospital. So one of the general surgeons stood up and said, "We've got a celebrity in our bunch." He described the movie and the League and then said, "I can't believe the Mary that I've known all my life has got all this notoriety, and I never knew anything about it. So, why don't we get Mary to come up and tell us about playing ball?"

I almost fell off the chair. Well, I had to get up and talk. So I kept 'em amused for about forty minutes, and not many of 'em left. Everybody was sayin',' "Mary, how wonderful!" and such things. It was a very rewarding hour. Now they come up to me and say, "Mary, you got to tell us some more about the baseball."

Depending on personality, some of the players revel in the new fame, others enjoyed it at the beginning but will be glad when it's over. But regardless of their private opinions, all have fielded the questions just like they used to field grounders, with consistency, pride in their work and flashes of brilliance.

Four players representing the Players' Association were honored at Washington State University. Charlene "Shorty" Pryer Mayer reported in the newsletter,

Between games we were invited on the field and, as they called our names, we went out to the coach who put a WSU ball cap on our heads and hugged us. Except Penny [O'Brien Cooke]. When they called her name she ran out and slid into home plate. Everybody roared!

I asked the players which they valued most, their recognition by the Hall of Fame, or their celebrity status thanks to the movie. Marie Mansfield Kelley thought about it a while.

> It was because of the movie, not the display in Cooperstown, that everybody in the country now knows about the League. The Hall of Fame didn't make anybody else know about it, only us ballplayers and whoever we told. So it's a tough question.
>
> I guess as far as importance, I'd say the picture. But as far as personal satisfaction, I'd say the Hall of Fame.

Marilyn Jones Doxey had a slightly different slant on the choice I posed for her.

> I think it's tremendous to have the exhibit. I'd have to go for the exhibit being more important to me, even though less people know about it. Because it's us; it's not a story written about us.

A theme of this account of the All-American Girls Baseball League has been the clash of image and reality: the feminine image projected by the League versus the reality of playing a demanding physical sport; the middle-class image versus the working-class backgrounds of the girls; the post-League married-with-children image versus the fact that a majority of the players became independent single women or lesbians.

The existence of the movie adds a new dimension to this matter of image versus reality. While exposing millions of moviegoers to the fact that the League existed, the movie paints its own Hollywood version of what the League was like. Once upon a time no one except we privileged few knew about the League; now everyone knows about a fictional version of the League. The 1990s portrayal threatens to superimpose itself upon the reality of the 1940s and 1950s, eventually replacing Wrigley's vision with Penny Marshall's.

Even the players can get confused. Marilyn Jones Doxey blithely issues this statement which, if you think about it, is surreal: "It was exciting when the movie come out, and I found out I had been part of that." It used to be that when Helen Callaghan's major-league-playing son came up to bat, the television announcers said something like, "Here's Casey Candaele, whose mother once played in a women's professional baseball league in the 1940s." Just the other day I heard them say, "Here's Casey Candaele, whose mother was portrayed in the movie 'A League of Their Own.'"

The players are probably not as concerned about the movie replacing the reality of the League in the public's mind as I am. They know from their playing days that sports is a branch of the entertainment industry, and that image is important to the box office. If the movie image creates a public interest in the reality of the League, and if the players themselves can tell people how it really was, then hurrah for the movie. These women, after all, were willing to don skirts if someone would pay them to play ball. Now they're willing to don clip-on microphones if someone will let them talk about the real League.

The November/December 1992 issue of the newsletter included this letter from the director of the Texas Baptist Children's Home.

> I want to thank you for your time and the information you provided during our recent phone call. I did happen to see you on the Home Box Office behind-the-scenes television special about "A League of Their Own," and my girls were captivated that the AAGPBL was real. Just knowing that I had spoken to you made the girls feel special.
>
> One of my girls, Becky, is now wanting to get back into softball. She's a good athlete, but she felt awkward being able to beat the boys at their own game. Now she's telling me that she doesn't care what they think, and that she is going to play whatever sport she wants to.
>
> Thank you again and God Bless you.

◆◆◆

With all the hoopla of the movie, it is indeed a struggle to remember how it really was, how hard the girls played, how many games were piled one upon another upon another, how much the strawberries hurt, how long and hot the bus rides were, how sometimes only a few fans showed up. It's hard to remember how some rookies lasted less than a season, and how some teams folded and how almost everyone got traded.

Through it all the girls just kept playing hard, thinking ahead, hoping for a lucky break, working the pitcher, counting horses, eating tomatoes, enduring the losses and, thank you God, celebrating the victories.

Dottie Key has a way of describing the doggedness of herself and her teammates: "We were all mudders then," she says.

The 1950 championship series was postponed by rain once, had to be changed to a less soggy field twice, was played in a drizzle much of the time, and is always remembered by the players as "the time we played in all that rain." The 1950 Peaches and Daisies were mudders.

The last time I saw any All-Americans play baseball was in 1992 in Fort Wayne. The Indiana reunions have always featured an exhibition game between anyone who ever played for the Daisies and everyone else, collectively called the All-Stars. On this day, September 26, 1992, I joined a good crowd collected at a local stadium, excited to watch fifty- and sixty-some-year-old women play ball once again.

Just as the players were warming up, exercising creaky joints, stretching tight muscles and getting a feel for the ball, a slight rain began to fall. As the teams were being organized and the rules agreed to, the skies opened up. The players hunched into their jackets, looked around and saw all the fans who'd showed up, now huddled under coats and umbrellas. There was really no question of what they would do. Being the home team, the Daisies took the field. Dottie Collins pitched.

Getting down for those grounders was impossible, but fly balls were a cinch. Batting was so-so, running was slow, throwing was accurate. There was a lot of good chatter and laughter; the spirit was there.

But the field conditions were terrible; very soon there was standing water around the plate, the bases, and at shortstop. Only one woman actually fell down in the mud, a young umpire. But all were in danger, and sooner or later someone was going to get hurt. Sensible minds prevailed, and the game lasted only one inning. I didn't keep score, but I bet they did.

I doubt, though, that who won or lost mattered this time. They had played, like the All-Americans they are. I had gotten to see Dottie Kamenshek bat one more time. And, as we were all leaving the ballpark I overheard a dripping Dottie Collins say to a soaked teammate, "It's a good thing we played 'cause I heard a woman tell her husband, 'That was wonderful.'"

Afterword

I began this story of the All-American Girls Baseball League in a bittersweet mood and I need to end it in the same spirit. While public events have catapulted the women of the League into an exhilarating if sometimes exhausting prominence, there is a more somber side to their lives. Given their age, it is fitting that the newsletters are full of concerns about the serious illness of some teammates and the deaths of others.

Many of the people who played a part in the story of the 1950 Peaches and Daisies have died: Rockford's pitcher Lois Florreich, second baseman Charlene Barnett, left fielder Squirt Callow, utility player Jackie Kelley, chaperone Dottie Green, and manager Bill Allington; and Fort Wayne's left fielder Sally Meier and manager Max Carey.

The women of the League are aware of their own mortality, and they mourn the deaths of their buddies with imagery from their lives together. A teammate's eulogy for Mary "Windy" Reynolds, a Peoria Redwing from 1947 through 1951, read in part, "I'm sure Windy is up there in the Diamond in the Sky waiting for the rest of us, so we can start a new Heavenly League."

Another newsletter reported that, when the time was right, Jean Lovell Dowler, who played from 1948 to 1954, had planned exactly the funeral she wanted before she had herself taken off her kidney dialysis machine: "She ordered an arrangement of yellow roses with her catcher's mitt in the center, and when they closed the casket, the mitt went inside."

Pepper Paire Davis, who played from 1944 to 1953 and who composed the League's victory song, writes a regular column from California for the newsletter. Here Pepper is eulogizing Philomena Gianfrancisco Zale, a player from 1945 to 1949, wishing for her what all the players would most wish for themselves, could they really work miracles.

So sorry to hear of "Frisco's" sudden passing...I'm sure Frisco has reported for "Spring Training" and joined our "Heavenly Team" up there on "Cloud Nine." Think about it Gals! They'll be running, swinging that bat, and circling those bases! All the aches and pains will be gone! The sound of pure laughter will fill the air! Sure, we miss them, but—God Bless them—they'll be young again. So let's be glad for them!

Pepper reminds her readers—who of course don't need reminding—of the reality they all face: "Get together all you can, gals. Time is slipping away from us."

Once the women who played baseball in the 1940s and 1950s are gone, what will become of their history? Their experience may easily slip back into obscurity, the fact that women once played baseball unknown and disbelieved. The hold on public comprehension is fragile even now. Terry Donahue, who played from 1946 to 1949, reported a recent experience that does not inspire confidence in our ability to retain knowledge that contradicts stereotypes. Donahue, hospitalized for some heart problems, reported,

> I was in my room watching "A League of Their Own." One of the nurses asked what it was about, so I explained it was about the AAGPBL, and I was one of the original players. I also said I had met Madonna and some of the other stars of the movie. She looked at me so strangely as if to say, "that poor lady, they should be checking her head, not her heart." Two other nurses came and started questioning me. They watched the movie a few minutes and said they had never heard of any girls playing baseball in skirts. They gave me a strange look and left.

The development that would ensure that our culture remembers the All-American Girls Baseball League would be the creation of a new baseball league for women. If women played baseball today, we would have less trouble believing that they played baseball yesterday. Current players would be carrying on a time-honored, hallowed sports tradition of which the Bloomer Girls and the All-Americans were simply pioneers. The first, not the only.

Is it not sad for all of us that women playing baseball is regarded as a miracle, a fluke of history if you will, instead of being enjoyed as a routine part of our daily life?

I for one want more. I want to be able to cheer for my Rockford

Peaches now, not just remember them then. I want to go to the ballpark and watch women playing baseball. I want to root for the home team. I want to see their games on television. I want to wait for the scores on the evening news. I want to read about them in the sports pages every morning. And, yes, I want to get their autographs and keep them for the next forty years.

I want us to take women's baseball for granted. If that became a reality, it would be the All-Americans' proudest legacy. And they would, I know, watch every game from their box seats in the sky.

TEAM ROSTERS

Rockford Peaches and Fort Wayne Daisies

1950 Season

Rockford Peaches

Amy Irene "Lefty" Applegren: pitcher. Also played first base and right field. Had a long, successful career in baseball, in both the underhand and overhand eras. Years: 1944 to 1953. Home town: Peoria, Illinois.

Charlene "Barnie" Barnett: batted fifth and played second base. A critical part of Rockford's fine infield. Years: 1947 to 1950. Home town: near Chicago, Illinois.

Eleanor "Squirt" Callow: batted sixth and played left field. Lighthearted, and liked to hassle rookies. Years: 1948-54. Hometown: Winnipeg, Manitoba, Canada.

Dorothy "Snookie" Doyle: batted second and played shortstop. A team leader and frequent All-Star. Years: 1944-50 and 1952. Home town: Los Angeles, California.

Louise "Lou" Erickson: pitcher. 16 wins, 10 losses in 1950. One of three principal Rockford starters. Years: 1948 to 1950. Hometown: Arcadia, Wisconsin.

Lois Florreich: pitcher. Rockford's ace, threw an intimidating fastball. 20 wins, 8 losses during 1950 season, but injured during championship series. Years: 1943 to 1950. Home town: Midwest, near southern Illinois.

Helen Nichol "Nickie" Fox: batted eighth and pitched Rockford's first, fourth, fifth (in relief) and seventh games. Lifetime earned-run average of 1.89. Years: 1943-52 plus home games in 1953 and 1954. Home town: Ardley, Alberta, Canada.

Rose "Rosie" Gacioch: batted clean-up and played right field. Linked the early professional "Bloomer Girl" teams with the All-American League. Record for assists from right field. Later pitched. Years: 1944-54. Home town: Wheeling, West Virginia.

Marilyn "Jonesy" Jones: batted seventh, a rookie and backup catcher. Got her chance to play in the 1950 playoffs and championship. Later, after being traded, pitched a no-hitter against the Peaches. Years: 1950-54. Home town: Providence, Rhode Island.

Dorothy "Kammie" Kamenshek: led off and played first base. The best first baseman in the League, some think the best all-around player. Led League in batting 1946, 1947. Years: 1943-53. Home town: Cincinnati, Ohio.

Jackie "Babe" Kelley: batted third and played third base. Utility player who could play anywhere, and pitch. Replaced Alice Pollitt in the championship series and played well. Years: 1947-53. Home town: Lansing, Michigan.

Dorothy "Dottie" Ferguson Key: batted ninth and played center field. Determined to make the League. Adept at being hit by pitches to get on base. Effective base-stealer. Years: 1945-54, all for Peaches. Home town: Virden, Manitoba, Canada.

Marie "Boston" Mansfield: pitcher. A rookie in 1950, backed up Gacioch in right field, but soon became a pitcher. Years: 1950 to 1954. Home town: Jamaica Plain, Massachusetts.

Alice "Al" Pollitt: third base. A fine fielder, injured toward end of regular season and sat on the bench during the championship series. Years: 1947 to 1953. Home town: Lansing, Michigan.

Ruth "Richie" Richard: catcher. Injured at end of regular season, Richard, a perennial All-Star, sat out the 1950 championship series. Years: 1947 to 1954. Home town: Argus, Pennsylvania.

Helen "Sis" Waddell: utility infielder. Useful supporting player, a rookie in 1950. Years: 1949-1951. Home town: Lemoyne, Pennsylvania.

Manager and Chaperone

Bill Allington: Manager. The winningest manager in the history of the League, an excellent baseball stategist and a firm disciplinarian.

Allington's Rockford Peaches won two pennants and four championships from 1945 to 1950, and his Fort Wayne Daisies won two pennants in 1953 and 1954. Managed: 1944 to 1946; 1948 to 1954. Home town: Los Angeles, California.

Dorothy "Dottie" Green: Chaperone. After an injury ended her playing career as the regular Peaches catcher, Green became their chaperone in 1948. Greatly respected in both roles. Years: 1943 to 1947; Chaperone 1948, 1950 to 1953. Home town: Natick, Massachusetts.

Fort Wayne Daisies

Kay "Swish" Blumetta: pitcher. Long career with five different teams. Years: 1944 to 1954. Home town: North Plainfield, New Jersey.

Wilma "Willie" Briggs: batted second and played right field. A team player whose job was to move the runner along. Years: 1948-54. Officer of Players' Association. Home town: East Greenwich, Rhode Island.

Dorothy "Dottie" Wiltse Collins: pitcher. Adapted easily from underhand to overhand pitching. Four-time 20-game winner. One season kept pitching while four months pregnant. Treasurer of Players' Association. Years: 1944 to 1948 and 1950, all for the Daisies. Home town: Los Angeles, California.

Millie Deegan: pitcher. 1950 regular-season record of 16 wins, 9 losses, but roughed up in championship series. Years: 1943 to 1952. Home town: Brooklyn, New York.

Thelma "Tiby" Eisen: leadoff batter and centerfielder. A base-stealing threat, Tiby's knowledge of the game enabled her to manage several teams for short periods of time. Years: 1944-52. Home town: Los Angeles, California.

Betty Weaver Foss: batted fourth, "clean-up," and played third base. A rookie in 1950 who won the batting crown that year with a .346 average. Won again the next year. One of three ball-playing Weaver sisters. Years: 1950-54. Home town: Metropolis, Illinois.

Frances "Fran" Janssen: relief pitcher. Useful in replacing starters when they tired. Active in Players' Association. Years: 1948 to 1952. Home town: Remington, Indiana.

Vivian "Kelly" Kellogg: batted seventh and played first base. Played entire career with Daisies. A power hitter. Years: 1944-50. Home town: Jackson, Michigan.

Helen Ketola: utility infielder. A rookie in 1950, Helen was inspired to play baseball by Mary Pratt, her junior high teacher and an earlier All-American. Years: 1950 only. Home town: Quincy, Massachusetts.

Maxine "Max" Kline: batted ninth and pitched the first, fourth and sixth games of the 1950 championship series. Fort Wayne's ace. All-Star pitcher five of the seven years she played: 1948-54. Home town: Addison, Michigan.

Betty Luna: pitcher. Luna was traded for Sally Meier during the 1950 season. Years: 1944 to 1950. Home town: Los Angeles, California.

Ruth Matlock: left-handed pitcher, in relief role in 1950, her rookie season. Excellent hitter with 13 hits in 36 at-bats. Years: 1950 only. Home town: Cornwells Heights, Pennsylvania.

Naomi "Sally" Meier: batted fifth and played left field. Acquired in trade during 1950 season. Decided third game of championship series with a bases-loaded double. Home town: Fort Wayne, Indiana.

Norma Metrolis: catcher, backup to both Rountree and Vonderau. A steady player, Metrolis got little chance to play and was traded during the season. Years: 1946 to 1950. Home town: Orlando, Florida.

Mary Rountree: batted eighth and played catcher. Played ball for the money to enter medical school. Years: 1946-52. Home town: Miami, Florida.

Edna "Bunny" Scheer: pitcher. Largely used in relief role. Years: 1950 only. Home state: Wisconsin.

Dorothy "Dottie" Schroeder: batted sixth and played shortstop. Many felt the most graceful player in the League. Signature pigtails. Years: 1943-54, the only woman to play all twelve seasons. Home town: Sadorus, Illinois.

Kathryn "Kate" Vonderau: catcher. Backup to Rountree, Vonderau actually caught the championship series after Game Two. Officer of Players' Association. Years: 1946 to 1953. Home town: Fort Wayne, Indiana.

Evelyn "Evie" Wawryshyn: batted third and played second base. 1950 was her All-Star year. Hit .520 in the championship series. Years: 1946-51. Home town: Tyndall, Manitoba, Canada.

Joanne "Jo" Weaver: Betty Foss' younger sister, Jo was only fifteen years old in 1950 and legally couldn't play. Fort Wayne didn't want to lose her, however, so she hung out with the team all season, learning. Became a batting and base-stealing champion. Years: 1951 to 1954. Home town: Metropolis, Illinois.

Trois Wood: utility player. A rookie in 1950. Home state: Pennsylvania.

Manager and Chaperone

Max Carey: Manager. Carey played twenty years of major league baseball for the Pittsburgh Pirates (1910-1926) and the Brooklyn Dodgers (1926-1929). For ten of those years he lead the majors in stolen bases. Inducted into the Hall of Fame in 1961.

Carey was President of the All-American League from 1945 to 1949 and managed two teams, the Milwaukee Chicks (who won the pennant in 1944), and the Fort Wayne Daisies (in 1950 and 1951). Home town: Terre Haute, Indiana.

Doris Tetzlaff: Coach-chaperone. Tetzlaff played infield for several teams from 1944 to 1949. She became Fort Wayne's chaperone in 1950 and also acted as an assistant coach to manager Max Carey. Years: 1944 to 1949; Chaperone 1950 to 1953. Home town: Watertown, Wisconsin.

Notes

Preface

1. The term "girls," sensibly regarded since the emergence of the modern feminist movement as pejorative unless it describes females under age eighteen or so, was not so regarded by the players themselves at the time. Nor do the players now think of themselves as having been "women." They were girls then and they are proud to be girls now. I have thus stayed true to their spirit and use the two words, girls and women, interchangeably.

2. The most important research decision involved choosing who to interview. According to a 1992 Newsletter of the All-American Girls Professional Baseball League Players' Association, five hundred fifty-eight women played in the twelve years of the League, and fourteen different cities at one time or another fielded teams. Thus, writing about the League is a large and complex undertaking.

Since I wanted to learn the players' stories in depth, and to pay special attention to their relationships with each other and to the specifics of playing the game, I chose to focus on one year, 1950. Nearly all of the women who played for the Peaches and Daisies in 1950 who are available to be interviewed—twenty-six of twenty-nine players—agreed to in-depth interviews. I talked with each player for anywhere from one to three hours, either in their homes, at the 1992 mini-reunion in Fort Wayne, or by phone.

Both the manager and chaperone of any team are, of course, central to that team's experience and performance. Because Bill Allington and Max Carey, the managers of Rockford and Fort Wayne respectively, have died, I interviewed another manager, Leo Schrall. Now eighty-five years old, Leo guided the Peoria (Illinois) Redwings for fourteen games at the end of the 1947 season ("We had 11 wins and 3 losses"), and for the full seasons of 1948 and 1949. I also had to search beyond the two teams for a chaperone to interview. I found Millie Lundahl, who played this critical role during the Peaches' 1947 and 1948 seasons.

The roster of each of these teams listed seventeen players plus the manager and chaperone. A few other players qualified as members of these two teams because of trades during the season. The total pool of players, managers and chaperones I thus wanted to locate was forty. Of the nineteen Peaches, six have died (four players, the chaperone and the manager). I was unable to make contact with one living player. I conducted interviews with the twelve remaining Peaches, nine in person and three over the phone.

There were twenty-one Daisies on the 1950 team, including the manager and chaperone. The manager and one player are known to be dead, two players have not been located and one was located too late to be interviewed. Two Daisies whom I contacted did not want to be interviewed. I conducted interviews with fourteen Daisies, five in person, eight by phone, and one by written questionnaire.

I thus was able to talk at some length with twenty-six of the forty participants on these two teams. All the interviews were conducted from September to December, 1992.

I conducted interviews with the following players:

Rockford: Amy Irene Applegren, Alice Pollitt Deschaine, Marilyn Jones Doxey, Dorothy Harrell Doyle, Helen Nichol Fox, Rose Gacioch, Dorothy Kamenshek, Marie Mansfield Kelley, Dorothy Ferguson Key, Ruth Richard, Louise Erickson Sauer and Helen Waddell Wyatt.

The Peaches who were unavailable to be interviewed were: Edna Scheer, not located; and the six who are deceased: manager Bill Allington, chaperone Dorothy Green, pitcher Lois Florreich, second baseman Charlene Barnett, leftfielder Eleanor Callow, and utility infielder Jackie Kelley.

Fort Wayne: Wilma Briggs, Dorothy Wiltse Collins, Thelma Eisen, Betty Weaver Foss, Frances Janssen, Vivian Kellogg, Helen Ketola LaCamera, Norma Metrolis, Evelyn Wawryshyn Litwin Moroz, Maxine Kline Randall, Mary Rountree, Dorothy Schroeder and Kathryn Vonderau. Kay Blumetta sent information by questionnaire.

The Daisies unavailable for interviewing were: deceased, manager Max Carey and leftfielder Naomi "Sally" Meier; located too late for an interview, pitcher Ruth Matlock Sagrati; not located, utility player Trois Wood, and outfielder Betty Luna; and, declining to be interviewed, pitcher Millie Deegan and chaperone Doris Tetzlaff.

For a variety of reasons, I interviewed six other individuals: 1951 Fort Wayne rookie, Joanne Weaver, Peoria Redwings manager Leo Schrall, earlier Peaches chaperone Mildred Lundahl, League historian Sharon

Roepke, Peaches fan and "farm team" player, Colleen Holmbeck, and Minneapolis, earlier Fort Wayne and Peoria player Faye Dancer.

3. Whenever I quote an individual, the source is the interview I conducted with them, unless otherwise indicated.

4. Throughout most of this book I use the names under which the women played in 1950. In Chapters Six and Seven, where I discuss the players' current lives, I use married names for those women who got married. Thus, for example, Helen Waddell becomes Helen Waddell Wyatt at the end of the book.

History

5. The League underwent several name changes in the course of its history. In 1943 it was the All-American Girls Softball League, but this name was changed during the first season. By 1954 it was called the American Girls Baseball League. The current Players' Association refers to the League as the All-American Girls Professional Baseball League. I have chosen to call the League by the name I knew it as in 1950: the All-American Girls Baseball League.

6. Handwritten (undated) description of the early history of the League by Ken Sells, its first president. Available at the League's official archives, the All-American Girls Professional Baseball League Collection, Northern Indiana Historical Society, South Bend, Indiana.

7. All-American Baseball League Manual (Management Corporation, All-American Girls' Baseball League, 550 Wrigley Building, Chicago, Illinois, undated), p. 8.

8. The comparable dimensions for the men's game of baseball are: 90-foot base paths, 60 feet 6 inches from pitcher's rubber to plate, and a ball 9 to 9-¼ inches in circumference. Both overhand and sidearm pitching are allowed.

9. Barbara Gregorich, *Women at Play: The Story of Women in Baseball* (New York, Harcourt Brace & Co., 1993), p. 129. The account of the game is from Jack Fincher, "The 'Belles of the Ball Game' were a hit with their fans," *Smithsonian*, Vol. 20, No. 4 (July, 1989).

10. Rickey Henderson holds the major league single-season record with 130 bases stolen in 1982. By the end of the 1993 season, Henderson also led the majors with his career total 1,095 steals. Henderson has played for fifteen years, while Kurys compiled her record in a career that lasted nine years.

11. According to statistics available in *The Baseball Encyclopedia*, the best single-season batting average in the history of professional league baseball (for players with at least 300 at-bats) is that of Dobie Moore who, in 1924, hit .453 (307 at-bats) for the Negro League Kansas City Monarchs. Joanne Weaver's .429 average ties her for fourth overall, behind only Moore, Hugh Duffy (.438 in 539 at-bats, 1894) and Tip O'Neill (.435 in 517 at-bats, 1887), and tied with Ross Barnes (.429 in 322 at-bats, 1876).

The highest batting average for a male major-league player this century is Rogers Hornsby's .424 (536 at-bats), accomplished in 1924. The last male major-leaguer to bat over.400 was Ted Williams, who hit.406 (in 456 at-bats) in 1941. Negro League player Artie Wilson, of the Birmingham Black Barons, hit .402 (in 333 at-bats) in 1948.

Game One

12. Dick Day, *Rockford Register-Republic*, September 1, 1950. Both Rockford and Fort Wayne had two newspapers in 1950. We thus have available the observations and accounts of four different sportswriters of the time, Dick Day of the *Rockford Register-Republic*, Harry D. Milnes of the *Rockford Morning Star*, Bob Reed of the *Fort Wayne Journal-Gazette*, and Phil Olofson of the *Fort Wayne News-Sentinel*. Used with permission of the *Rockford Register Star*, the *Fort Wayne Journal Gazette* and the *Fort Wayne News-Sentinel*.

13. Dick Day, *Rockford Register-Republic*, September 5, 1950.

14. Bob Reed, *Fort Wayne Journal-Gazette*, September 6, 1950.

15. Dick Day, *Rockford Register-Republic*, September 9, 1950.

Early Innings

16. The common appelation "tomboy" has a frustrating etymology, or rather lack thereof. *Brewer's Dictionary of Phrase and Fable*, 14th Edition (1989) simply defines tomboy as "a romping girl."*The Oxford Dictionary of English Etymology* (1983 printing) defines tomboy as a "bold boy or woman; wild romping girl." Neither source offers anything about the origins of the peculiar word except by implication, as the word appears along with a list of other "tom" words, like tomfoolery and tom cat. The prefix "Tom", is used to indicate an anonymous man or boy, like John Doe, as in "every Tom, Dick and Harry." It comes from the British practice of using Thomas Atkins as the official generic name in their Army manuals. But if "tom" is a generic male name, why isn't the word "tomgirl"?

17. Most of the women played for more than one team and for several years in the course of their All-American career. When I describe someone as, for example, the Fort Wayne shortstop, I mean she held this position in the year we are focusing on, 1950.

18. Of the twenty-six players I talked to, nine did come from rural areas or very small towns (population 1,000 or less), but four came from small cities (with a population under 50,000), seven were raised in or on the outskirts of medium-sized cities (around 100,000), and six were from major metropolitan areas: three from Los Angeles, two from Boston, and one from Cincinnati.

19. Eighteen of the twenty-six players I interviewed had older brothers. Five of the girls were born second to a single older brother. The others were born third or later, with one or more older brothers. Ten players were either the youngest in a family that included older brothers (eight girls) or second to the youngest in large families of eight and ten children respectively (two girls).

By contrast, only nine of the players had older sisters. Only one player, Irene Applegren, had one older sister (and a twin sister) and no older brothers.

Four of the players were only-children.

20. Allen Guttman, *A Whole New Ball Game* (Chapel Hill, North Carolina: University of North Carolina Press, 1988), pp. 56-59. The quotes that follow come from the same source.

21. Ten women categorized their families as working-class, three as working-class tending toward poorer than that, and five as unquestionably poor. Only three players consider their families to have been middle-class. Five of the girls were from family farms, a category all its own when one is considering class background.

22. Blanche Wiesen Cook, *Eleanor Roosevelt*, Vol. I (New York: Viking Penguin, 1992), p. 493.

23. Susan Brownmiller, *Femininity* (New York: Ballantine Books, 1985), p. 148.

Game Two

24. The second-highest All-Star vote-getter was Doris Satterfield, a Grand Rapids outfielder, with seventy-eight votes.

25. Lois Browne, *Girls of Summer*, (Toronto, Canada: Harper Collins Publishing Ltd., 1992) p. 149.

Wilma Briggs

26. Browne, p. 139.

27. According to the Columbia University College of Physicians and Surgeons, a "charley horse" occurs under these conditions: "When a ligament suffers an acute strain or sprain due to sudden stretching, the muscle fibers tear and blood may collect in a small area under the skin. Tenderness, pain and local swelling usually are present." *Complete Home Medical Guide* (New York: Crown Publishers, 1985), p. 562.

28. An "assist" is an official statistical category meaning the fielding or throwing of a baseball in such a way that a teammate is able to put out a runner. In the case of the Peaches, Gacioch would throw from right field to Kamenshek at first for the out. Gacioch is credited with the assist, Kamenshek with the put-out.

Playing to Win

29. The average salary for a white male National or American League player at the time was the government-imposed wage freeze of $6,400 for a 154 game season, approximately $250 a week. Salaries for African-American men in the Negro Leagues in the early 1940s averaged about $1,250 for a five-month season or $57 a week.

30. Andy Seiler, *The Courier-News*, Plainfield, New Jersey, June 28, 1992.

31. By 1954, the last year of the League, the ball was 9 to 9-¼ inches, the mound 60 feet from home, and the basepaths 85 feet long.

32. *Rockford Register-Republic*, May 9, 1950.

33. Greg Cote, *The Miami Herald*, July 11, 1991.

34. Quoted by Barbara Gregorich in an interview with umpire Emil Pietrangeli, *The Milwaukee Journal*, June 28, 1992.

Life Off the Field

35. All-American Girls Baseball League Chaperone's Contract (between Dottie Green and the Rockford Girls Professional Ball Club, Wilbur E. Johnson, President), March 19, 1948.

36. Browne, p. 194.

37. For instance, Sue Macy reports that an African-American woman, Toni Stone, in 1953 played around fifty games for a men's Negro League

team, the Indianapolis Clowns. *A Whole New Ball Game*, (New York, Henry Holt & Co., 1993). p. 53.

38. Barbara Gregorich, *Women at Play*, p. 153.

39. The wording is from Dottie Green's Chaperone's Contract, 1948.

40. "Rules of Conduct of the 1954 Peaches," Rockford Girls' Baseball Club, Inc., p. 2.

Game Four

41. Phil Olofson, "Our Daisies," Fort Wayne Daisies Program and Score Book, 1950, p. 9.

42. This apparently low number of home runs was enough to tie her with teammate Dottie Schroeder for second place in the League home run standings for 1950 (Rockford's Eleanor Callow and Racine's Sophie Kurys tied for first with seven home runs), evidence of the fact that the All-Americans were not long-ball hitters.

43. *Fort Wayne News-Sentinel*, July 31, August 12 and 30, 1950.

44. *Rockford Register-Republic*, May 15 and 24, 1950.

45. All descriptions are from the *Fort Wayne News-Sentinel*, July 12, 19, 31, and August 12 and 29, 1950.

Looking Like Girls, Playing Like Men

46. Herb Graffis, "Belles of the Ball Game," *Liberty* magazine, October 16, 1943.

47. All the quotes in this section specifying the League's code of conduct come from the All-American Girls Baseball League Manual.

48. *Liberty*, October 21, 1944; *World Herald*, undated, from Ann O'Dowd papers, AAGPBL Collection, Northern Indiana Historical Society; *Holiday*, June, 1952.

49. *Rockford Register-Republic*, August 17, 1943; *South Bend Tribune*, August 17, 1943.

50. *South Bend Tribune*, May 31, 1943.

51. Browne, p. 27.

52. Sue Macy, "Diamonds and Lace," *Los Angeles Daily News*, January 22, 1984.

53. All-American Girls' Professional Baseball League Players' Association Newsletter, April, 1992, p. 27.

54. Susan M. Cahn, "No Freaks, No Amazons, No Boyish Bobs," *Chicago History*, Spring 1989, p. 35.

55. *Rockford Register-Republic*, September 4, 1950.

Dorothy Kamenshek

56. From an article quoting the United Press International wire-service account, in Irene Applegren's files. Undated, but appeared during the 1950 season.

57. Quoted in the *Rockford Register-Republic*, May 16, 1950.

58. United Press International wire-service account, *op. cit.*

The Play of the Game

59. At the beginning major-league men's baseball also changed its rules. Some things, however, have never changed. When the National League was formed in 1876, the basepaths were 90 feet long and have remained so to this day. Likewise baseball has retained the stipulations of nine men in the field, three strikes to record an out, and three outs to retire a side.

Pitching, however, was underhand at the game's beginning. In 1889 overhand pitching was introduced, the pitching distance was increased to 50 feet, and 4 balls qualified as a walk (4 balls had been considered a hit before). In 1893 the pitcher's rubber and the raised mound were instituted, and the pitching distance was increased again, to 60 feet 6 inches, where it has remained until this day.

While, like the female players of the 1940s and 1950s, the early professional male players had to adapt to changes, after the first seventeen years the male game stabilized. Presumably, had the All-American League continued, it would have reached a similar equilibrium.

60. The following chart of AAGPBL Rules and Equipment Changes is taken from Sue Macy, *A Whole New Ball Game*, p. 111. Macy's source for the chart was Merrie A. Fidler's Master's Thesis, "The Development and Decline of the All-American Girls Baseball League, 1943-1954," University of Massachusetts Department of Physical Education, September, 1976, p. 110.

AAGPBL RULES AND EQUIPMENT CHANGES

Year	Circumference of Ball	Length of Basepaths	Pitching Distance	Pitching Style
1943	12 inches	65 feet	40 feet	Underhand
1944	11½ inches	68 feet	"	"
1945	"	"	42 feet	"
1946	11 inches	72 feet	43 feet	Underhand and Sidearm

Year	Circumference of Ball	Length of Basepaths	Pitching Distance	Pitching Style
1947	"	"	"	Sidearm Only
1948	10⅜ inches	"	50 feet	Overhand and Sidearm*
1949	10 inches	"	55 feet	"
1950	"	"	"	"
1951	"	"	"	"
1952	"	"	"	"
1953	"	75 feet	56 feet	"
1954	9 to 9¼ inches	85 feet**	60 feet***	"

* Same as in major-league baseball
** 5 feet shorter than major-league baseball
*** 6 inches shorter than major-league baseball

61. Ken Sells, "History," Northern Indiana Historical Society, Official Archives of the AAGPBL, handwritten notes. Undated, but Sells was describing the 1943 and 1944 seasons.

62. A classic example of impossible comparisons in the men's major leagues was the 1887 rule that counted bases on balls as hits, producing twenty.400 hitters. Batting averages for the year have since been recalculated to eliminate the effects of this rule, but the current *Baseball Enclyclopedia* objects to the practice: "For that year such records were official and latter-day statisticians violated historical canons by revamping them." *The Baseball Encyclopedia*, Ninth Edition (New York: Macmillan, 1993), p. 4.

63. The distinction and the description of the different styles come from *The Baseball Encyclopedia*, p. 5.

Rose Gacioch

64. Quoted in an article by Susan Smiley in *The Chronicle*, a Detroit suburban newspaper, July 22, 1992.

65. An excellent account of the early history of women and baseball can be found in Barbara Gregorich's *Women at Play* . Much of the information about Rose's early playing years comes from this book.

66. In 1931 Bert Niehoff was coaching the men's minor-league Chattanooga Lookouts who in March had signed a woman player, pitcher Jackie Mitchell. In an exhibition game that spring against the New York Yankees, Bert replaced his starting pitcher in the first inning after the Yankees' first two batters had hit a double and single and scored a run. Jackie Mitchell took the mound and struck out the number three hitter, Babe Ruth, and the number four, Lou Gehrig. Jackie walked the next batter, and Bert then reinstated his starting pitcher. Almost immediately the Commissioner of Baseball voided Mitchell's contract on the grounds that baseball was "too strenuous" for a woman. See the account in Gregorich,*Women at Play*, pp. 66 to 72.

67. The incident is reported in Gregorich, *Women at Play*, p. 117.

The Years After Baseball

68. *Kalamazoo Gazette*, September 8, 1954.

69. Browne, p. 146.

70. The statistic on marriage rates for women throughout the United States is supplied by Sue Macy, *A Whole New Ball Game* , p. 53.

71. Fincher, p. 96.

72. Mary Rountree remembers reading somewhere that there have been 125 father-son combinations in men's major-league baseball, and only one mother-son combination. Helen Callaghan Candaele St. Aubin played from 1944 through 1948 for the Minneapolis Millerettes and Fort Wayne Daisies. She married twice and had five sons.

Two of these sons have been important to baseball. Son Casey Candaele plays major-league baseball for the Houston Astros. Son Kelly produced and directed a 1986 documentary about his mother's league that was shown on public television and was the stimulus for Penny Marshall's 1992 movie "A League of Their Own."

73. Recent developments suggest that women's team sports may be achieving more acceptance. Thanks to legislation which requires schools receiving federal funding to provide equal facilities and funding

for male and female athletes, women's college team sports are receiving increased financial and fan support. Women's basketball and volleyball are especially successful. Amateur women's soccer and softball are both popular. And there are plans for professional women's leagues in both fast-pitch softball and baseball.

Game Seven

74. Sports Roundup, Fort Wayne Journal-Gazette, September 19, 1950.

75. Sue Macy, A Whole New Ball Game, p. 62.

A New Generation of Fans

76. The registrar of the official AAGPBL archives is Diane Barts assisted by Carol Pickerl, Northern Indiana Historical Society, 808 W. Washington, South Bend, Indiana 46601, phone (219) 284-9664.

77. More precisely, Jackie Robinson integrated baseball in 1945, when Brooklyn Dodgers President Branch Rickey signed him to play for the Dodgers' farm team in Montreal. Two years later he began playing for the parent team and won Rookie of the Year honors in the National League.

78. Greg Cote, The Miami Herald, July 11, 1991.

79. The Hall of Fame defines major leagues to mean the National and American Leagues (plus four other short-lived men's leagues), thereby excluding from the Hall anyone outside these leagues. African-American men who played in the negro leagues have been included in the Hall since 1971 on the reasoning that their skill level was such that they could have played in the major leagues had they not been discriminated against. Interview with Ted Spencer, curator, National Baseball Hall of Fame, July 21, 1993.

This reasoning—or some other appropriate rationale—has not yet been extended to women players.

80. Newsletter of the All American Girls Professional Baseball League Players' Association, April, 1993.

81. Time, July 6, 1992.

82. Entertainment Weekly, June 2, 1992.

Photo Acknowledgments

Page ix: from the Northern Indiana Historical Society; **page x:** courtesy of Helen Waddell Wyatt; **page xviii:** courtesy of Dorothy Key; **page 2 (upper):** courtesy of Irene Applegren; **page 2 (lower):** courtesy of Maxine Kline Randall; **page 10 (upper):** courtesy of Marilyn Jones Doxey; **page 10 (lower):** courtesy of Susan E. Johnson; **page 23:** from Susan E. Johnson's collection; **page 24:** courtesy of Dorothy Doyle; **page 29, 35:** from the Northern Indiana Historical Society collection; **page 44 (upper):** courtesy of Dorothy Key; **page 44 (lower):** from the Northern Indiana Historical Society collection; **page 50 (upper):** from Sharon L. Roepke, © 1984, 1986, AAGBL Cards; **page 50 (lower):** photograph by Leith A. Rohr, from the Northern Indiana Historical Society collection; **page 64:** courtesy of Helen Waddell Wyatt; **page 69:** *People and Places*, Volume 8 (12); **page 73, 84:** from the Northern Indiana Historical Society collection; **page 90 (upper and lower):** courtesy of Alice Pollitt Deschaine; **page 97:** from the Northern Indiana Historical Society collection; **page 99:** courtesy of Susan E. Johnson; **page 102 (upper):** courtesy of Maxine Kline Randall; **page 102 (lower):** *Rockford Register Star*; **page 107:** from the Northern Indiana Historical Society collection; **page 121:** from the Northern Indiana Historical Society; **page 122, 128 (upper):** courtesy of Maxine Kline Randall; **page 128 (lower):** from the Northern Indiana Historical Society collection; **page 137:** courtesy of Maxine Kline Randall; **page 138 (upper):** from the Northern Indiana Historical Society collection; **page 138 (lower):** courtesy of Maxine Kline Randall; **page 146, 149, 158:** from the Northern Indiana Historical Society collection; **page 164 (upper):** courtesy of Rose Gacioch; **page 164 (lower):** courtesy of Susan E. Johnson; **page 176, 186:** from the Northern Indiana Historical Society collection; **page 189:** from Sharon L. Roepke, © 1984, 1986, AAGBL Cards; **page 190:** courtesy of Dorothy Key; **page 197:** from Susan E. Johnson's collection; **page 198 (upper):** from the Northern Indiana Historical Society collection; **page 198 (lower):** American Girls Baseball League Official 1952 Program, from Susan E. Johnson's collection; **page 204 (upper):** from the Northern Indiana Historical Society collection; **page 204 (lower):** courtesy of Susan E. Johnson; **page 208:** courtesy of Rose Gacioch; **page 216:** courtesy of Susan E. Johnson; **page 234:** photograph by Leith A. Rohr, from the Northern Indiana Historical Society collection; **page 236:** from the Northern Indiana Historical Society collection; **page 244 (upper):** from Sharon L. Roepke, © 1984, 1986, AAGBL Cards; **page 244 (lower):** courtesy of Evelyn Warwryshyn Litwin Moroz; **page 249:** from the Northern Indiana Historical Society collection; **page 254:** photograph by Leith A. Rohr, from the Northern Indiana Historical Society collection.

More About the League

The first history of the League was Sharon Roepke's pamphlet *Diamond Gals* (Marcellus, Michigan: AAGBL Cards, 1986). With the growing national recognition of the League, several full-length books have been published.

Lois Browne's *Girls of Summer* (Toronto, Canada: HarperCollins, Ltd., 1992) is an account of League history that focuses on management decisions, foibles and mishaps. Many player anecdotes are included.

Diana Star Helmer's *Belles of the Ballpark* (Brookfield, Connecticut: The Millbrook Press, 1993) is a book for young adults that describes the League and highlights the Racine Belles.

Barbara Gregorich's history of women and baseball, *Women at Play* (San Diego, New York and London, Harcourt Brace & Co., 1993), includes a substantial discussion of the All-American Girls League as well as wonderful material about the "Bloomer Girl" teams who preceded the All-Americans.

Sue Macy's excellent *A Whole New Ball Game* (New York: Henry Holt & Co., 1993) combines great accuracy with accessibility; it is written for young adults.

Other references of interest:

The Baseball Encyclopedia, Ninth Edition (New York, Macmillan Publishing Co., 1993), pp. 2837–2845. For the first time in the history of the *Encyclopedia* (this standard reference work has been published since 1969), information about the All-American Girls Baseball League is included. The material provides a short history, the teams and the years they played, the rule changes, the final yearly standings and league champions, and a complete (at the time of printing) player roster that includes name, maiden name, and years played.

Susan M. Cahn, "No Freaks, No Amazons, No Boyish Bobs," *Chicago History*, Spring 1989, pp. 26–41, an intelligent and fascinating discussion of the feminine image issue in the era of the League and in women's sports in general.

Merrie A. Fidler, "The Development and Decline of the All-American Girls Baseball League, 1943–1954," Master of Science Thesis, University of Massachusetts-Amherst Department of Physical Education, 1976. An article-length version of this thesis is the chapter "The All-American Girls' Baseball League, 1943–1954," in Reet Howell (ed.), *Her Story in Sport* (West Point, New York: Leisure Press, 1982).

Jack Fincher, "The 'Belles of the Ball Game' were a hit with their fans," *Smithsonian*, Volume 20, Number 4 (July 1989), pp. 88-97.

Nancy Randle, "Their Time at Bat," packed with accurate information and good stories, *Chicago Tribune Magazine*, July 5, 1992, pp.10–15.

Karen H. Weiller and Catriona T. Higgs, "Living the Dream: A Historical Analysis of Professional Women Baseball Players 1943–1954," *Canadian Journal of the History of Sport*, Volume 23, Number 1 (May 1992). This article reports information collected via written questionnaire from fifty-two AAGPBL members.

Two documentaries have been produced that cover various aspects of the League. Kelly Candaele and Kim Wilson used archival footage of actual games plus contemporary interviews at a 1986 reunion for their documentary "A League of Their Own," 1987, directed by Mary Wallace (Columbia Tristar Home Video, 1992), available for rent or purchase at your local video store.

Janis L. Taylor's documentary "When Diamonds Were a Girl's Best Friend" (1987) also contains contemporary interviews and footage of the players at the time. Taylor's second documentary, "When Dreams Come True," recorded events at the 1988 opening of the Hall of Fame exhibit. Both tapes can be obtained by writing 909 Meadow Ridge Drive, Cincinnati, OH 45245.

Constance Wolfe

Susan E. Johnson grew up in Rockford, Illinois and was a loyal fan of the Rockford Peaches. She is a sociologist and has taught at several universities around the country. She is a member of the Society for American Baseball Research and lives in Anchorage, Alaska.

Sports and Outdoors Titles from Seal Press

THE CURVE OF TIME by M. Wylie Blanchet. $12.95, 1-878067-27-3. This is the fascinating true adventure story of a woman who packed her five children onto a twenty-five-foot boat and explored the coastal waters of the Pacific Northwest summer after summer in the late 1920s.

WATER'S EDGE: *Women Who Push the Limits in Rowing, Kayaking and Canoeing* by Linda Lewis. $14.95, 1-878067-18-4. An inspiring book that takes us inside the world of competitive rowing, kayaking and wilderness canoeing through ten candid profiles of women who have made their mark in these sports—from pioneering rower Ernestine Bayer to Arctic distance canoer Valerie Fons.

DOWN THE WILD RIVER NORTH by Constance Helmericks. $12.95, 1-878067-28-1. In 1965, Connie Helmericks announced to her two teenage daughters: "We are going to make a canoe expedition to the Arctic Ocean." This is their remarkable story of a wilderness adventure down the Peace, Slave and Mackenzie river systems in a sturdy twenty-foot canoe.

LEADING OUT: *Women Climbers Reaching for the Top* edited by Rachel da Silva. $16.95, 1-878067-20-6. Packed with riveting accounts of high peak ascents and fascinating narratives by some of the world's top climbers, this exciting collection is an inspiring testament to the power of discipline and desire.

RIVERS RUNNING FREE: *Canoeing Stories by Adventurous Women* edited by Judith Niemi and Barbara Wieser. $14.95, 1-878067-22-2. This spirited collection spans a century of women's canoeing adventures. Whether they embark on back country wilderness expeditions or leisurely canoeing trips, these women eloquently record the personal boundaries canoeing has inspired them to explore and push beyond.

UNCOMMON WATERS: *Women Write About Fishing* edited by Holly Morris. $14.95, 1-878067-10-9. A wonderful anthology that captures the bracing adventure and meditative moments of fishing in the words of thirty-four women anglers—from finessing trout and salmon in the Pacific Northwest to chasing bass and catfish in the Deep South.

SEAL PRESS, founded in 1976 to provide a forum for women writers and feminist issues, has many other books of fiction, non-fiction and poetry. You may order directly from us at 3131 Western Avenue, Suite 410, Seattle, Washington 98121 (add 15% of total book order for shipping and handling). Write to us for a free catalog.